Camping Michigan

Help Us Keep This Guide Up to Date

Every effort has been made by the author and editors to make this guide as accurate and useful as possible. However, many things can change after a guide is published—trails are rerouted, regulations change, techniques evolve, facilities come under new management, etc.

We appreciate hearing from you concerning your experiences with this guide and how you feel it could be improved and kept up to date. While we may not be able to respond to all comments and suggestions, we'll take them to heart and we'll also make certain to share them with the author. Please send your comments and suggestions to the following address:

Globe Pequot Press
Reader Response/Editorial Department
246 Goose Lane, Suite 200
Guilford, CT 06437

Thanks for your input!

Camping Michigan

A Comprehensive Guide to Public Tent and RV Campgrounds

Second Edition

Kevin Revolinski

FALCONGUIDES

GUILFORD, CONNECTICUT

An imprint of The Rowman & Littlefield Publishing Group, Inc.
4501 Forbes Blvd., Ste. 200
Lanham, MD 20706
www.rowman.com
Falcon and FalconGuides are registered trademarks and Make Adventure Your Story is a trademark of The Rowman & Littlefield Publishing Group, Inc.

Distributed by NATIONAL BOOK NETWORK

Photos by Kevin Revolinski unless otherwise noted
Maps by The Rowman & Littlefield Publishing Group, Inc.

British Library Cataloguing in Publication Information available

Library of Congress Cataloging-in-Publication Data available

ISBN 978-1-4930-5666-8 (paper: alk. paper)
ISBN 978-1-4930-5667-5 (electronic)

♾™ The paper used in this publication meets the minimum requirements of American National Standard for Information Sciences—Permanence of Paper for Printed Library Materials, ANSI/NISO Z39.48-1992.

Contents

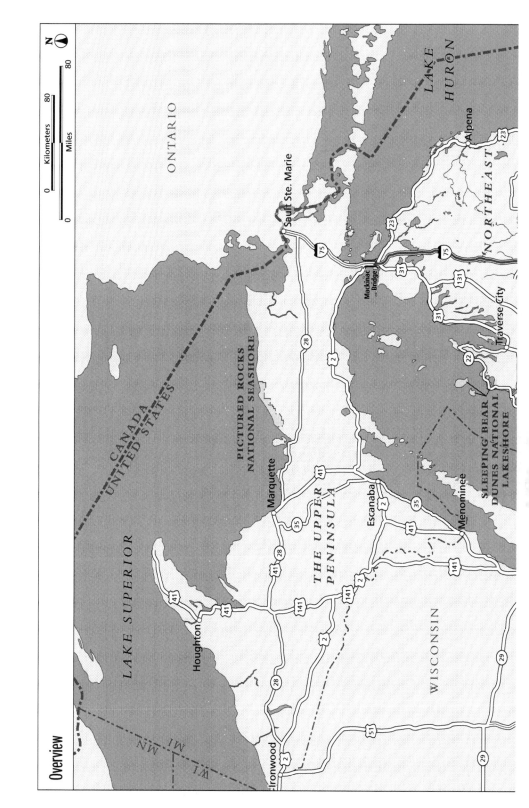

Overview

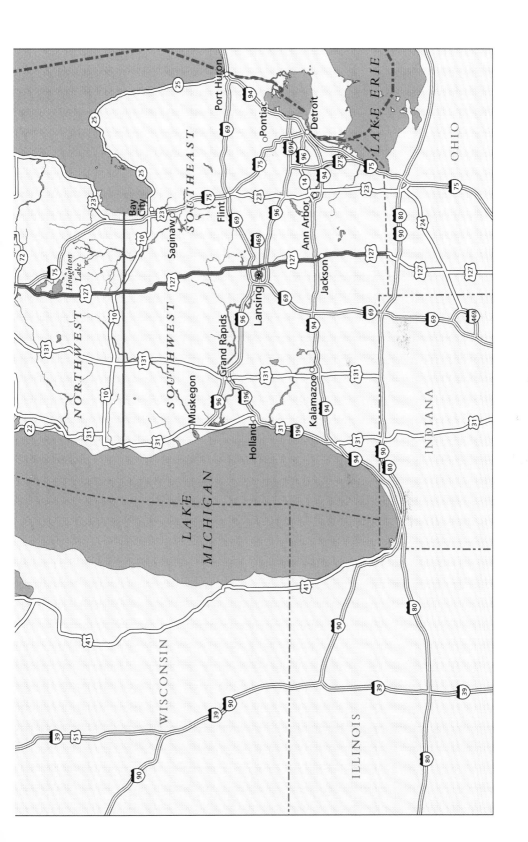

Acknowledgments

As always, I must express my deepest gratitude to the people who keep these wild places wild. The rangers, naturalists, administrators, camp hosts, and other personnel of all the parks—national, state, county, or local—are instrumental in preserving and maintaining Michigan's incredible bounty of parks, lakeshores, rivers, trails, and forests for all to enjoy.

A big thanks to Dave Lorenz at Travel Michigan for always being there when I need him, as well as to Michelle Begnoche for more of the same. Thanks to the Green Grass Hotel for the workspace and to Dan for footing the bill for a moment.

And hats off to a few good lumber barons. While one might have expected these men would have just cleared the land and been done with it, many of them and their descendants ended up donating pristine plots of pine or hardwood that would become the kernels for a number of Michigan's parks.

Thanks to Lake Superior for reminding me of the importance of really good and well-placed tent stakes. A shout-out to the deer, foxes, eagles, and ospreys I encountered on this journey, always nice reminders that we are really camping and not just in a clump of trees down the street.

I appreciate my father for passing on his love of the outdoors and the skills to read a map, and my grandparents for more of the same. And I am forever grateful to Preamtip Satasuk, without whose help and indulgence I would have struggled with such a large project. I thank her for putting up with The Grumpy Man when book deadlines hung like a dark storm coming in off Lake Superior.

Introduction

Michigan may be more remarkable than most people imagine. With a nickname like The Great Lakes State, you are likely to expect great things from Michigan. Its cup runneth over with natural attractions, bordered as it is by Lakes Superior, Michigan, Huron, and Erie—four of the five Great Lakes. With all that coastline, Michigan has more lighthouses than any other state, by a wide margin.

But the Great Lake moniker may also refer to the more than 11,000 inland lakes. In fact, you are never more than 6 miles from a lake or more than 85 miles from one of the Great Lakes no matter where you are in the state. Being unusually composed of two peninsulas, Upper and Lower, Michigan has character from two regions as well: Midwestern and Northern. Despite the big-city shoes of Detroit, Grand Rapids, and Lansing, and college towns such as Ann Arbor, Kalamazoo, and Marquette, there is also an abundance of the down-to-earth small-town culture of those middle states, and the hardiness of people who adapt each year to four seasons up north.

In some parts of the Lower Peninsula (L.P.), as you leave town on a country highway, you pass a mix of rolling farmland, woods, and more small towns, as if you are never very far from civilization or from wilderness. In the Upper Peninsula (U.P.), however, it seems a town ends and the wilderness runs right up to the shoulder. And that's all there is for the next hour or so until you find the next community. Back roads may or may not appear on a map and may be with or without the correct road name.

But perhaps the numbers say it best for outdoors lovers. There are sixteen National Wild and Scenic Rivers, eleven alone in the Upper Peninsula, totaling 625 miles of paddling paradise. Four national forests, Ottawa and Hiawatha in the U.P. and the combined Huron and Manistee in the L.P., have protected massive sections of forests that have either recovered from the lumber days or remain tracts of virgin, old-growth pine and hardwoods. Each peninsula has its own National Lakeshore: Sleeping Bear Dunes along Lake Michigan in the L.P. and Pictured Rocks up north along Lake Superior. Both National Lakeshores should be on the short list of places to see before you die.

Michigan's Department of Natural Resources manages over 100 state parks and recreation areas, over 740 boat launches on public lakes and waterways, and over 13,000 miles of trails, including over 2,400 miles of rail trails and over 3,600 miles for ATVs and other off-road vehicles. Double that for snowmobiles. That's a lot of land preserved for the public and future generations.

Michigan has more than 1,150 miles of the North Country National Scenic Trail, a hiking pathway that extends from Vermont to North Dakota. Nearly a quarter of the entire trail stretches within the two peninsulas of Michigan, and many of its completed segments pass through or close to many of the campgrounds in this book. Michigan's own Shore-to-Shore Trail, shared by horseback riders and hikers, runs 220 miles between Empire on Lake Michigan and Oscoda on Lake Huron right across the Lower Peninsula.

The state arrived in its present geological form about 12,000 years ago, when the last of the giant sheets of ice—at times as much as 10,000 feet thick—melted and withdrew, leaving the two peninsulas and the Great Lakes carved out of ancient riverbeds. The weight of them had their way with the landscape, both eroding and depositing what remains today: glacial lake plains around Detroit, deposits such as moraines in the U.P., and the drifted sand deposits that make up the dunes along Lake Michigan. Detroit and the suburbs north and west once were under an ancient lake. The notable exception is the western half of the U.P., which still shows the remaining nubs of some of the oldest mountains on the planet.

And then there's the wildlife. Birders have recorded more than 420 species in Michigan, and anyone with a life list should know that the rare and elusive Kirtland's warbler resides here. Migration routes love the lakes and the islands in the Great Lakes. Shorebirds have no lack of territory; neither do the avian residents of forest, wetlands, and prairie. The big critters include deer, black bear, wolves, coyotes, foxes, bobcats, the occasional moose, and even the rare cougar. Campers will see otters in the rivers, possums in the trees, and raccoons in their picnic baskets if they're not diligent. The largest free herd of elk east of the Mississippi makes its home in the Pigeon River Country in the northeastern quadrant of the state. Anglers will delight in the abundance of trout hot spots and salmon runs as well as steelhead, northern pike, muskie, walleye, bluegill, perch, and bass.

All of this awaits the camper in Michigan. Inside these pages are 324 places to make base camp, offering a wide range of comforts, from urban parks to the serious roughing-it sites.

Great efforts were taken to ensure the accuracy and usefulness of the information in this book. Despite all efforts, guidebooks are static things about places that are always changing—for better or for worse. This can mean more electric sites at a campsite than you had thought, or maybe they started taking reservations this year. Or budget cuts can mean this summer's restrooms at the campground might not be getting cleaned frequently enough or that sections of a camp may be closed or showing some wear and tear. Forest fires prior to the publication of this book eliminated a couple of sites entirely. Management of a federal campground may be taken up by a local community, prices may rise, and things may fall apart over time. Use this as your general guide, but be prepared for the unexpected.

How to Use This Guide

This book focuses on public campgrounds. People interested in exploring the natural wonders that Michigan has to offer really need look no further than the public park systems. This is not to pass judgment on private campgrounds or camping resorts, but those may be the subject of a different book. Much care has been taken to include nearly all public campgrounds in the state of Michigan, with one stipulation: that you can drive up directly to your site, whether with an RV, car, or motorcycle. Excluded are backcountry campsites (other than those mentioned within parks that also have drive-up camping) as well as campgrounds that offer only one or two sites or cater specifically to equestrian campers. That said, the varying levels of comfort range from very modern camps with full hookups for RVs to completely rustic with nothing but vault toilets and a hand pump for water (or less than that!).

For the purposes of this book, I have divided the state of Michigan into five regions: Southeast, Southwest, Northeast, Northwest, and the Upper Peninsula. The lines are rather arbitrary, and it's worth noting that toward the center of the state there are many great camping options over the line, in another section of the book, that are just as close as what you may be considering. Each campground has its own unique number in this book, so the count crosses from section to section, ending at #324 in the Upper Peninsula.

For each of the five regions covered in *Camping Michigan,* the following information is provided:

- A map of the region
- Tables listing all the campgrounds in subdivisions of the region and their most important attributes
- A brief overview of the region
- A description of each of the public campgrounds within the region

Maps of the regions: Each map shows the location of the campgrounds within it, with the number on the map corresponding to the number of the campground description within the text.

The maps in this book are not drawn to scale, and campground locations are approximate. However, by using the maps and the instructions in the "Finding the campground" section of each campground description, you should have no difficulty reaching many of the sites. You may need additional maps—or in the Upper Peninsula, a local's kindly suggestions—to find some of the more remote campgrounds, especially as forest roads that may appear on maps may be either torturous washboards or simply no longer roads (as learned from experience).

Quick-reference tables: A table at the beginning of each section lists all the campgrounds in the area and highlights their most important attributes. If you are looking for specific recreation opportunities, such as fishing, boating, or hiking, you can use these tables to narrow your selection of campgrounds.

Overview: Highlights and points of interest within the tour region are discussed briefly here.

Campground descriptions: Each campground description is numbered to correspond with the campground's location on the map. The following information is provided:

- **Location.** This is the name of a city or town near the campground, the driving distance in miles from that city to the campground, and the general direction of travel to reach it.

- **Season.** This will indicate when the campground is open. Some parks remain open year-round but close to camping in the fall. Some campgrounds also remain open year-round but may limit camping to a handful of sites. Water and flush toilets are commonly not available in the off-season, and roads within, or even to, the park might not be plowed when the snow comes. Season dates are approximate and can change each year based on weather, floating holidays, or even park budget.

- **Sites.** This information provides the number of campsites available and whether hookups are available. An increasing number of public campgrounds are remodeling at least some of their sites to offer hookups. This is especially true of state and county parks.

- **Maximum length.** This indicates the largest size (measured in feet) of an RV or vehicle/trailer combo that should be accommodated at the camp at least at a few sites. Be aware that some sites can handle a big rig, but the road leading in may have low clearance or tight turns.

- **Facilities.** This describes the facilities and amenities provided, including any recreational facilities available at the campground. A note on water: Water is listed within facilities, and frankly most camps offer it, whether from city supply, wells, or hand pumps. A note has been added in the camp descriptions in case you didn't notice its absence in the listed facilities. But a "no drinking water" notation does not necessarily mean there is no water at the site. Nonpotable water may be available at the campground or from a nearby stream or lake. In either case, the water should be filtered, boiled, or otherwise treated before use.

- **Fee per night.** A general guideline using dollar signs, this helps you sort sites by budget. In cases where campgrounds offer both modern and rustic facilities, you may find a combination such as $$–$$$$ to note the two-tiered pricing. See the Amenities Charts Key below for price levels. The fees shown here are current as of the date of this writing. Don't forget that Michigan state parks have daily vehicle fees in addition to camping fees. An annual "Recreation Passport," which can be purchased at any park and grants a vehicle access to ninety-eight state parks and recreation areas as well as use of state boat landings, quickly pays for itself. Fees are slightly more for nonresidents. Michigan residents can get a discount if they purchase one at the same time they renew their license plates.

- **Management and Contact.** The authority in charge of the campground as well as the specific camp's website and a phone number are listed. These can be used to confirm information and in some cases to make reservations. In the case of individual state parks, web addresses are notoriously long and complicated and tend to change from time to time, so the main page for the parks is listed instead. Go there and search for the specific site name.

- **Finding the campground.** Detailed instructions are furnished for driving to the campground from the nearest city, town, or major highway. Although it is possible to find most of the campgrounds in this book using these directions and the corresponding map, the task will be easier with the help of USDA Forest Service maps and/or a good state road map or GPS device.

- **GPS coordinates** are provided for the tech-savvy.

- **About the campground.** This is information that differentiates a particular campground from others or highlights special features. For example, if a campground is located on the water, this fact is noted. Specific fishing, hiking, or wildlife-watching information may be noted as well as a comment or two on shade, site size, or even a mention of a particularly good site.

Amenities Charts Key

Max RV Length: given in feet
Hookups: W = Water, E = Electricity, S = Sewer
Toilets: F = Flush toilets, NF = Nonflushing toilets
Showers: N = None, Y = Yes
Drinking Water: N = None, Y = Yes
Dump Station: N = None, Y = Yes
Recreation: H = Hiking, S = Swimming, F = Fishing, B = Boating, L = Boat Launch, O = Off-road driving, R = Horseback riding, C = Cycling

Fee:

$	up to $10 per night
$$	$11–$20
$$$	$21–$30
$$$$	more than $30

Reservations: N = None, Y = Yes

Key to Abbreviations

I have tried to minimize the use of abbreviations in this book. The few that have crept in are shown below, as well as some that may be encountered on maps or in other travel references.

ATV: all-terrain vehicle

CR: County Road, as in CR 405 for directions

DNR: Department of Natural Resources

FR: Forest Service Road. These letters precede numbers, as in FR 4235, and designate roads in national forests maintained by the forest service. They always appear on forest service maps, but they may not always be posted along the road.

MI: Michigan State Highway, as in MI 20

NPS: National Park Service

ORV: off-road vehicle. This usually refers to a campground or a trail for the primary use of those who wish to drive trail motorcycles, all-terrain vehicles, four-wheel-drive vehicles, and snowmobiles. It does not include mountain bikes.

U.P.: Why, the Upper Peninsula of course! The people of the U.P. often refer to themselves as Yoopers.

USDA: United States Department of Agriculture

Conscientious Camping

Careful planning plus appreciation and respect for the natural world are key components of a great outdoor experience. The listings below will guide you toward a fun camping trip that's easy on you and the environment, and keeps you safe.

Respecting the Environment

Zero-impact camping should be everyone's goal. When you leave a campground, it should look better than when you arrived.

Campfires: Heed all regulations concerning campfires, smoking, and wood gathering. Keep fires in the fire rings. To prevent the spread of the emerald ash borer insect, you should know the rules restricting the transportation of firewood. If you are traveling in Michigan, you may not move firewood from site to site; in fact, in some cases it is illegal. Most campgrounds offer some nearby options for purchasing firewood or permission to gather it in the surrounding woods. Visit www.emerald ashborer.info to see what parts of the Midwest have firewood quarantines. Visit the Michigan DNR website for more information: www.michigan.gov/invasives. And it's not just ash borers; beech bark disease, Dutch elm disease, and gypsy moths all threaten Michigan's forests.

Courtesy: Please keep your campground clean and show respect for other campers who want to enjoy a tranquil atmosphere. Keep the sound level low, especially during quiet hours. Generally, people don't camp in order to listen to your music or to your generator at all hours. In fact, some camps don't even allow generators in certain areas. With cutbacks at many parks, fewer staff are on hand to patrol the grounds and ask people to keep the noise down. As a result, campers must regulate themselves.

Storing food: During times you're away from the site and during the night, store food in your car; otherwise, squirrels, raccoons, chipmunks, or even bears will come for your provisions. If you don't have a car at the campsite, keep food in your tent *unless you're in bear country*. Then *don't* bring food inside the tent but rather hang it from a tree out on a long branch.

Garbage: If no trash containers are provided, pack it out. At night and when you are away from the campsite, stash your trash in your vehicle. Never toss garbage into the vault toilets or leave it behind in the firepit.

Sanitation: Bathing and dishwashing should be done well away from lakes and streams and away from the campground's water supplies.

Smoking: To prevent fires, use extreme care when smoking. Dispose of butts properly or pack them out.

Pets: Keep your animal at your site, restrained and quiet. On trails, pets must be leashed at all times to protect wildlife and habitat and the pets themselves.

Stay limits: Public campgrounds typically have stay limits. In the case of state parks, you may camp up to fifteen consecutive days in each separately administered campground. Some county or local campgrounds offer longer stays, including weekly, monthly, or seasonal rates.

Getting Geared Up

Clothing: Since Michigan is surrounded by the temperamental Great Lakes and is a short stretch from Canada, its climate can vary considerably. As one would suspect, the normal camping season is extended in the south (as are the hot and sticky days of midsummer) and is a bit shorter in the north. While camping during spring and fall, you want to be prepared for a full spectrum of weather conditions.

Wool makes the most versatile clothing and works great for cold, wet, changeable weather. It retains heat even when it's wet and does not absorb smells as readily as other fabrics. Cotton is the fabric for warm summer days. Shorts are great for warm summer days too, but you'll likely want a pair of long pants in the evening when the mosquitoes emerge. Always bring along a rain jacket.

Footwear: Sneakers are appropriate for most activities while camping in Michigan. Where there's likely to be mud or more rugged trails—in the Hiawatha National Forest, for example—boots are a better option. They provide support and protection from the elements and rocky surfaces.

Equipment: Your quantity and variety of camping gear will depend on the time of year, your destination, and the level of comfort that you prefer. Along with a tent, sleeping bags, food, and a flashlight, you may want to bring items such as a gas stove, lantern, and large water container. Some campers bring extra items that add to their comfort: a hammock, a small weather radio, and a tarp to hang above the picnic table to block the rain and sun. If you plan to hike, be sure to bring a daypack with padded straps to carry items such as snacks, water, rain gear, an extra sweater, keys, money, sunglasses, a camera, and binoculars.

Once you start wading through the options for camping gear, you'll encounter a bewildering number of possibilities. One rule of thumb is to keep the packing list simple. When it's easy to pack and make your escape, you're likely to do it more often. Bring just enough gear to make your stay safe and comfortable. While that list will be different for everyone, keep in mind that bringing too much stuff tends to complicate the experience and may defeat the purpose of escaping to the woods.

Staying Safe

Many of these campgrounds are in fairly remote areas, sometimes a good distance from towns, hospitals, and stores. Campers should be prepared with a first-aid kit and a supply of food and water. It's likely that you'll have cell reception at most Lower Peninsula campgrounds, but you may not always be able to count on it in the more remote areas of the Upper Peninsula. While cell phones are convenient, they are no replacement for being thoroughly prepared.

Drowning: When enjoying the lakes and rivers, always be aware of children's whereabouts and swimming skills. But also remember that drownings can happen to anyone. Dozens drown each year in the Great Lakes alone. Check color-coded beach flags: green means safe to swim, yellow recommends caution, and red means stay out of the water. If caught in a current, especially a riptide, do not fight it. Swim parallel to shore until out of the current and then swim back in.

Hypothermia: Hypothermia occurs when your body temperature drops to a dangerous level. Common causes are exposure to cold, physical exhaustion, and too little food. Contributing factors may include exposure to wind, rain, and snow; dehydration; and wearing damp or wet clothes. Falling in cold water on a cool day is one of the fastest ways to make your body temperature plummet. The waters of the Great Lakes, particularly Lake Superior, can be seriously cold even in July some years, especially when the weather turns.

Poison ivy: A nasty encounter with poison ivy can put a damper on your outdoor vacation. Poison ivy is a very common plant throughout most of Michigan. It occurs as a vine or groundcover, three leaflets to a leaf, and contains urushiol, an oily and toxic irritant that is responsible for the skin rash. After contact, raised lines or blisters will occur on the skin. Do not scratch them. Wash and dry the surface, then apply calamine lotion to dry it out. If the case is severe, consult a doctor.

Stings and bites: Most often, mosquitoes and other biting insects are more of a nuisance than a danger. Using insect repellent, wearing pants and long sleeves, and avoiding areas where insects congregate are strategies to keep from getting bitten.

If you're spending ample time outdoors, you should know about the diseases spread by some insects. Individuals can become infected by the West Nile virus if bitten by an infected mosquito. Culex mosquitoes, the primary varieties that can transmit West Nile virus to humans, thrive in urban rather than natural areas. Insect repellent and protective clothing are the best preventive measures. Remember to follow the instructions on the insect repellent, especially when applying it to children.

Ticks are often found on brush and tall grass waiting to catch a ride on a warm-blooded passerby. While they're most active in early and midsummer, you should keep an eye peeled for them throughout spring, summer, and fall. Deer ticks, the primary carrier of Lyme disease, are very small, sometimes only the size of a poppy seed. For hikers, one of the most common places to find ticks is inside the top edge of your sock (ticks need some type of backstop to start drilling into the skin). Some people wear light clothing so they can spot ticks right away. Insect repellent containing DEET is an effective deterrent. Most importantly, be sure to visually check yourself, especially if you're out on a hike. If it's prime tick season, you'll want to check your exposed skin (particularly your legs, if you're wearing shorts) every hour or so, and then do a more thorough examination back in your tent or in the shower. For ticks that are already embedded, tweezers work best for removal.

Map Legend

══🛡94🛡══	Interstate Highway
──(10)──	US Highway
──(25)──	State Highway
────────	Local Road
─ ─ ─ ─ ─	Trail
▬ ▪ ▬ ▪ ▬ ▪ ▪	International Border
─ · ─ · · ─ · ·	State Border
▬▬▬▬▬▬▬	Region Boundary
～～～	River or Creek
⬭	Body of Water
▭	National Forest/Park
⬚	State/County/Preserve/Wilderness
❶	Campground
✪	Capital
○	Town

Southeast Michigan

This corner of the state is most often associated with Detroit and its suburbs, as well as the university town of Ann Arbor and a great number of nice small towns. Most people wouldn't imagine this region would have much to offer for the outdoor enthusiast. But that couldn't be further from the truth.

The auto industry and music (hello, Motown!) have left their mark on this southeastern portion of Michigan, but many natural places still exist from the border with Ohio to the south on up into The Thumb of Michigan's mitten. In fact, the Lower Peninsula's largest state park is here: Waterloo Recreation Area, with almost 21,000 acres. Fishing lakes such as Lake Hudson are abundant and provide public boat landings or swimming beaches. Pontiac Lake has a nationally rated mountain bike trail.

Perhaps it is hard to imagine just a short drive from downtown Detroit you can be trout fishing on the Huron River. You can stay right on the other side of Lake St. Clair, where you can watch the big ships sail by between Lakes Huron and Erie, or head downtown for a Tigers game or a visit to one of the museums. Or follow the river south and check out Sterling Park, the only park on the shores of Lake Erie.

Alternatively, head north up into The Thumb, the peninsula on the peninsula that rises out past the mouth of the St. Clair River as it empties Lake Huron south toward Lake Erie. This is the Blue Water Area, with attractive charm to be found in Port Huron, Thomas Edison's childhood home and the site of the Blue Water Bridge to Sarnia, Canada (bring your passport!). Beyond this is the long shoreline of Huron. Visit the four lighthouses. One of the better stretches of sandy beach lies at the top of The Thumb within Sleeper State Park, named for the state governor who signed the legislation that created the state park system.

In the notch between The Thumb and the rest of The Mitten lies Big Bay, which has its own recreation area on Lake Huron. This is Saginaw Bay, and near the state park is Tobico Marsh. These coastal wetlands are a bit of a rarity along the Great Lakes in modern times, but they're also home or a stopover for myriad birds, especially waterfowl.

Nonnatural attractions are numerous as well, including the handsome state capitol over in Lansing, and the foodie culture of Ann Arbor as well as its "Big House"

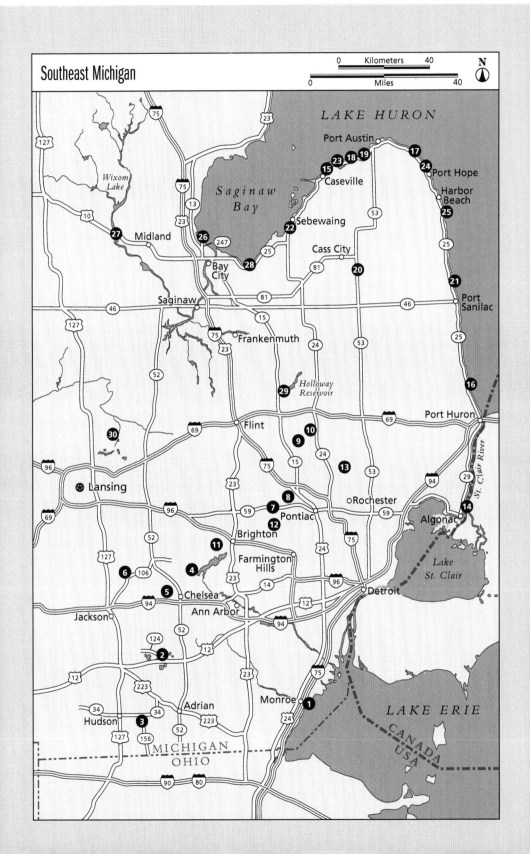

A heron waits patiently for its dinner in Sterling Lake. MATT FORSTER

stadium for the University of Michigan's Wolverines and annual folk music festival. The Michigan International Speedway is just west of Hayes State Park. Chelsea has the Purple Rose Theatre, founded by Michigan native Jeff Daniels. You can see an original Hudson at Ypsilanti Automotive Heritage Museum. Then head back to camp and sleep under the stars.

Detroit–Ann Arbor Area

	Hookup Sites	Total Sites	Max. RV Length	Hookups	Toilets	Showers	Drinking Water	Dump Station	Recreation	Fee	Reservations
1 Sterling State Park (Wm. C. Sterling State Park)	256	256	50	E	F	Y	Y	Y	HSFC	$$$–$$$$	Y
2 W. J. Hayes State Park	185	185	40	E	F	Y	Y	Y	HFL	$$$	Y
3 Lake Hudson State Recreation Area	50	50	40	E	NF	N	Y	N	FSL	$$	Y
4 Pinckney Recreation Area	186	221	50	E	F	Y	Y	Y	HSFLRC	$$–$$$	Y
5 Waterloo Recreation Area	300	350	45	E	F	Y	Y	Y	HSFLR	$$–$$$	Y
6 Pleasant Lake County Park and Campground	60	60	N/A	WE	F	Y	Y	Y	SFC	$$$	Y
7 Highland Recreation Area	0	25	N/A	E	NF	N	Y	N	HSFLR	$$	Y
8 Pontiac Lake Recreation Area	176	200	50	E	F	Y	Y	Y	HSFLR	$$–$$$	Y
9 Ortonville Recreation Area	0	25	N/A	N/A	NF	N	Y	N	HSLRC	$$	Y
10 Metamora-Hadley Recreation Area	214	214	50	E	F	Y	Y	Y	HSF	$$–$$$	Y
11 Brighton Recreation Area	144	213	50	E	F/NF	Y	Y	Y	HSFBLR	$$–$$$	Y
12 Proud Lake Recreation Area	130	130	50	E	F	Y	Y	Y	HFLRC	$$$	Y

See Amenities Charts Key on page xiii.

1 Sterling State Park

Location: About 4 miles east of Monroe
Season: Year-round
Sites: 256 sites with electrical hookups
Maximum RV length: 50
Facilities: Flush toilets, showers, grills, water, tables, picnic shelter, picnic area, dump station, boat launch, hiking/biking trails, beach, beach house, playground, nature center, fishing pier, fish-cleaning station, vending machines
Fee per night: $$$–$$$$
Management: Michigan DNR
Contact: (734) 289-2715; www.michigandnr.com/parksandtrails
Finding the campground: From I-75 go east on Dixie Highway and turn left (south) on State Park Road less than a mile from the interstate.
GPS coordinates: N 41 55.275' / W 83 20.460'

About the campground: This is the only state park on the shores of Lake Erie, and it includes 1 mile of beach. The campground has no shade whatsoever and feels more like a large parking lot, but its proximity to the beach and lake is the value here. On the opposite side of the campground are lagoons. Hikers and bikers have 7 miles of mostly paved trails. Birders will note this is on a major flyway for migratory species.

2 W. J. Hayes State Park

Location: About 40 miles southwest of Ann Arbor
Season: Year-round
Sites: 185 sites with electrical hookups
Maximum RV length: 40
Facilities: Flush/vault toilets, showers, grills, water, tables, dump station, playground, boat launch, picnic shelter, cabin rentals, fishing pier, beach
Fee per night: $$$
Management: Michigan DNR
Contact: (517) 467-7401; www.michigandnr.com/parksandtrails
Finding the campground: From US 12 heading west from Ann Arbor, take MI 124/Wamplers Lake Road right (north) less than a mile to the park entrance.
GPS coordinates: N 42 04.085' / W 84 08.203'
About the campground: This 654-acre state park set amid the rolling landscape of the Irish Hills region offers good fishing lakes that are also good for swimming and boating. The modern campground doesn't offer much in the way of privacy, and more than half of the sites have no shade, but all sites have electric hookups. The campgrounds are walking distance to the water though not in sight of it. Hayes is one of the oldest Michigan state parks and named for a former senator. Two historic towers stand together in the park. Big attractions outside the park are Cambridge Junction Historical State Park and the Michigan International Speedway.

3 Lake Hudson State Recreation Area

Location: About 7 miles east of Hudson
Season: Year-round
Sites: 50 sites with electrical hookups
Maximum RV length: 40
Facilities: Vault toilets, grills, water, tables, picnic shelter, picnic area, boat launch, beach, volleyball court
Fee per night: $$
Management: Michigan DNR
Contact: (517) 445-2265; www.michigandnr.com/parksandtrails
Finding the campground: From Hudson go east on MI 34/Carleton Road and turn right (south) onto MI 156/Morey Highway. At 1.5 miles turn right (west) into the park.
GPS coordinates: N 41 49.488' / W 84 15.579'

About the campground: Set amid farmland and not far from the border of Ohio, this 2,796-acre recreation area is a bit of a fishing mecca, and anglers are most interested in Lake Hudson's muskie, walleye, and bass populations. Hunting is also allowed, and there is a swimming beach for bathers. The campground is laid out in 2 loops that are separated from the lake by trees yet have only partial shade in a limited number of sites. The park is noted for being a very good place to observe the night sky. Modern amenities, from food and laundry to entertainment, are a 10-minute drive to Hudson.

4 Pinckney Recreation Area

Location: About 10 miles north of Chelsea
Season: Year-round
Sites: 186 sites with electrical hookups, 25 sites with no hookups, 10 walk-in sites
Maximum RV length: 50
Facilities: Flush/vault toilets, showers, grills, water, tables, picnic shelter, picnic area, dump station, boat launch, hiking/mountain biking/equestrian trails, beach, beach house, playground, fishing pier, volleyball court, horseshoe pits
Fee per night: $$–$$$
Management: Michigan DNR
Contact: (734) 426-4913; www.michigandnr.com/parksandtrails
Finding the campground: From Chelsea take MI 52 north to Werkner Road to the right (north). Go left (north) on Stofer Road and then right (east) on Territorial Road. Go left (north) on Dexter Townhall Road and the first left (west) is Silver Hill Road, which takes you to the park office.
GPS coordinates: N 42 24.715' / W 83 57.894'
About the campground: Here's an expansive park with something for everyone. At 11,000 acres the recreation area includes a chain of lakes and boat access on Bruin, Halfmoon, South, North, Joslin, Portage, Crooked, Gosling, and Hiland Lakes. Half the modern sites, all located at Bruin Lake, are unshaded and are close to the water.

The sites at Blind and Crooked Lakes campgrounds are all rustic and cost half what the modern sites do per night. The Blind Lake sites are walk-in, but the Crooked Lake sites have a drive-up loop and a boat launch. Hikers have over 60 miles of trails to explore, while mountain bikers have 24, and horses 8. A cabin and yurt are rentable.

5 Waterloo Recreation Area

Location: About 13 miles west of Chelsea
Season: Year-round
Sites: 300 sites with electrical hookups, 25 sites with no hookups, 25 equestrian sites
Maximum RV length: 45
Facilities: Flush/vault toilets, showers, grills, water, tables, picnic shelter, picnic area, dump station, boat launch, hiking/mountain biking/equestrian trails, beach, beach house, playground, nature center, fishing pier, concessionaire

Fee per night: $$–$$$ (rustic-modern)

Management: Michigan DNR

Contact: (734) 475-8307; www.michigandnr.com/parksandtrails

Finding the campground: From I-94 take exit 156 and go north on Kalmbach Road for 1 mile. Turn right (northeast) on Glazier Road and go 1 mile. Turn right (north) on Ridge Road until McClure Road to turn left (west). Park headquarters will be on the right (north) side of the road at 0.3 mile.

GPS coordinates: N 42 20.000' / W 84 06.368'

About the campground: With nearly 21,000 acres, this is one of the largest parks in Michigan (and the largest in the Lower Peninsula). Campground options are several: 2 modern camp-grounds, Portage Lake and Sugarloaf, divide the electrical sites, while the rustic sites are split between an equestrian camp and Green Lake campground. There are also 4 cabins and a yurt for rental. Hikers have many miles to explore, including the 22-mile Pinckney Trail. The Gerald E. Eddy Discovery Center offers educational information about the area's geology and wildlife. One launch and a fishing pier are accessible. The park is quite spread out, and directions are to the park office to get you started.

6 Pleasant Lake County Park and Campground

Location: About 13 miles north of Jackson

Season: Memorial Day Weekend through Labor Day Weekend

Sites: 60 sites with electrical and water hookups

Maximum RV length: None

Facilities: Flush toilets, showers, grills, water, tables, picnic shelter, picnic area, dump station, beach, playground

Fee per night: $$$

Management: Jackson County Government

Contact: (517) 769-6401; www.co.jackson.mi.us/Facilities/Facility/Details/Pleasant-Lake-County-Park-Campground-19

Finding the campground: From I-94 take exit 139 and go 5 miles north on MI 106 to Merid-ian Road. Turn left (north) on Styles Road and follow it 0.5 mile to the park entrance on the left (south) side of the road.

GPS coordinates: N 42 24.123' / W 84 20.807'

About the campground: Set on 22 acres next to a small lake, this county park offers 60 modern sites with just a few scattered shade trees and grassy areas for tents. A sandy beach graces the swimming area, and the lake offers fishing. Three picnic shelters are available by reservation. Han-kered Hills, an 18-hole golf course, lies less than a mile away.

7 Highland Recreation Area

Location: About 15 miles west of Pontiac

Season: Year-round

Sites: 25 sites with no hookups
Maximum RV length: None
Facilities: Vault toilets, water, firepits, tables, hiking/mountain biking/equestrian trails, beach house, boat launch, picnic area and shelter, dog trial area, horseshoe pits, volleyball court
Fee per night: $$
Management: Michigan DNR
Contact: (248) 889-3750; www.dnr.state.mi.us/parksandtrails
Finding the campground: Take MI 59 east from I-75 about 17 miles and look for Haven Road on the left (south) side of the road, which heads right into the park.
GPS coordinates: N 42 39.007' / W 83 32.616'
About the campground: Don't let the "equestrian" label scare you off if you only have a tent. While these rustic sites are horse-friendly, the park has more miles of trails for hikers (17 miles) and mountain bikers (16 miles) than for the riders (12 miles). For a place so close to the urban world, the 5,900 acres have much to offer in environments ranging from swamp forest to mixed hardwood, as well as a variety of unusual plants and critters. Wildflower viewing and birding are popular in the spring. Fishing and boating enthusiasts have access to 4 lakes.

8 Pontiac Lake Recreation Area

Location: About 9 miles west of Pontiac
Season: Year-round
Sites: 176 sites with electrical hookups, 24 sites with no hookups
Maximum RV length: 50
Facilities: Flush/vault toilets, showers, grills, water, tables, picnic shelter, picnic area, dump station, boat launch, hiking/mountain biking/equestrian trails, beach, beach house, playground, fishing pier, concessionaire, shooting range
Fee per night: $$-$$$
Management: Michigan DNR
Contact: (248) 666-1020; www.michigandnr.com/parksandtrails
Finding the campground: From US 24 (Dixie Highway) turn left (west) on Andersonville Road and left (southwest) again on White Lake Road. Go left (south) on Teggerdine Road and take the first left (east) on Maceday Road, following it 0.9 mile to the campground.
GPS coordinates: N 42 41.190' / W 83 28.370'
About the campground: The modern campgrounds are separated into 2 major loops, with many of the sites unshaded. The westernmost sites in the western loop offer some bigger shade trees. The rustic sites are farther east on Maceday Road and are shared by equestrian campers. Pontiac Lake offers a beach and boating with a long shoreline and good fishing, and the recreation area is far from the campgrounds but connected by a 1.9-mile hiking trail. Additionally, there are equestrian trails, and the 11-mile mountain bike trail has been ranked as one of the Top 100 in the United States.

A boardwalk trail in Highland Recreation Area MATT FORSTER

9 Ortonville Recreation Area

Location: About 30 miles north of Pontiac
Season: Year-round
Sites: 25 sites with no hookups
Maximum RV length: None
Facilities: Vault toilets, firepits, water, tables, picnic shelter, picnic area, boat launch, hiking/ mountain biking/equestrian trails, beach, beach house, playground, volleyball court, horseshoe pits, shooting range

Fee per night: $$
Management: Michigan DNR
Contact: (810) 797-4439; www.michigandnr.com/parksandtrails
Finding the campground: From I-75 head north on MI 15 for 8 miles and turn right (east) on Oakwood Road. Go left (north) on Hadley Road and turn left (west) 2.2 miles later at Fox Lake Road. The campground is on the right (north) side almost 1 mile down.
GPS coordinates: N 42 53.750' / W 83 24.792'
About the campground: The recreation area is a combined 5,400 acres of high wooded hills spread out around several lakes. The rustic campground, located closest to the tiny Webster Lake and just off Fox Lake Road, is off the beaten path and allows equestrian users. There are over 6 miles of horse trails in the park. Day users will spend more time at Big Fish Lake, where most of the facilities are. Hunters may enjoy the shooting range inside the park. There is also fishing access at Algoe, Davidson, Round, and Today Lakes. A 3.5-mile hiking and mountain biking trail is toward the southern portion of the recreation area at Bloomer #3 State Park. One rustic cabin is also available.

10 Metamora-Hadley Recreation Area

Location: About 54 miles north of Detroit
Season: Year-round
Sites: 214 sites with electrical hookups
Maximum RV length: 50
Facilities: Flush/vault toilets, showers, firepits/grills, water, tables, picnic shelter, picnic area, dump station, boat launch, hiking trails, beach, beach house, playground, accessible fishing pier, boat rental, concessionaire, cabins
Fee per night: $$–$$$
Management: Michigan DNR
Contact: (810) 797-4439; www.michigandnr.com/parksandtrails
Finding the campground: From MI 24 turn left (west) on Pratt Road and 2.3 miles later turn left (south) onto Herd Road. The second left is the park entrance.
GPS coordinates: N 42 56.707' / W 83 21.529'
About the campground: The campground loops are set up to the west of the lake and offer some sparse shade from older trees. The sites farthest south to the back of the loops have the best amount of tree cover, and the sites in the first loop are right by the water. Across the water from the campgrounds is the beach area, so day-trippers and campers are separated. You can rent boats and paddleboats, and hikers have 6 miles of trail to explore. This is just over an hour from the farthest reaches of the Detroit metro area. Rates are discounted in the off-season.

11 Brighton Recreation Area

Location: About 6 miles west of Brighton
Season: Year-round

Sites: 144 sites with electrical hookups, 69 sites with no hookups, 19 equestrian sites, 5 rustic cabins; wheelchair-accessible sites available

Maximum RV length: 50

Facilities: Flush/vault toilets, water, tables, grills, picnic area/shelter, dump station, beach, beach house, boat launch, cabins, hiking/equestrian/mountain biking trails, playground, boat rentals, vending machines, fishing pier

Fee per night: $$–$$$

Management: Michigan DNR

Contact: (810) 229-6566; www.michigandnr.com/parksandtrails

Finding the campground: From I-96 take exit 147 at Brighton. Go west about 6 miles to Chilson Road, then drive south 1.5 miles to Bishop Lake Road to reach the park gate.

GPS coordinates: N 42 30.401' / W 83 51.534'

About the campground: With a number of lakes spread throughout its 4,947 acres, Brighton Recreation Area is great for fishing and other water activities. A range of hills and forest around the lakes, as well as some marshy lowlands, offer miles of hiking, mountain biking, and horse trails. The 2 rustic campgrounds are close to lakes and are well separated from the modern, electrical sites, which tend to be shadeless and popular with RVs. The water draws a variety of bird species, and the beach is popular with families.

12 Proud Lake Recreation Area

Location: About 14 miles northwest of Farmington Hills

Season: Year-round

Sites: 130 sites with electrical hookups

Maximum RV length: None

Facilities: Flush/vault toilets, showers, grills, water, tables, picnic shelter, picnic area, dump station, boat launch, hiking/mountain biking/equestrian trails, beach, beach house, playground, boat rental, concessionaire

Fee per night: $$$

Management: Michigan DNR

Contact: (248) 685-2433; www.michigandnr.com/parksandtrails

Finding the campground: From I-96 west of Farmington Hills, go north on Wixom Road and the park entrance will be on the right (east) side of the road.

GPS coordinates: N 42 34.226' / W 83 33.567'

About the campground: About 4,700 scenic acres of woodlands and water make up this park. The campground runs a long, narrow loop from east to west and offers only a modest smattering of a few shade trees. It also has a boat launch on Proud Lake exclusively for campers. Canoes and kayaks can be rented for the lake and the Huron River, which is popular for trout fishing. Horse and mountain biking trails total almost 9 miles, while hiking trails are just over 6 miles. The park is also popular for geocaching. Two cabins are available for rent as well.

Port Huron Area and The Thumb

	Hookup Sites	Total Sites	Max. RV Length	Hookups	Toilets	Showers	Drinking Water	Dump Station	Recreation	Fee	Reservations
13 Addison Oaks County Park	170	170	50	E	F	Y	Y	Y	HFBRC	$$$$	Y
14 Algonac State Park	296	296	60	E	F/NF	Y	Y	Y	HSFBL	$$-$$$	Y
15 Caseville County Park	172	230	N/A	WES	F	Y	Y	Y	SFL	$$$$	Y
16 Lakeport State Park	250	250	50	E	F	Y	Y	Y	HSF	$$$	Y
17 Lighthouse County Park	105	110	45	E	Y	Y	Y	Y	HL	$$$-$$$$	Y
18 Oak Beach County Park	55	55	45	E	Y	Y	Y	N	SF	$$$$	Y
19 Port Crescent State Park	142	142	50	E	F	Y	Y	Y	HSFL	$$$$	Y
20 Evergreen Park	163	173	35	E	F	Y	Y	N	HFL	$$$-$$$$	Y
21 Forester Park	170	190	40	E	F	Y	Y	Y	HSFB	$$$-$$$$	Y
22 Sebewaing County Park	54	64	35	E	Y	Y	Y	N	N/A	$$-$$$$	Y
23 Sleeper State Park	226	226	50	E	F	Y	Y	Y	HSF	$$$	Y
24 Stafford County Park	43	73	50	WES	F	Y	Y	Y	SFB	$$$-$$$$	Y
25 Wagener County Park	96	96	40	WES	F/NF	Y	Y	N	HFL	$$-$$$$	Y

See Amenities Charts Key on page xiii.

13 Addison Oaks County Park

Location: About 9 miles north of Rochester
Season: May 18 to October 21
Sites: 170 sites with electrical hookups and water on-site
Maximum RV length: 50
Facilities: Flush toilets, showers, fire ring, water, tables, dump station, boat launch, hiking/mountain biking/equestrian trails, beach, playground, fishing pier, fish-cleaning station, volleyball court, ball field, disc golf course, boat/bike rental, concessionaire
Fee per night: $$$$
Management: Oakland County
Contact: (248) 693-2432; www.oakgov.com/parks/parksandtrails/Addison-Oaks/Pages/default .aspx
Finding the campground: From Rochester take Main Street north out of the city (it will become Rochester Road). At just over 8 miles look for Romeo Road and go left (west) 1.7 miles to find the road into the park on the right (north) side of the road before the big turn.
GPS coordinates: N 42 47.947' / W 83 10.086'

An ore ship on the St. Clair River

About the campground: This 1,139-acre park contains 2 lakes, making the obvious draws boating, swimming, and fishing. But the activities on land are even more numerous, making this a good choice for families with kids. The campsites are spread out into 4 loops, A through D. Most sites offer little or no shade; the best bet might be Section D. The sites are to the north of the larger Buhl Lake, while the park activities and day-use area are to the south.

14 Algonac State Park

Location: About 3 miles north of Algonac
Season: Year-round
Sites: 296 sites with electrical hookups, 1 site with no hookups
Maximum RV length: 60
Facilities: Flush/vault toilets, showers, grills, tables, picnic shelter, picnic area, dump station, hiking trails, playground, shooting range
Fee per night: $$–$$$
Management: Michigan DNR
Contact: (810) 765-5605; www.michigandnr.com/parksandtrails
Finding the campground: Head north from Algonac on MI 29/St. Clair River Drive. Watch for State Park Road on your left (west).
GPS coordinates: N 42 38.830' / W 82 30.872'

About the campground: Watch big freighters sail past the park on the St. Clair River, where the parallel loops of the unshaded riverfront section of campsites are located. The view across the water is Canada. But you also have much to look at in the park itself. The habitats are rare and are home to a variety of wildflowers, trees, butterflies, and larger critters. The wagon-wheel loop of sites, while still unshaded, is at least backed up by the surrounding trees.

15 Caseville County Park

Location: Right inside Caseville
Season: April 15 to October 31
Sites: 58 sites with water and electrical hookups, 172 sites with full hookups
Maximum RV length: None
Facilities: Flush toilets, showers, grills, water, tables, picnic shelter, picnic area, dump station, boat launch, beach, beach house, playground, boat rental, concessionaire, Wi-Fi
Fee per night: $$$$
Management: Caseville County
Contact: (989) 856-2080 or (888) 265-2583 for bookings; www.huroncountyparks.com/caseville-county-park
Finding the campground: Come into Caseville on MI 25 and it becomes Main Street. Toward the north end of town, watch for County Harbor Drive on the west side of the road to get into the park.
GPS coordinates: N 43 56.829' / W 83 16.273'
About the campground: This park packs in a lot of RVs. The loops can be a little cramped for bigger rigs, but there are some shade trees throughout and the ground is grassy, which is nice for tents. The beach, which looks out at Saginaw Bay, lies beyond the camp to the west, so it's good for sunsets. It is wide and deep and an easy walk from the sites. The campground has Wi-Fi as well.

16 Lakeport State Park

Location: About 11 miles north of Port Huron
Season: Early April through late October
Sites: 250 sites with electrical hookups
Maximum RV length: 50
Facilities: Flush toilets, showers, firepits, tables, picnic shelter, picnic area, dump station, beach, beach house, playground, volleyball nets, horseshoe pits, concessionaire
Fee per night: $$$
Management: Michigan DNR
Contact: (810) 327-6224; www.michigandnr.com/parksandtrails
Finding the campground: From Port Huron take MI 25 north along Lake Huron toward Lakeport. On the north side of Lakeport, watch for the park road on your right (east).
GPS coordinates: N 43 07.383' / W 82 29.830'

The lighthouse just north of Port Huron, down the highway from several parks

About the campground: Lakeport is divided into 2 parts, so don't get confused. The southernmost unit, south of the Village of Lakeport, is the day-use area. Go north for camping, where you'll find 2 loops in the woods. The southernmost of these has a lot of shade trees spread throughout the site. The northern one has the advantage of being closer to the beach, though just a few of the sites themselves may lack some shade.

17 Lighthouse County Park

Location: About 6 miles north of Port Hope
Season: May 1 to October 15
Sites: 105 sites with electrical hookups, 5 sites with no hookups
Maximum RV length: 45
Facilities: Flush toilets, showers, tables, picnic area, dump station, boat launch, hiking trails, playground, Lighthouse Museum
Fee per night: $$$-$$$$
Management: Huron County Parks
Contact: (989) 428-4749 or (888) 265-2583 for bookings; www.huroncountyparks.com/lighthouse-county-park
Finding the campground: Follow MI 25 north from Port Hope, and just past 6 miles watch for Lighthouse Road on the right (east). Drive in, and as the road curves to the west, look for Park

Road on your right (north). This will take you through the woods to the lakefront and Gulick Road. Follow that right (south) to get to the campground.

GPS coordinates: N 44 01.076' / W 82 47.664'

About the campground: One of the highlights of this park is a visit to the museum inside the historic 1857 Pointe aux Barques Lighthouse. The campground is set up right next to the lakeshore, which affords a view of the sunrise over Lake Huron. Sites are grassy, but the meager scattering of trees offers little shade. Rates are reduced in early May and starting in September when schools are back in session.

18 Oak Beach County Park

Location: About 9 miles east of Caseville
Season: May 1 to October 15
Sites: 55 sites with electrical hookups
Maximum RV length: 45
Facilities: Flush toilets, showers, water, picnic shelter, grills, picnic area, beach, horseshoe pits, playground
Fee per night: $$$$
Management: Oak Beach County
Contact: (989) 856-2344 or (888) 265-2583 for bookings; www.huroncountyparks.com/oak-beach-county-park
Finding the campground: From Caseville take MI 25 east along the coast to Oak Beach Road. The campsites are to the right (south); the beach is to the left (north).
GPS coordinates: N 43 59.762' / W 83 07.584'
About the campground: This park is situated between Caseville and Port Austin on the shores of Lake Huron. The campgrounds are actually across the highway from the beach—still walkable, but there are no water views here. The sites are arranged in rows parallel to the beach and getting farther away as you go—maybe a good thing to sacrifice beach proximity for a site farther from potential road noise. Some mature trees are spread throughout the camp, offering some intermittent shade among the sites. Holidays and special events incur a surcharge on the daily rate, and weekly and seasonal rates are available.

19 Port Crescent State Park

Location: About 6 miles west of Port Austin
Season: Year-round
Sites: 142 sites with electrical hookups
Maximum RV length: 50
Facilities: Flush/vault toilets, firepits, showers, water, tables, picnic shelter, picnic area, dump station, hiking trails, beach, beach house, boat launch, playground, fishing pier, observation platform
Fee per night: $$$$
Management: Michigan DNR

Contact: (989) 738-8663; www.michigandnr.com/parksandtrails
Finding the campground: From Port Austin take MI 25 west along the lakeshore and in 4 miles you will see the campground entrance on your right (west).
GPS coordinates: N 44 00.413' / W 83 03.097'
About the campground: Set between a river and Saginaw Bay on Lake Huron, this park offers some simple trails, a boardwalk with scenic overlooks, and a nice stretch of beach. The campgrounds lie at the eastern end of the park, occupying the narrowest point of the park with lake on one side, highway on the other. Most of the sites have a good amount of shade, and some sites even have views of Saginaw Bay or the Old Pinnebog River channel. All of it is a short walk to the beach and a slightly longer one to the day-use area. Birding is notable here. Attention stargazers: the park has one of seven "dark sky preserves" in Michigan.

20 Evergreen Park

Location: About 7 miles southeast of Cass City
Season: May 1 to December 1
Sites: 163 sites with electrical hookups, 10 rustic sites
Maximum RV length: 35
Facilities: Flush toilets, showers, firepits, tables, picnic shelter, picnic area, boat launch, hiking trails, playground, horseshoe pits, ball field, Wi-Fi
Fee per night: $$$–$$$$
Management: Sanilac County Parks
Contact: (989) 872-6600; www.sanilaccountyparks.com/evergreen/index.php
Finding the campground: From Cass City take MI 81 east until MI 53. Go right (south) and at 3.5 miles find the entrance to the park on your right (west).
GPS coordinates: N 43 33.111' / W 83 05.706'
About the campground: Don't just think that The Thumb of Michigan is only about water. This park lies in the heart of the forest alongside the Cass River. The sites line up in a long loop in a grassy area with good shade trees. The road is unpaved and can get a bit muddy in rain. Sites are spacious enough, though not really private. Fishing is good in the river. The park is nice for kids, and there are activities planned. Pull-through sites are available, and there are discounts during hunting season.

21 Forester Park

Location: About 6 miles north of Port Sanilac
Season: May through October
Sites: 170 sites with electrical hookups, 20 sites without hookups
Maximum RV length: 40
Facilities: Flush toilets, firepits, showers, water, picnic shelter, picnic area, dump station, hiking trails, beach, playground, volleyball court, horseshoe pits, concessionaire, basketball court, recreation field, Wi-Fi hot spots

Fee per night: $$$-$$$$
Management: Sanilac County Parks
Contact: (810) 622-8715; www.sanilaccountyparks.com/forester
Finding the campground: From Port Sanilac take MI 25 north up the coast about 6 miles and the park entrance is on your right (east).
GPS coordinates: N 43 30.709' / W 82 34.490'
About the campground: Another option for some Port Huron shoreline. These campsites are spacious and spread out just a bit with loops throughout the park. Trees are abundant, so at least partial shade is common. The least shaded may be the most southern of the loops. The sandy beach is OK for swimming but has a lot of rocks, and sunrises are over the lake. Kids have much to do here. The park is quite wheelchair accessible, including the showers and beach area. Hymn sing-alongs are conducted on summer season weekends.

22 Sebewaing County Park

Location: Right inside Sebewaing along the river
Season: May 1 to October 15
Sites: 54 sites with electrical hookups, 10 sites with no hookups
Maximum RV length: 35
Facilities: Flush toilets, showers, firepits, tables, picnic area, playground
Fee per night: $$$-$$$$
Management: Huron County
Contact: (989) 883-2033 or (888) 265-2583 for bookings; www.huroncountyparks.com/sebewaing-county-park
Finding the campground: MI 25 passes right through Sebewaing. Find where Center Street intersects with it at an angle toward the southwest. Take Center Street southwest to Union Street and turn right (west) and follow it to the end and the entrance to the park.
GPS coordinates: N 43 44.204' / W 83 27.439'
About the campground: Located on the banks of the Sebewaing River just before it empties into Saginaw Bay, this campground is also in the middle of town. Right across the river is the local airstrip, in fact. Many of the sites have a full or partial view of the river, but only a few of the sites have shade trees. Tents can also set up in a sunny field in the back corner of the park, surrounded by trees but set back from the river. Despite the proximity of the lake, there isn't any good access here. Holidays and special events incur extra daily charges, and there are weekly and seasonal rates. The private Sebewaing River Campground is right next door and easily confused with the county park.

23 Sleeper State Park

Location: About 5 miles east of Caseville
Season: Year-round
Sites: 226 sites with electrical hookups

The beach at Sleeper State Park

Maximum RV length: 50
Facilities: Flush/vault toilets, firepits, showers, tables, picnic shelter, picnic area, dump station, hiking/mountain biking trails, beach, beach house, volleyball, playground, concessionaire, Wi-Fi
Fee per night: $$$
Management: Michigan DNR
Contact: (989) 856-4411; www.michigandnr.com/parksandtrails
Finding the campground: From Caseville take MI 25 east for 5 miles and the campground entrance is on the right (south) side of the highway.
GPS coordinates: N 43 58.819' / W 83 12.621'
About the campground: Named for Albert E. Sleeper, the state governor and Huron County resident who signed the legislation that made Michigan state parks possible, this park is very popular for its beachfront. Day users come to swim and play volleyball on the beach, which faces north into Lake Huron at the top of The Thumb of Michigan's mitten. This orientation allows visitors to see both the sunrise and sunset. Steps and boardwalk connect the parking lot with the beach beyond the modest dunes. The campground is located across the highway to the south of the day-use area. Divided into 2 big loops, the sites are well shaded and spacious but are not sheltered from each other.

24 Stafford County Park

Location: At the center of Port Hope on the lakeshore
Season: May 1 to October 15
Sites: 43 sites with full hookups, 10 sites with electrical hookups, 20 rustic sites
Maximum RV length: 50
Facilities: Flush toilets, water, showers, picnic shelter, picnic area, dump station, boat launch, hiking/mountain biking/equestrian trails, beach, beach house, playground, volleyball net, horseshoe pits, tennis court, ball field, pavilion
Fee per night: $$$–$$$$
Management: Huron County Parks
Contact: (989) 428-4213 or (888) 265-2583 for bookings; www.huroncountyparks.com/stafford-county-park
Finding the campground: MI 25 passes right through Port Hope. At State Street turn right (east) and take that to the lakeshore to turn left on Huron Street, and the park is on either side.
GPS coordinates: N 43 56.732' / W 82 42.675'
About the campground: Set right in the heart of Port Hope on the eastern side of Michigan's Thumb, this beachfront campground sees sunsets over the beach. Summer is very active here, with softball tournaments and beach users. An 1858 sawmill chimney still stands next to the park pavilion. The best of the sites are on the beach and have a bit of shade. The 2 big loops across the street from the beach have no shade and generally serve RVs. Holidays and special events incur extra daily charges, and there are weekly and seasonal rates.

25 Wagener County Park

Location: About 5 miles south of Harbor Beach
Season: May 1 to October 15
Sites: 59 sites with electrical hookups, 29 sites with full hookups, 9 rustic sites, 6 rustic cabins
Maximum RV length: 40
Facilities: Flush/vault toilets, showers, water, picnic area, boat launch, hiking trails, playground, pavilion
Fee per night: $$$–$$$$
Management: Wagener County
Contact: (989) 479-9131 or (888) 265-2583 for bookings; www.huroncountyparks.com/wagener-county-park
Finding the campground: From Harbor Beach head south on MI 25 and at 5 miles find the park road on the left (east) side of the road.
GPS coordinates: N 43 46.303' / W 82 37.388'
About the campground: The campground is set back from the lakeshore and surrounded by forest (though not really shaded by it at midday). Park roads are unpaved. The park has nice colors that enhance the several miles of hiking trails in fall. A boat launch and sandy beach allow visitors to enjoy Lake Huron; these are about a quarter-mile stroll from camp. Holidays and special events incur extra daily charges, and there are weekly and seasonal rates.

Saginaw–Bay City Area

	Hookup Sites	Total Sites	Max RV Length	Hookups	Toilets	Showers	Drinking Water	Dump Station	Recreation	Fee	Reservations
26 Bay City State Recreation Area	193	193	50	E	F/NF	Y	Y	Y	HFSC	$$$	Y
27 Black Creek State Forest Campground	0	23	40	N/A	NF	N	Y	N	HFL	$$	N
28 Vanderbilt County Park and Campground	24	32	40	E	NF	N	Y	N	H	$$–$$$	Y
29 Wolverine Campground and Buttercup Beach	144	191	N/A	E	F	Y	Y	Y	SL	$$$	Y
30 Sleepy Hollow State Park	181	181	45	E	F	Y	Y	Y	HSFLR	$$$	Y

See Amenities Charts Key on page xiii.

26 Bay City State Recreation Area

Location: About 6 miles north of Bay City

Season: Year-round

Sites: 193 sites with electrical hookups

Maximum RV length: 50

Facilities: Flush/vault toilets, showers, grills, water, tables, picnic shelter, picnic area, dump station, boat launch, hiking/biking trails, beach, beach house, playground, nature center, fishing pier

Fee per night: $$$

Management: Michigan DNR

Contact: (989) 684-3020; www.michigandnr.com/parksandtrails

Finding the campground: From Bay City take MI 13 (Euclid Avenue) north, and where MI 13 bends left, stay straight on Euclid Avenue (now MI 247) for 2.6 miles until State Park Drive where you turn right (east). The camp entrance is 0.3 mile east on the right (south) side of the road.

GPS coordinates: N 43 40.036' / W 83 54.348'

About the campground: The park road separates the campgrounds from the lakeshore, where you can find Tobico Marsh, one of the largest surviving coastal wetlands on the Great Lakes. Birding here is notably good. The campsites have good shade cover from tall hardwood trees, but there isn't much privacy between them. Beach lovers have a nice sandy stretch along Lake Huron's Saginaw Bay. The Saginaw Bay Visitor Center is an award-winning educational facility at the park.

The wetlands boardwalk at Bay City State Park

27 Black Creek State Forest Campground

Location: About 29 miles west of Bay City
Season: Mid-April through mid-November
Sites: 23 sites with no hookups, 15 sites accommodate longer vehicles/trailers
Maximum RV length: 40
Facilities: Vault toilets, fire rings, water, tables, boat launch
Fee per night: $$
Management: Michigan DNR
Contact: (989) 539-3021; www.michigandnr.com/parksandtrails
Finding the campground: From US 10 west of Bay City, take the River Road exit and go right (north) 1.5 miles and turn left (west) on Mier Road. The campground is on the left (south) side of the road.
GPS coordinates: N 43 42.739' / W 84 23.862'
About the campground: This rustic campground is popular with anglers who come to Black Creek and 2 nearby lakes in search of walleye, bass, perch, pike, and panfish. Sites are spacious and shaded, and are assigned on a first-come-first-served basis. The creek runs just west of the site loops. The field office is in Sanford, and there is a self-pay system in place. Hiking opportunities are a short drive away, including 10 miles of trail at Pine Haven, 20 miles of paved trail at Pere Marquette, and access to the 280-mile Midland County to Mackinaw City Trail. Boat access is at Sanford or Wixom Lake.

28 Vanderbilt County Park and Campground

Location: About 12 miles east of Bay City
Season: April 15 through November 30
Sites: 24 sites with shared electrical hookups, 8 sites with no hookups
Maximum RV length: Up to 40 feet at 15 sites
Facilities: Vault toilets, grills, fire rings, water, tables, picnic shelter, picnic area, playground, volleyball court, nature trail
Fee per night: $$–$$$
Management: Tuscola County
Contact: (989) 325-2037; www.tuscolacounty.org/parks
Finding the campground: From Bay City take MI 25 about 10 miles east and turn left (north) on Quanicassee Road, which bends right and becomes Vanderbilt Road. Watch for the park on the right (north) side of the road after you pass the Bath Road junction.
GPS coordinates: N 43 35.585' / W 83 39.599'
About the campground: The campground allows some partial shade from tall hardwoods over mowed grass. There is no understory to provide privacy. Bring your own drinking water, as the water on-site, while safe to drink, is not recommended due to an above-average amount of salt. There are no pull-through sites, and the park itself does not have any direct lake access, though the shore of Lake Huron is not far off. Expect a camp host in high season.

29 Wolverine Campground and Buttercup Beach

Location: About 18 miles northeast of Flint
Season: Memorial Day Weekend through Labor Day Weekend
Sites: 144 sites with electrical hookups, 47 rustic sites
Maximum RV length: None
Facilities: Flush toilets, showers, fire rings, grills, water, tables, picnic shelter, picnic area, dump station, boat launch, beach, playground
Fee per night: $$$
Management: Genesee County Parks
Contact: (810) 736-7100; www.geneseecountyparks.org/wolverine/
Finding the campground: From I-75 take the Mt. Morris Road exit. Drive east on Mt. Morris Road 14.5 miles to Baxter Road and turn right (south).
GPS coordinates: N 43 07.344' / W 83 28.151'
About the campground: The campground lies in pine forest along the shore of the 2,000-acre Holloway Reservoir. Site fees vary according to whether the site is lakefront, pull-through, or non-lakefront. Sites closer to the water are better shaded than many of the pull-through sites, which are totally exposed, with no nearby shade trees. Weekly, monthly, and senior rates are available. The beach is sandy and popular with day users. The park is staffed during camping season.

30 Sleepy Hollow State Park

Location: About 22 miles north of Lansing
Season: Year-round
Sites: 181 sites with electrical hookups
Maximum RV length: 45
Facilities: Flush/vault toilets, showers, fire rings, grills, water, tables, picnic shelter, picnic area, dump station, boat launch, hiking/mountain biking/equestrian trails, beach, beach house, playground, fishing pier, boat rental, concessionaire, disc golf course
Fee per night: $$$
Management: Michigan DNR
Contact: (517) 651-6217; www.michigandnr.com/parksandtrails
Finding the campground: From US 127 north of Lansing, take the Price Road exit and go right (east) 5.7 miles to the park entrance on the left (north) side of the road.
GPS coordinates: N 42 55.519' / W 84 24.576'
About the campground: Encompassing 410-acre Lake Ovid, this state park is a popular mid-Michigan escape. The campground is divided into 2 sections, each with 2 long loops of sites. There is no understory, so sites are not very private, though they are spacious enough and some shade is provided. A short walking trail connects the camping area to the beach area. Kayaks, pontoons, and paddleboats are available for rent, and there is a nice disc golf course at the park. Hikers and bikers have 11 miles of trails, while horse riders have 6 miles. Lake Ovid is good for a swim and attracts anglers for muskie, largemouth and smallmouth bass, perch, and various panfish. Birders have recorded over 220 species here.

Southwest Michigan

If you're coming from the Chicagoland area, Michigan makes quite a first impression. The Lake Michigan coast is a show stealer with endless miles of sandy beaches and the dominant formation along those shores—the dunes.

These sands are the by-product of a lot of glacial grinding thousands of years ago. Over time and amid changing lake levels, these towering sands like frozen waves piled up along the eastern shore of the lake. Sleeping Bear Dunes are up north, but you don't need to drive that far for some sweeping mountains of sand. Warren Dunes State Park is just over 15 miles from the Indiana border and quite a sight to behold if you've never seen these inland dunes before. One of them reaches a height of 260 feet.

The naked dunes are joined by their overgrown brethren, such as the grassy dunes near Muskegon or the forested portions of Hoffmaster State Park. The beaches of Benton Harbor and Holland are spectacular and consequently quite popular.

But while the Lake Michigan coastline is impressive, don't overlook the treasures to the east, which shows a mix of forest and rolling farmland as well as popular swimming and fishing lakes and rolling hills that are great for hiking and biking. Yankee Springs offers a bit of the North Country National Scenic Trail and some of its own challenging trails, including a look down into the glacially formed Devil's Soup Bowl.

Kalamazoo and Grand Rapids are attractions in their own right. Holland hosts an annual tulip festival that is attended by hundreds of thousands of visitors in spring. Hikers can enjoy many miles of hiking trails within just an hour's drive in any direction from Grand Rapids at the top of this section, including segments of the North Country National Scenic Trail. The Lake Express car ferry from Milwaukee arrives at Muskegon and is just minutes from the state parks.

Go blueberry picking in the summer and visit some of the wineries or breweries. Pick-your-own fields of berries and vegetables are common throughout the area; roadside stands tout the bounty of this corner of the state. At the north end of this region, the southern reaches of the Huron-Manistee National Forests provide some rustic camping options.

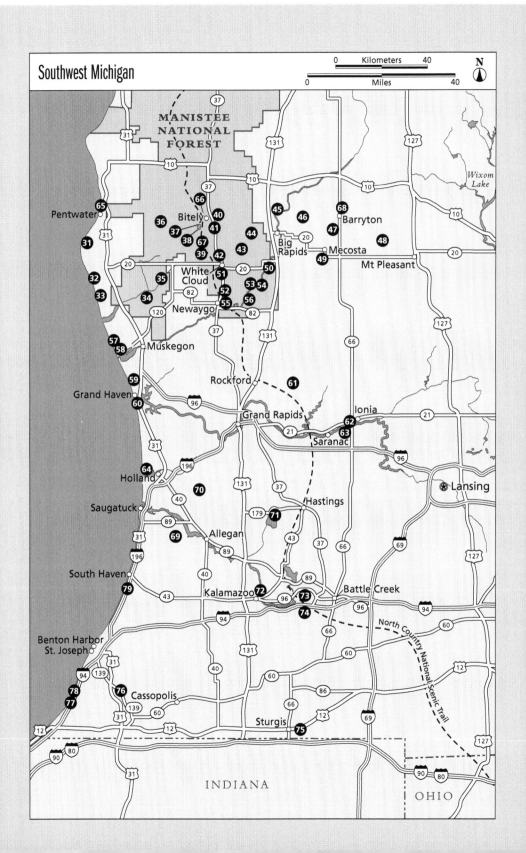

Whether you prefer big campgrounds that feel like summer festivals, such as Grand Haven, or secluded little rustic sites along internal lakes, such as a handful of sites along Minnie Pond, you have options here.

Grand Rapids Area

	Hookup Sites	Total Sites	Max RV Length	Hookups	Toilets	Showers	Drinking Water	Dump Station	Recreation	Fee	Reservations
31 Silver Lake State Park	200	200	40	E	F	Y	Y	Y	FHLOS	$$$$	Y
32 Claybanks Township Park	68	68	40	E	F	Y	Y	Y	S	$$$	Y
33 Meinert Park Campground (Muskegon County Parks)	67	67	45	WES	F	Y	Y	Y	S	$$$$	N
34 Blue Lake County Park	25	25	40	WE	F	Y	Y	Y	SFB	$$$$	N
35 Pines Point Campground—Huron-Manistee National Forests	0	29	40	N/A	F/NF	N	Y	N	HFC	$$	N
36 Black Lake County Park	11	14	35	E	NF	N	Y	N	SF	$-$$	N
37 Walkup Lake Campground	0	12	35	N/A	NF	N	Y	N	FBL	$	N
38 Nichols Lake South Campground	0	30	50	N/A	F	Y	Y	N	FSBL	$$	N
39 Minnie Pond Campground	0	11	25	N/A	NF	N	N	N	FBL	$	N
40 Shelley Lake Campground	0	8	25	N/A	NF	N	N	N	FBL	$$	N
41 Indian Lake Campground	0	6	25	N/A	NF	N	N	N	FBL	$$	N
42 Diamond Lake County Park	60	60	40	WES	F	Y	Y	Y	HSL	$$-$$$$	Y
43 Brush Lake Campground—Huron-Manistee National Forests	0	7	35	N/A	NF	N	N	N	FBL	$$	N
44 Hungerford Trail Camp—Huron-Manistee National Forests	0	48	80	N/A	NF	N	Y	N	HC	$$	N
45 Paris Park and Campgrounds	66	66	45	WE	F	Y	Y	Y	FBL	$$-$$$	Y
46 Haymarsh State Game Area and Campground	0	19	35	N/A	NF	N	Y	N	FL	$$	N
47 Tubbs Lake Campground	0	33	35	N/A	NF	N	Y	N	FL	$$	N
48 Coldwater Lake Family Park	95	95	45	W	F	Y	Y	Y	SFL	$$$	Y
49 School Section Lake Veteran's Park	162	162	45	WE	F	Y	Y	Y	FS	$$$-$$$$	Y
50 Brower Park	230	230	40	WES	F	Y	Y	Y	HSFL	$$$-$$$$	Y

	Hookup Sites	Total Sites	Max RV Length	Hookups	Toilets	Showers	Drinking Water	Dump Station	Recreation	Fee	Reservations
51 White Cloud Campground	76	80	40	E	NF	Y	Y	Y		HF	$$-$$$	Y
52 Twinwood Lake Campground	0	5	25	N/A	NF	N	N	N		FBL	$	N
53 Sandy Beach County Park	129	169	45	WES	F	Y	Y	Y		SL	$$-$$$$	Y
54 Newaygo State Park	0	99	40	N/A	NF	N	Y	Y		FLS	$$	Y
55 Ed H. Henning County Park	60	67	40	E	F	Y	Y	Y		HSFL	$$$$	Y
56 Croton Township Campground	151	159	40	E	F	Y	Y	Y		HL	$$-$$$	Y
57 Pioneer County Park	235	235	45	WE	F	Y	Y	Y		S	$$$$	N
58 Muskegon State Park	244	244	40	E	F	Y	Y	Y		FHLS	$$$$	Y
59 Hoffmaster State Park (P. J. Hoffmaster State Park)	293	293	40	WE	F	Y	Y	Y		HS	$$$-$$$$	Y
60 Grand Haven State Park	174	174	45	E	F	Y	Y	Y		FHS	$$$$	Y
61 Wabasis Lake Park	60	75	45	WES	F	Y	Y	Y		HSFL	$$$-$$$$	Y
62 Bertha Brock Park	0	23	25	N/A	NF	N	Y	N		H	$$	N
63 Ionia State Recreation Area	100	162	40	E	F	Y	Y	Y		FHLRS	$$$	Y
64 Holland State Park	309	309	50	WES	F	Y	Y	Y		FLS	$$$$	Y
65 Charles Mears State Park	175	175	40	E	F	Y	Y	Y		FHS	$$$$	Y
66 Highbank Lake Campground–Huron-Manistee National Forests	0	9	20	N/A	NF	N	Y	N		HL	$$	N
67 Benton Lake Campground	0	30	14x55	N/A	NF	N	Y		FHS		$-$$	N
68 Merrill-Gorrel Park	122	146	45	WE	F/NF	Y	Y	Y		SFL	$$-$$$	Y

See Amenities Charts Key on page xiii.

31 Silver Lake State Park

Location: About 30 miles south of Ludington

Season: March 30 to October 31

Sites: 200 sites with electrical hookups

Maximum RV length: 40

Facilities: Flush toilets, showers, grills, tables, picnic shelter, picnic area, dump station, boat launch, hiking/off-road trails, beach, beach house, lighthouse
Fee per night: $$$$
Management: Michigan DNR
Contact: (231) 873-3083; www.michigandnr.com/parksandtrails
Finding the campground: From Ludington head south on US 31 and take exit 149 toward Mears. Turn right (west) on Polk Road and left (south) on 56th Avenue 1.1 miles later. Turn right (west) on 4th Street/Fox Road and follow Fox 2.7 miles to turn left (south) on 34th Avenue. Follow this as it takes a curve right (west) onto Hazel Road and take Hazel until a traffic circle. Go left (south, third exit) onto Silver Lake Road and follow it to the camp entrance on the left (east) side of the road.
GPS coordinates: N 43 39.689' / W 86 29.752'
About the campground: Here are 3,000 acres of sand dunes and forest along a 4-mile stretch of beach on Lake Michigan. A 450-acre off-road vehicle area allows motorized dune climbing, while other areas are reserved for hikers. The nicely shaded campgrounds are set not on Lake Michigan but across the road from the day-use area on the eastern shore of Silver Lake behind the dunes. Get a ticket for the interpretive dune ride and see Little Sable Point light station. Other campground activities include hunting, metal detecting, and participating in the MI State Park Explorer Program. Alcohol is prohibited in the park.

32 Claybanks Township Park

Location: About 32 miles north of Muskegon
Season: May 1 to September 18
Sites: 68 sites with electrical hookups
Maximum RV length: 40
Facilities: Vault toilets, showers, water, tables, picnic shelter, dump station, beach, playground, volleyball court, horseshoe pits, firepits
Fee per night: $$$
Management: Claybanks Township
Contact: (231) 861-8885; www.claybankstownship.org/claybanks-township-park
Finding the campground: From US 31 about 20 miles north of Muskegon, take the Winston Road exit toward Rothbury. Go left (west) on Winston and take the first left (south) on 72nd Avenue. About 1 mile later go right (west) on Webster Road; 4.5 miles later it turns north and becomes Scenic Drive. The park entrance is 2.8 more miles on your left (west).
GPS coordinates: N 43 31.842' / W 86 29.108'
About the campground: Two long loops of sites run parallel to each other and Lake Michigan, but the campground is separated from the beach and lake by a narrow band of forest. Sites are generally out in the sun, with just a few sites that offer either a shade tree or two or very good tree cover.

The Little Sable Lighthouse at Silver Lake MATT FORSTER

33 Meinert Park Campground

Location: About 25 miles north of Muskegon
Season: May through September
Sites: 67 sites with full hookups
Maximum RV length: 45
Facilities: Flush toilets, tables, showers, picnic area, dump station, beach
Fee per night: $$$$
Management: Muskegon County Parks
Contact: (231) 744-3580 or (231) 894-4881; https://parksandrec.heresjoe.com/meinert-park
Finding the campground: Take US 31 to the Fruitvale Road exit and go right (west) on Fruitvale Road to Old 31; turn right (north) and follow Old 31 1 mile to Meinert Road; turn left (west). The park entrance is about 5 miles more at Lake Michigan.
GPS coordinates: N 43 27.552' / W 86 27.053'
About the campground: Lake Michigan shores are always a big attraction, and this county park offers a great stretch of sand and a parabolic dune while remaining a bit under the radar as compared to bigger state parks. Sites are arranged in 2 sections, 1 slightly closer to the lake than the other, but both a short walk to the beach. There are both shaded and sunny sites. Little Flower Creek flows to the lake here, and climbing the dune is allowed for a great scenic overlook.

34 Blue Lake County Park

Location: About 19 miles north of Muskegon
Season: May 15 to first Sunday after September 15
Sites: 25 sites with water and electrical hookups
Maximum RV length: 40
Facilities: Flush toilets, showers, picnic area, dump station, boat launch, beach, playground, shelter, ice, firewood, ranger service and security
Fee per night: $$$$
Management: Muskegon County Parks
Contact: (231) 894-5574; https://parksandrec.heresjoe.com/blue-lake-park
Finding the campground: From US 31 just north of Muskegon, take MI 120 north through Twin Lake. In town go left (north) on Main Street, which continues north out of town as Blue Lake Road. Five miles north take a left (west) on Owasippe Road and follow it 1 mile to the first right (north) on Nichols Road. A quarter mile takes you to Lake Street on the left (west) and the park entrance.
GPS coordinates: N 43 26.933' / W 86 11.585'
About the campground: Located along the southeast shore of Big Blue Lake, the 25-acre park has 600 feet of shoreline and open mowed-grass spaces for picnicking. The closest boat launch is at the north side of the lake at Deremo Access Site. It is good for fishing, but there is also water-skiing going on. The sites offer some partial shade or are completely sunny.

35 Pines Point Campground– Huron-Manistee National Forests

Location: About 8 miles southwest of Hesperia
Season: May 10 to October 7
Sites: 29 sites with no hookups
Maximum RV length: 40
Facilities: Flush/vault toilets, grills, water, tables, picnic area, lantern posts
Fee per night: $$
Management: Baldwin/White Cloud Ranger District
Contact: (231) 745-4631 or (877) 444-6777 for reservations; www.fs.usda.gov/recarea/hmnf/recreation/wateractivities/recarea?recid=18662&actid=83
Finding the campground: From MI 20 1 mile south of Hesperia turn right (west) on Garfield Road and drive 5 miles. Go left (south) on 168th Avenue 1.5 miles and the road becomes FR 5637, which takes you right to the site.
GPS coordinates: N 43 31.691' / W 86 07.230'
About the campground: This is a prime canoeing and tubing spot with a carry-in landing on the White River. Sites are shaded well by tall white pine, and in fact the clearance is medium. There are asphalt pads at each. Consider Kellogg Canoe Livery and Happy Mohawk Livery for canoe rentals. Anglers may find trout and salmon in the river.

36 Black Lake County Park

Location: About a 35-mile drive southeast of Ludington
Season: May 15 until October 1
Sites: 11 sites with electrical hookups, 3 sites with no hookups
Maximum RV length: 35
Facilities: Tables, picnic area, beach, playground, fire ring, boat launch
Fee per night: $–$$
Management: Oceana County
Contact: (231) 288-3285; www.oceana.mi.us/parks/black-lake-county-park
Finding the campground: About 15 miles south of Ludington on US 31, take the exit for Monroe Road and go east to the end at 144th Avenue. Go left (north) to Madison Road and head right (east) until 176th Avenue. Go right (south) here and the park entrance will be 1.8 miles on your right (west).
GPS coordinates: N 43 44.762' / W 86 07.109'
About the campground: Set on 100 acres alongside Black Lake, not far from Huron-Manistee National Forests, this is a really quiet spot, and even on summer weekends there are often spaces available. The sites are mostly shaded, and the fishing on the lake isn't bad. There is a playground for the kids and a swimming area. RVs still fit in, and a few recognize this little gem for what it's worth and book it for the season.

37 Walkup Lake Campground

Location: About 21 miles north of White Cloud
Season: Year-round
Sites: 12 sites with no hookups
Maximum RV length: 35
Facilities: Vault toilets, tables, water, lantern posts, trash can, boat ramp
Fee per night: $
Management: Baldwin/White Cloud Ranger District
Contact: (231) 745-4631; www.fs.usda.gov/recarea/hmnf/recreation/wateractivities/recarea?recid=18890&actid=78
Finding the campground: From White Cloud go north 16.5 miles on MI 37. Turn left (west) on 14 Mile Road and continue a mile to turn left (south) on Bingham Avenue. Take the third right (west) on Main Street/Cleveland Drive to the park entrance on the right (north) side of the road.
GPS coordinates: N 43 43.992' / W 85 54.324'
About the campground: A decent rustic campground, the sites are on a gravel loop and offer good shade. A gravel boat ramp gives access for anglers with motorized and nonmotorized craft. While camping is possible year-round, the roads are not plowed in winter. The lake has private land on one side, so it is not a lost-in-the-woods lake. Use the self-pay tube for fees. This is just north of Nichols Lake and Nichols Lake South Campground and the North Country Trail.

38 Nichols Lake South Campground

Location: About 21 miles north of White Cloud
Season: Mid-May through September
Sites: 30 sites with no hookups
Maximum RV length: 50
Facilities: Flush/vault toilets, tables, fire rings, water, hiking trails, fishing pier, boat ramp
Fee per night: $$
Management: Baldwin/White Cloud Ranger District
Contact: (231) 745-4631; www.fs.usda.gov/recarea/hmnf/recarea?recid=18896
Finding the campground: Travel north from White Cloud 13 miles on MI 37. Go left (west) on 11 Mile Road for 4.2 miles and the campground is on the right.
GPS coordinates: N 43 42.774' / W 85 54.428'
About the campground: Part of Huron-Manistee National Forests, this is a popular spot for family campers located on the south side of Nichols Lake. Camping pull-ins are paved, and sites offer good shade. Fishing is especially nice, and those with kids appreciate that the shoreline trails and the pier offer easy non-boat access for fishing. Both motorized and nonmotorized boats are permitted. The North Country National Scenic Trail passes right through here.

39 Minnie Pond Campground

Location: About 13 miles northwest of White Cloud
Season: Year-round
Sites: 11 sites with no hookups
Maximum RV length: 25
Facilities: Vault toilets, lantern posts, boat ramp, picnic area
Fee per night: $
Management: Baldwin/White Cloud Ranger District
Contact: (231) 745-4631; www.fs.usda.gov/recarea/hmnf/recreation/wateractivities/recarea?recid=18870&actid=82
Finding the campground: Go north from White Cloud on MI 37 and take MI 20 (1 Mile Road) left (west) 7.4 miles to turn right (north) on Luce Avenue. Take this for 3 miles and turn right (east) on 4 Mile Road, continue 0.5 mile and turn left (north) on Alger Avenue. At 1 mile past the entrance for the day-use area on the right (east), cross Mena Creek and take the next forest road right (east) and follow it into the camping area.
GPS coordinates: N 43 37.657' / W 85 53.959'
About the campground: Tucked into the forest near a small lake—and a bit tricky to find—is this small rustic site best suited for anglers and those looking to really get away from it all. The roads are undeveloped and the services very limited. A footbridge over Mena Creek connects the camping area to the day-use area to the south. Fishing is for bass, bluegill, and pike. Both motorized and nonmotorized boats are permitted.

40 Shelley Lake Campground

Location: About 13 miles north of White Cloud
Season: Year-round
Sites: 8 sites with no hookups
Maximum RV length: 25
Facilities: Vault toilets, trash can, boat ramp
Fee per night: $$
Management: Baldwin/White Cloud Ranger District
Contact: (231) 745-4631; www.fs.usda.gov/recarea/hmnf/recreation/wateractivities/recarea?recid=18882&actid=78
Finding the campground: Go north 10 miles on MI 37 and turn right (east) on FR 5450. The primitive road to the sites is 0.5 mile down the forest road. Follow the primitive road to the sites.
GPS coordinates: N 43 42.764' / W 85 48.661'
About the campground: Many of the lakes in this section of the book have at least some development on them, but not this one. If you are looking for your own private fishing hole, this 15-acre lake surrounded by national forest might do. This is primitive camping, and campers must bring their own water. Be aware the roads are primitive as well, and the boat launch is carry-in. Long or low-clearance vehicles are not recommended. Sites are shaded by maples and oaks. Fishing is for bass and bluegill. Both motorized and nonmotorized boats are permitted.

41 Indian Lake Campground

Location: About 7 miles north of White Cloud
Season: Year-round
Sites: 6 sites with no hookups
Maximum RV length: 25
Facilities: Vault toilets, boat ramp
Fee per night: $$
Management: Baldwin/White Cloud Ranger District
Contact: (231) 745-4631; www.fs.usda.gov/recarea/hmnf/recarea?recid=18868
Finding the campground: From White Cloud go north on MI 37 about 10 miles, then turn left (west) on Center Street. Take the immediate first left (south) and follow it as it curves west. Watch for Nagek Drive on the left (south) side of the road and take that right into the campground.
GPS coordinates: N 43 40.358' / W 85 49.426'
About the campground: These are very primitive numbered sites in a wooded area at the edge of Huron-Manistee National Forests. The lake is clear and excellent for bass fishing. Be aware there is no water at the campground. It's a great rustic experience and especially nice for anglers. Both motorized and nonmotorized boats are permitted.

42 Diamond Lake County Park

Location: About 6 miles northwest of White Cloud
Season: About mid-May through September
Sites: 24 sites with water, sewer, and electrical hookups; 36 sites with electrical hookups
Maximum RV length: 40
Facilities: Flush/vault toilets, showers, picnic area, dump station, boat launch, hiking trails, beach, playground, volleyball court, horseshoe pits, boat rental, shelter
Fee per night: $$-$$$$
Management: Newaygo County Parks
Contact: (231) 689-7340; www.countyofnewaygo.com/ParksAndRecreation.aspx
Finding the campground: From White Cloud take MI 37 north from town and follow it as it curves west. Just after 5 miles, before it turns north again, take Foss Avenue left (south) 0.3 mile until a T-juncture. Turn right (northwest) and continue 0.3 mile to Mundy Avenue. Turn right (north) and follow it 1 mile to the camp entrance on the left (west) side of the road.
GPS coordinates: N 43 36.874' / W 85 48.683'
About the campground: This park has 156 wooded acres with a lot of shoreline on Diamond Lake. Bordering land is national forest. Sites are arranged in 3 loops from the entrance with a few random sites spread throughout. They are all set back away from the water, well shaded. Some of them offer more privacy than others, though all are rather spacious. Sites 17–26 in their own exposed loop are the least shaded and are often given to a couple rows of larger campers/RVs.

43 Brush Lake Campground– Huron-Manistee National Forests

Location: About 14 miles west of Big Rapids
Season: Year-round
Sites: 7 sites with no hookups
Maximum RV length: 35 or less
Facilities: Vault toilets, boat launch
Fee per night: $$
Management: Baldwin/White Cloud Ranger District
Contact: (231) 745-4631; www.fs.usda.gov/recarea/hmnf/recreation/wateractivities/recarea?recid=18854&actid=82
Finding the campground: From US 131/MI 20 on the west side of Big Rapids, take 15 Mile Road/Perry Avenue west 5 miles (it becomes 9 Mile Road) and then keep left at a fork in the road as it turns onto Cypress Avenue. Go another mile south then turn right (west) on 8 Mile Road, continuing another mile to go left (south) on Elm Avenue. Take this 2 miles to turn right (west) on 6 Mile Road, driving 2.6 miles to go left (south) on FR 5534 on your left (south). Follow this into the campground.
GPS coordinates: N 43 38.329' / W 85 41.392'
About the campground: This campground, surrounded by national forest, is most popular with the hunting and fishing crowd. The boat launch here is small for carry-in, but a larger ramp is located on the east side of the river. Both motorized and nonmotorized boats are permitted. Most sites offer good shade with a little sunshine coming through at midday. The season is annual, but management is only here May through September.

44 Hungerford Trail Camp– Huron-Manistee National Forests

Location: About 9 miles west of Big Rapids
Season: April 13 to November 1
Sites: 48
Maximum RV length: 80
Facilities: Vault toilets, water, hiking/mountain biking/equestrian trails, picket poles, manure disposal area, wheelbarrows, garbage service
Fee per night: $$
Management: Baldwin/White Cloud Ranger District
Contact: (231) 745-4631; www.fs.usda.gov/recarea/hmnf/recarea/?recid=18752
Finding the campground: From Big Rapids head west on MI 20 for 8.5 miles and go right (north) on Cypress Avenue for 0.5 mile. Go right (east) on Hungerford Lake Drive for 0.5 mile. Turn left (north) on FR 5134 and drive 1 mile and the camp is on the left.
GPS coordinates: N 43 42.087' / W 85 37.327'

About the campground: Horse riders and mountain bikers know this camp, and in summer it can be quite busy. A big loop tucked in among the trees of the national forest, the campground meets the trailheads for both interests. There are over 35 miles of horse trails in the Hungerford Recreation Area. Bikers have 2 loops totaling 10 miles. The camp, like the trails, is sheltered by oak, maple, aspen, and red and white pine.

45 Paris Park and Campgrounds

Location: About 8 miles north of Big Rapids
Season: May through September
Sites: 66 sites with water and electrical hookups
Maximum RV length: 45
Facilities: Flush toilets, showers, tables, picnic shelter, picnic area, dump station, boat launch, playground, fishing pier, volleyball court, horseshoes, firepits, bicycle rental
Fee per night: $$–$$$
Management: Mecosta County Parks
Contact: (231) 796-3420; www.mecostacountyparks.com/paris-park.html
Finding the campground: From Big Rapids take US 131 north to exit 142 and go right (east) on 19 Mile Road (Business US 131). At 1.2 miles go left (north) on Northland Drive for 3.1 miles and the park entrance is on the right (east) side of the road.
GPS coordinates: N 43 47.227' / W 85 30.168'
About the campground: These 40 acres were once a state fish hatchery along the Muskegon River. The sites have good shade cover and are set along 3 contiguous loops. The park has access to the river, which is nice for paddling, as well as the White Pine Trail that goes right past the entrance. There are also 3 cabins. It's a busy park, so reservations are a good idea.

46 Haymarsh State Game Area and Campground

Location: About 11 miles northeast of Big Rapids
Season: April to October
Sites: 19 sites with no hookups
Maximum RV length: 35
Facilities: Vault toilets, water, boat launch, hiking trails
Fee per night: $$
Management: Mecosta County
Contact: (231) 832-3246; www.mecostacountyparks.com/haymarsh-lake.html
Finding the campground: From Big Rapids take MI 20 east to 165th Avenue and turn left (north). Stay on this as it curves a bit, becoming Sumac Drive, and straightens out north once again as 160th Avenue. Turn right (east) on 21 Mile Road and stay on that, turning right when it forks with 140th Avenue, and then turning right (south) on 140th Avenue a short distance later, where 140th will take you right into the park.
GPS coordinates: N 43 45.777' / W 85 21.790'

About the campground: Once a chain of 6 lakes, Haymarsh Lake was created in 1949 by a dam and now offers 375 acres of surface water. Anglers love the lake; hunters come for the good game. (Hunting permitted beginning October 1.) These nicely shaded rustic sites are spread out north to south along the west shore of the lake. The boat launch is at the southern end of the park, but be aware some of the park roads can be rough and potholed. No reservations taken, and you have to use the self-pay station.

47 Tubbs Lake Campground

Location: About 7 miles southwest of Barryton
Season: Year-round
Sites: 33 sites with no hookups
Maximum RV length: 35
Facilities: Vault toilets, fire rings, water, tables, boat launch
Fee per night: $$
Management: Michigan DNR
Contact: (231) 775-9727; www.michigandnr.com/parksandtrails
Finding the campground: From Barryton go south 2.8 miles on MI 66 and turn right (west) on 17 Mile Road, traveling 1.5 miles to 45th Avenue. Turn left (south) and take the first right (west) on Madison Road. Go 1.2 miles to Birch Haven Drive and turn right (north) and follow to the campground.
GPS coordinates: N 43 42.550' / W 85 11.655'
About the campground: Beavers were the first to flood this area, and the DNR followed suit in the 1950s, building a dam to flood 1,420 acres and create the Martiny Chain of Lakes on the Chippewa River. Sites are either on the mainland or an island connected by a narrow strip to the rest of the park. The park is set back from the larger lake, which has a large private campground on its southern shore and private development. While still on the narrow water channels, this is not a deep-woods experience. Tubbs Lake has naturally occurring wild rice, a rarity these days. Wildlife viewing is a favorite pastime here.

48 Coldwater Lake Family Park

Location: About 14 miles northwest of Mt. Pleasant
Season: May to September/mid-October
Sites: 95 sites with hookups, 8 pull-through sites
Maximum RV length: 45
Facilities: Flush toilets, showers, grills, tables, picnic shelter, picnic area, dump station, boat launch, beach, playground, volleyball court, horseshoe pits, concessionaire, beach pavilion, basketball court
Fee per night: $$$
Management: Isabella County
Contact: (989) 317-4083; www.isabellacounty.org/departments/parks-recreation

Finding the campground: Take MI 20 west from Mt. Pleasant 7 miles to Winn Road. Go right (north) 4 miles and turn left (west) on Jordan Road. At 1.9 miles go right (north) on Littlefield Road and go 0.8 mile to the park entrance on the left (west).

GPS coordinates: N 43 39.873' / W 84 56.927'

About the campground: A nice family-friendly park, Coldwater is on the eastern shores of the lake of the same name. Sites 11–22 are closest to the water. The playground is grand like a fortress and the beach is nice for kids. The sites are under mature trees for good shade. A few small cabins are spread throughout the sites as well.

49 School Section Lake Veteran's Park

Location: About 4 miles south and west of Mecosta

Season: May through September

Sites: 162 sites with water and electrical hookups

Maximum RV length: 45

Facilities: Flush toilets, showers, tables, picnic shelter, picnic area, dump station, boat launch, beach, playground, fish-cleaning station, volleyball court, horseshoe pits, boat rental, concession-aire, firepits, basketball court, disc golf, baseball diamond, Ping-Pong table

Fee per night: $$$-$$$$

Management: Mecosta County Parks

Contact: (231) 972-7450; www.mecostacountyparks.com/school-section-lake-veterans-park.html

Finding the campground: From Mecosta head south 1.6 miles on MI 20/Cass Street, turn right (west) on 9 Mile Road and follow it 2 miles right into the park.

GPS coordinates: N 43 35.874' / W 85 15.894'

About the campground: You'll pass an old schoolhouse at the entrance as the park road curves around a recreation field with a couple of ball diamonds. For a campground, this sure has a lot of extra activities, and the camp office even has some equipment that campers can borrow for free. The sites are partly shaded, as is the picnic area. The sandy beach is a short walk from the sites and curves around a small bay on School Section Lake.

50 Brower Park

Location: About 14 miles south of Big Rapids

Season: April through October

Sites: 230 sites with water and electrical hookups

Maximum RV length: 40

Facilities: Flush toilets, firepits, showers, tables, picnic area, dump station, boat launch, beach, playground, fishing pier, fish-cleaning station, volleyball court, horseshoe pits, basketball court, tennis court, ball field, disc golf, concessionaire

Fee per night: $$$-$$$$

Management: Mecosta County

Contact: (231) 823-2561; www.mecostacountyparks.com/brower-park.html
Finding the campground: From west of Big Rapids take US 131/MI 20 south 7.4 miles and take exit 131. Go right (west) on MI 20/8 Mile Road and then take the first left (southwest) on Old State Road; 1.9 miles later it continues as Polk Road going due west and heads straight into the park.
GPS coordinates: N 43 33.726' / W 85 32.660'
About the campground: The park has 280 acres right along the Muskegon River above the Hardy Dam. The river is the main attraction, good for fishing, boating, paddling, and even waterskiing. The campsite has shade trees spread throughout the sites, offering at least partial shelter from the sun. The sites are right along the river at a bend in its path.

51 White Cloud Campground

Location: Right in White Cloud
Season: Year-round
Sites: 76 sites without electrical hookups, 4 with no hookups
Maximum RV length: 40
Facilities: Vault toilets, water, tables, picnic area, playground, fire rings
Fee per night: $$–$$$
Management: Newaygo County Parks
Contact: (231) 689-7340; www.countyofnewaygo.com/ParksAndRecreation.aspx
Finding the campground: From the intersection of MI 20/Wilcox Avenue and MI 37/Charles Street at the center of White Cloud, go west on Wilcox Avenue 0.7 mile and the park is on the left (south) side of the road.
GPS coordinates: N 43 33.003' / W 85 47.106'
About the campground: Situated along the little meandering White River, this collection of wooded sites was once actually a state and then a city park before being taken up by the county park system. The sites vary in size, and they are all wide open, so you can always see the neighbors and, in fact, most of the other campers. The 89 acres are convenient for their location right next to White Cloud, and the River Walk offers nice strolls with the sound of running water. The park connects to the North Country National Scenic Trail via a feeder trail. White Cloud itself is a great jumping-off point for an abundance of area campgrounds, all of it within about an hour of Grand Rapids. Hunting is permitted in season.

52 Twinwood Lake Campground

Location: About 5 miles south of White Cloud
Season: Year-round but partially maintained during winter
Sites: 5 sites with no hookups
Maximum RV length: 25
Facilities: Vault toilets, tables, boat ramp, lantern posts, trash can
Fee per night: $

Management: Baldwin/White Cloud Ranger District

Contact: (231) 745-4631; www.fs.usda.gov/recarea/hmnf/null/recarea?recid=18886&actid=42

Finding the campground: From White Cloud head south on MI 37 just under 5 miles and go left (east) on 40th Street. Take the first right (south) on Basswood Drive and then the first left on FR 5448. The camp is 0.3 mile down this road.

GPS coordinates: N 43 28.564' / W 85 46.054'

About the campground: On a small lake in Huron-Manistee National Forests, this small collection of primitive campsites offers a quiet escape and plenty of wildlife viewing. The trees are mostly white pine, and the sites are shaded. Eagles have been known to nest in the area, and swans may show up on the water. Bigelow Creek flows into the lake nearby. The roads are primitive as well, so big rigs with low clearance are not a good idea here. The boat ramp is gravel. Fishing is for bass and bluegill. Both motorized and nonmotorized boats are permitted.

53 Sandy Beach County Park

Location: About 13 miles northeast of Newaygo

Season: May to October

Sites: 26 sites with full hookups (19 pull-through), 75 sites with water and electrical hookups, 28 sites with electrical hookups, 40 sites with no hookups

Maximum RV length: 45

Facilities: Flush toilets, showers, tables, picnic area, dump station, boat launch, beach, playground, dock rentals

Fee per night: $$–$$$$

Management: Newaygo County Parks

Contact: (231) 689-1229; www.countyofnewaygo.com/ParksAndRecreation.aspx

Finding the campground: From MI 37 just 4 miles north of Newaygo, take 40th Street east 4.6 miles; follow it as it curves left (north) and then right (east) again, becoming 36th Street. At 1.9 miles from the curve, turn left (north) on Elm Avenue; go 0.8 mile and take the first right (east) on 30th Street. Follow this right to the campground.

GPS coordinates: N 43 30.010' / W 85 37.797'

About the campground: This county park is set on the western shore of the Hardy Dam Pond, a 6-mile-long body of water on the dammed Muskegon River. Most of the sites offer at least partial shade. The rustic sites are backed up against the trees on the west side of the park, the farthest from the water (though it isn't far anyway). Newaygo State Park lies straight across the water from here.

54 Newaygo State Park

Location: About 15 miles northeast of Newaygo

Season: April 1 to October 31

Sites: 99 sites with no hookups

Maximum RV length: 40

Facilities: Vault toilets, fire ring, tables, dump station, picnic area, boat launch, beach, playground
Fee per night: $$
Management: Michigan DNR
Contact: (231) 856-4452; www.michigandnr.com/parksandtrails
Finding the campground: From Newaygo go north on MI 37/Evergreen Drive for 4.4 miles and turn right (east) on 40th Street. At 4.6 miles it curves north on Pine Avenue for 0.3 mile, then curves right (east) again on 36th Street. Continue 2.2 miles and the road bends right (south) under the lake and up again. Go 1.5 miles more and turn left (north) on Beech Avenue and follow it to the park entrance.
GPS coordinates: N 43 29.840' / W 85 34.935'
About the campground: The Hardy Dam on the Muskegon River created this 6-mile "pond," which makes for some good fishing. Sites are spacious and private thanks to good distances and brush in between them, and the oak and poplar provide good shade. There are better choices for kids if they need distraction, but White Pine Trail State Park isn't far for hikers and bikers.

55 Ed H. Henning County Park

Location: Less than 1 mile east of Newaygo
Season: April 22 to October 16
Sites: 60 sites with electrical hookups, 7 tent-only sites 5 with no hookups
Maximum RV length: 40
Facilities: Flush toilets, showers, picnic area, dump station, boat launch, hiking/mountain biking/equestrian trails, beach, beach house, playground, nature center, fishing pier, fish-cleaning station, volleyball court, Wi-Fi, baseball, tennis court, soccer field
Fee per night: $$$-$$$$
Management: Newaygo County
Contact: (231) 689-7340; www.countyofnewaygo.com/ParksAndRecreation.aspx
Finding the campground: Head north out of Newaygo on MI 37/MI 82 and turn right (east) on State Road/Croton Drive. At 0.3 mile turn right (south) on Shaw Park Drive and it will take you right into the park.
GPS coordinates: N 43 25.314' / W 85 47.461'
About the campground: So close to town, the park is quite convenient. The sites area is arranged in 3 loops like the petals of a flower. They are rather open and sunny, though some shade is provided by intermittent trees and by the surrounding woods for the campsites on the north and east external sides of the loops. A boat launch grants access to the Muskegon River for paddlers, anglers, and even waterskiing.

56 Croton Township Campground

Location: About 8 miles east of Newaygo
Season: Mid-April through mid-October
Sites: 151 sites with electrical hookups, 8 sites without hookups

A dune overlook toward the lighthouse at Muskegon State Park

Maximum RV length: 40
Facilities: Flush toilets, fire rings, table, showers, water, picnic area, dump station, boat launch, hiking trails, beach, playground
Fee per night: $$-$$$
Management: Croton Township
Contact: (231) 652-4642; www.crotontownshipcampground.com
Finding the campground: From MI 37 in downtown Newaygo, take Croton Drive east for 8 miles. When you cross the lake causeway, look for the park entrance on the other side on your left (north).
GPS coordinates: N 43 26.791' / W 85 39.477'
About the campground: Situated above the dam at Croton Pond, this campground features 2 boat launches. Sites are spacious and shaded by abundant trees. The park offers many events and activities, and there are nearby options as well, such as Conklin Park, for a Frisbee golf course, tennis courts, a softball field, playground equipment, a volleyball court, the Muskegon River for boating and paddling, and several hiking trails, including the North Country Trail.

57 Pioneer County Park

Location: About 8 miles northeast of Muskegon
Season: Year-round
Sites: 235 sites with water and electrical hookups
Maximum RV length: 45
Facilities: Flush toilets, showers, tables, picnic shelter, picnic area, dump station, beach, playground, horseshoe pits, basketball court, tennis court, baseball field, volleyball court, tourist information, ranger service and security
Fee per night: $$$$
Management: Muskegon County Parks
Contact: (231) 744-3580; www.muskegoncountyparks.org/pioneer-park
Finding the campground: From just north of Muskegon, take US 31 to the Fremont/Big Rapids (MI 120) exit, go southwest on MI 120 to Giles Road, turn right (west) on Giles and follow it 5 miles to the end of the road. Turn right (north) on Scenic Drive and the park entrance is 0.3 mile on the left.
GPS coordinates: N 43 16.927' / W 86 21.710'
About the campground: This is Muskegon's most popular county park, and with 2,000 feet of beach on Lake Michigan, that's not surprising. There is a dune boardwalk with some scenic overlooks and stairs that lead down to the shoreline from the tops of the dunes. The campground has a lot of sites in one place, so privacy might not be enough for some campers, but tree coverage provides ample shade for hot summer days. There is an amusement park and many other activities nearby, and the magnificent Muskegon State Park is just to the south.

58 Muskegon State Park

Location: About 4 miles west of North Muskegon
Season: Year-round
Sites: 244 with electrical hookups
Maximum RV length: 40
Facilities: Flush toilets, showers, tables, picnic shelter, picnic area, dump station, boat launch, hiking trails, beach, beach house, playground, fishing pier, fish-cleaning station, luge run
Fee per night: $$$$
Management: Michigan DNR
Contact: (231) 744-3480; www.michigandnr.com/parksandtrails
Finding the campground: Just north of where MI 120 crosses the causeway (just north of the Business US 31 juncture), go left (southwest) on Lake Avenue. Follow this 0.6 mile and take the slight right onto Center Street and then the third left (southwest) onto Ruddiman Drive for 2.6 miles. It becomes Memorial Drive. Stay on Memorial (even as it bends right [north] and then left [west] again after 0.6 mile) and continue right into the park.
GPS coordinates: N 43 15.062' / W 86 19.931'
About the campground: A fantastic state park on Lake Michigan and Lake Muskegon, the 1,200-plus acres include 2 campgrounds, dunes, a sweeping beach on the big lake, and miles

Lost Lake at Muskegon State Park

of fantastic hiking. Channel Campground lies at the southern edge along a ship channel that connects the big lake to the small. Sites are partly shaded, and of the 2 loops the more eastern of them is a bit more private. This is also right under the rolling dunes and their trails. The Lake Michigan Campground is along the big lake and at the north end of the park. Sites are decently shaded and spacious. Metal detecting, wildlife viewing, and cross-country skiing are popular pastimes here. Alcohol is not permitted in the park.

59 Hoffmaster State Park

Location: About 10 miles south of Muskegon
Season: May 13 to September 8, October 3 to October 6
Sites: 293 sites with water and electrical hookups
Maximum RV length: 40
Facilities: Flush toilets, showers, grills, water, tables, picnic shelter, picnic area, dump station, hiking trails, beach, beach house, nature center, concessionaire, firepits, group use area, visitor center, observation platform, year-round interpretive programs

A beach trail to Lake Michigan at Hoffmaster State Park

The beach at Hoffmaster State Park

Fee per night: $$$$
Management: Michigan DNR
Contact: (231) 798-3711; www.michigandnr.com/parksandtrails
Finding the campground: From US 31 take Pontaluna Road west to the end where it curves north and becomes Lake Harbor Road. The first park entrance on your left (west) is for the day-use area. Continue a few hundred feet on Lake Harbor for the camping entrance.
GPS coordinates: N 43 08.209' / W 86 16.114'
About the campground: With some great dune trails and overlooks and 3 miles of shoreline on Lake Michigan, this is an excellent park for camping. Sites are well shaded and spread out nicely for a bit of privacy. The day-use beach access does not pass through the campgrounds. The Gillette Sand Dunes Visitor Center offers a good education about the dune environment. The hiking here is top-notch. Metal detecting, wildlife viewing, and cross-country skiing are popular pastimes here. Alcohol is prohibited in the park.

60 Grand Haven State Park

Location: Just outside Grand Haven, about 1 mile from US 31
Season: Year-round
Sites: 174 with electrical hookups
Maximum RV length: 45
Facilities: Flush toilets, showers, grills, tables, picnic shelter, picnic area, dump station, hiking trails, beach, beach house, playground, concessionaire, lighthouse, firepits
Fee per night: $$$$

The pier and beach at Grand Haven State Park

Management: Michigan DNR
Contact: (616) 847-1309; www.michigandnr.com/parksandtrails
Finding the campground: From US 31 through the center of Grand Haven, take Jackson Avenue west and follow it 1.7 miles as it curves south (becoming Harbor Drive). The park is on the right (west) side of the road right on the beach.
GPS coordinates: N 43 03.431' / W 86 14.765'
About the campground: The main attractions here are obviously Lake Michigan, the long pier, and the Grand Haven Lighthouse. The beach is beautiful and busy, and the park is right at the edge of town. However, the modern sites, set back from the beach but in sight of the water, feel more like a crowded, shadeless parking lot. This will be fine for some big rigs but less attractive for tents, especially when the asphalt heats up in summer. Metal detecting and cross-country skiing are popular pastimes here. Alcohol is not permitted in the park.

61 Wabasis Lake Park

Location: About 10 miles east of Rockford
Season: May through October
Sites: 15 sites with full hookups, 45 sites with electrical hookups, 15 sites with no hookups
Maximum RV length: 45
Facilities: Flush toilets, showers, grills, water, tables, picnic shelter, picnic area, dump station, boat launch, beach, playground, concessionaire, fire rings, basketball courts, ball diamonds, laundry facilities
Fee per night: $$$-$$$$

Management: Kent County Parks
Contact: (616) 691-8056; www.kentcountyparks.org/wabasislakecampground/index.php
Finding the campground: From Rockford go east for 7.6 miles on 10 Mile Road. Turn left (north) on Wabasis Avenue and continue 1.2 miles and turn right (east) on Springhill Drive. At 0.2 mile take another right (south) to stay on Springhill Drive, which takes you right to the park.
GPS coordinates: N 43 08.114' / W 85 23.551'
About the campground: Just a short drive from Grand Rapids, this campground on a small lake is a nice retreat from the city life. The modern sites include some with paved pads. The primitive campsites, next to a rentable cabin, are the closest to the lake and enjoy good tree cover. The walk-in sites are away from the lake and deeper into the woods. At midday most of the modern sites have pretty good sun exposure.

62 Bertha Brock Park

Location: About 3 miles west of Ionia
Season: Memorial Day Weekend through October
Sites: 23 sites with no hookups
Maximum RV length: 25
Facilities: Vault toilets, water, fire rings, tables, picnic area, hiking trails, playground, tennis court, baseball field, softball field, telephone, accessible table, disc golf course
Fee per night: $$
Management: Ionia County Parks
Contact: (616) 522-7275; www.ioniacounty.org/departments-officials/parks-recreation/bertha-brock-park
Finding the campground: From Ionia go west 3 miles on MI 21 and turn left (south) on Bertha Brock Drive.
GPS coordinates: N 42 58.613' / W 85 07.196'
About the campground: A nice county park in the woods, Bertha Brock also has a lot of non-camping activities. A disc golf course was added in 2012. The campsites are all rustic and well shaded, and they are spread out a bit for some privacy. The picnic area lies next to a trout stream. There are over 4 miles of hiking trails and 3 stone bridges, as well as a historic lodge.

63 Ionia State Recreation Area

Location: About 4 miles east of Saranac
Season: Year-round
Sites: 100 sites with electrical hookups, 46 sites without hookups, 16 rustic hike-in sites
Maximum RV length: 40
Facilities: Flush toilets, showers, grills, tables, picnic shelter, picnic area, dump station, boat launch, hiking/mountain biking/equestrian trails, beach, beach house, playground, fishing pier, horseshoe pits, ball field, dog trial area

Fee per night: $$$

Management: Michigan DNR

Contact: (616) 527-3750; www.michigandnr.com/parksandtrails

Finding the campground: From Saranac (just south of MI 21) take Mill Street east from downtown and it will become David Highway. At 4 miles look for the park entrance at Jordan Lake Road on the left (north) side of David Highway.

GPS coordinates: N 42 55.789' / W 85 08.047'

About the campground: The centerpiece of the park is Sessions Lake, created by damming a river. But the surrounding hills of woods and meadows offer a fine network of trails. The campsites, on the east side of the lake, are staggered a bit for some privacy, and some shade is also provided. It's a good park for active folks. Birders have nearly 200 species to look for here. The lake is popular with Canada geese, which can have a serious impact on how attractive the water is for swimming. Metal detecting, paddling, cross-country skiing, and snowmobiling are popular pastimes here. Hunting is permitted in season.

64 Holland State Park

Location: About 6 miles west of downtown Holland

Season: April through October (slightly shorter for the Beach Campground)

Sites: 278 sites with electrical hookups, 31 sites with full hookups

Maximum RV length: 50

Facilities: Flush toilets, showers, grills, tables, picnic shelter, picnic area, dump station, boat launch, beach, beach house, playground, fishing pier, fish-cleaning station, concessionaire, firepits, lighthouse

Fee per night: $$$$

Management: Michigan DNR

Contact: (616) 399-9390; www.michigandnr.com/parksandtrails

Finding the campground: From US 31 through Holland, take the Lakewood Boulevard exit and go west on Lakewood. Stay on this as it becomes Douglas Avenue and then Ottawa Beach Road before arriving at the Macatawa Lake camp entrance about 6.7 miles from the highway on the right (north) side of the road.

GPS coordinates: N 42 46.750' / W 86 11.934'

About the campground: This Lake Michigan state park is divided into 2 campgrounds. The modern sites at the Beach Campground situated north of the channel between Lake Macatawa and Lake Michigan are closer to the bigger lake's beach but offer less shade and more of a packed-in, parking lot experience. Lake Macatawa has more shade trees among its 211 sites (especially in the Pines Loop to the north), and its beach, which is right across Ottawa Beach Road, is actually on the smaller lake. Lake Michigan is a long walk or hike, or a short drive to the other side. Metal detecting is a popular pastime here. Alcohol is prohibited in the park.

The red lighthouse at Holland State Park

65 Charles Mears State Park

Location: Right inside Pentwater on Lake Michigan
Season: Year-round
Sites: 175 sites with hookups
Maximum RV length: 40
Facilities: Flush toilets, showers, grills, fire circles, water, tables, picnic shelter, picnic area, dump station, hiking trails, beach, beach house, playground, concessionaire, lighthouse
Fee per night: $$$$
Management: Michigan DNR
Contact: (231) 869-2051; www.michigandnr.com/parksandtrails
Finding the campground: US 31 passes by Pentwater to the east. Follow Business US 31 into Pentwater and find Lowell Street heading west just north of Pentwater Lake. Follow this right to the park.
GPS coordinates: N 43 46.913' / W 86 26.354'
About the campground: This is a popular park due to its fine sand beaches and easy access. The campground is 4 parallel loops with paved sites set back from the beach area, and not all sites are very well shaded. The park becomes very busy in summer, when an ample number of events are hosted here. Reservations are a must. Hikers have a 1-mile interpretive trail. Metal detecting is a popular pastime here.

66 Highbank Lake Campground– Huron-Manistee National Forests

Location: About 20 miles north of White Cloud
Season: May through September
Sites: 9 sites with no hookups
Maximum RV length: 20
Facilities: Vault toilets, water, fire rings, hiking trails, beach, boat ramp, lantern posts
Fee per night: $$
Management: Baldwin/White Cloud Ranger Station
Contact: (231) 745-4631; www.fs.usda.gov/recarea/hmnf/recarea/?recid=18864
Finding the campground: From White Cloud head north on MI 37 about 17 miles and turn left (west) on 15 Mile Road. A half mile later turn right (north) on Bingham Avenue and take the first slight left (northwest) on Roosevelt Drive going 1 mile, and then watch for another left (west) turn to stay on Roosevelt. This becomes Jerome Drive, but it's only 0.5 mile to the camp entrance on the right (west) side of the road.
GPS coordinates: N 43 46.355' / W 85 53.209'
About the campground: Set on 20-acre Highbank Lake, this is a popular site for anglers, and use is heavy. Sites are first come, first served. Tucked into the national park, these 9 rustic sites are private, with abundant shade. The road in is gravel, the clearance is low, and the sites are too

small for much more than a small trailer. The swimming beach has a sandy bottom, and the lake offers panfish, bass, and bluegill.

67 Benton Lake Campground

Location: About 15 miles north and west of White Cloud
Season: May to mid-September
Sites: 20 sites with no hookups, 10 rustic walk-in sites
Maximum RV length: 40
Facilities: Vault toilets, grills, lantern posts, water, tables, picnic area, fishing pier, boat launch, beach
Fee per night: $-$$
Management: American Land and Leisure
Contact: (801) 226-3564; https://www.fs.usda.gov/recarea/hmnf/recreation/camping-cabins/recarea/?recid=18894&actid=29
Finding the campground: From White Cloud head north on MI 37 and go left (west) on 9 Mile Road for 0.3 mile. Take the second left to Pierce Drive and continue nearly 4 miles and the park entrance is on the right (north) side of the road.
GPS coordinates: N 43 40.081' / W 85 53.659'
About the campground: There is no private land around the perimeter, and the simple back-in launch is the only access to this 33-acre lake surrounded by national forest. Anglers have bass and panfish to go after. A trailhead to the North Country National Scenic Trail is 2 miles east of the camp, and nature fans can enjoy Loda Lake National Wildflower Sanctuary as well. This site is notably busy during hunting season.

68 Merrill-Gorrel Park

Location: About 3 miles north of Barryton
Season: May through September
Sites: 122 sites with water and electrical hookups, 24 rustic sites
Maximum RV length: 45
Facilities: Flush toilets, showers, firepits, water, tables, picnic shelter, picnic area, dump station, boat launch, beach, playground, sand volleyball, horseshoe pits, basketball court, baseball diamond, concessionaire
Fee per night: $$-$$$
Management: Mecosta County
Contact: (989) 382-7158; www.mecostacountyparks.com/merrill-gorrel-campground.html
Finding the campground: From Barryton head north on MI 66. Turn left (west) on Evergreen Road and follow it right to the camp entrance.
GPS coordinates: N 43 48.317' / W 85 09.210'

About the campground: This 90-acre county park is set right between 2 lakes: Merrill to the north and Gorrel to the south, which has a swimming beach. Sites are divided into 2 main areas, one on either lake, and connected by a walking trail. Gorrel is closer to all the activities and has good lake access. Rustic sites are set apart and offer a bit more privacy but are farthest from the water on either side. This is good for families, and paddling is nice and relaxing on the lakes. There are also 4 cabins available.

Kalamazoo Area

	# of Hookup Sites	Total Sites	Max RV Length	Hookups	Toilets	Showers	Drinking Water	Dump Station	Recreation	Fee	Reservations
69 Ely Lake Campground	0	73	25	N/A	NF	N	Y	Y	HSL	$$	Y
70 Silver Creek Park and Campground	0	75	35	N/A	NF	N	Y	N	HL	$$	N
71 Yankee Springs Recreation Area	200	303	40	E	F	Y	Y	Y	FHLRS	$$-$$$$	Y
72 Markin Glen County Park	38	38	50	E	F	Y	Y	Y	SF	$$$$	Y
73 Fort Custer Recreation Area	219	219	60	E	F	Y	Y	Y	FHRS	$$$	Y
74 Cold Brook County Park	29	43	N/A	E	F	Y	Y	Y	HF	$$-$$$	Y
75 Cade Lake County Park and Campground	44	62	N/A	E	F/NF	Y	Y	Y	HSFB	$$$-$$$$	Y
76 Shamrock Park	101	113	50	WES	F	Y	Y	Y	FL	$$$-$$$$	Y
77 Warren Dunes State Park	182	219	40	E	F	Y	Y	Y	HS	$$$-$$$$	Y
78 Weko Beach Campground	40	61	40	E	F	Y	Y	Y	S	$$$$	Y
79 Van Buren State Park	220	220	40	E	F	Y	Y	Y	SC	$$$	Y

See Amenities Charts Key on page xiii.

69 Ely Lake Campground

Location: About 11 miles west of Allegan
Season: Year-round
Sites: 73 sites with no hookups, 16 open for equestrian camping
Maximum RV length: 25
Facilities: Vault toilets, fire rings, grills, water, tables, picnic shelter, picnic area, dump station, boat launch, hiking/mountain biking/equestrian trails, beach, beach house, playground, nature center, fishing pier, fish-cleaning station, volleyball court, horseshoe pits, boat rental, concessionaire, cross-country skiing
Fee per night: $$
Management: Allegan County Parks/Michigan DNR
Contact: (269) 686-9088; http://cms.allegancounty.org/sites/Office/Parks/SitePages/ElyLake .aspx
Finding the campground: From MI 40/MI 89 on the west side of Allegan, take Monroe Road west. This will become 118th Avenue after 6 miles, but continue on 2 more miles to turn left (south)

on 48th Street. After 1 mile turn right (east) on 116th Avenue and the park entrance is 1.1 miles farther on the left (south) side of the road.

GPS coordinates: N 42 32.131' / W 86 02.166'

About the campground: Located inside the Allegan State Game Area, this park centers on Ely Lake and is operated jointly by the state's DNR and Allegan County. These well-shaded and private sites lie on the north and south sides of the lake, and hiking trails run throughout the park between them. A swimming beach gives lake access, and only nonmotorized boats are allowed. Equestrian camping is available for those here to use the horse trails, and the park is connected into the Allegan County Equestrian Trail System. There is a self-pay tube for fees and a host on-site in the summer season.

70 Silver Creek Park and Campground

Location: About 12 miles north of Allegan

Season: Year-round

Sites: 75 sites with no hookups

Maximum RV length: 40

Facilities: Vault toilets, fire rings, water, tables, hiking/equestrian trails

Fee per night: $$

Management: Allegan County Parks

Contact: (269) 686-9088; http://cms.allegancounty.org/sites/Office/Parks/SitePages/Silver Creek.aspx

Finding the campground: From MI 40/MI 89 on the west side of Allegan, take 36th Street north 4.4 miles and turn left (west) on 128th Avenue. At 38th Street, turn right (north) and follow for 3 miles. Turn left (west) on 134th Street, continue 0.4 mile, and the park is on the left (south).

GPS coordinates: N 42 39.975', W 85 55.687'

About the campground: Primarily an equestrian park as it connects into 30 miles of riding trails, this 320-acre park hosts a primitive campground. The namesake spring-fed trout stream runs right alongside. Day visitors have access to the picnic area and grills, but the rest of the land is mostly forested and popular with color seekers in fall. Sites are generally well shaded, though not all will accommodate the maximum RV length.

71 Yankee Springs Recreation Area

Location: About 12 miles west of Hastings

Season: Early April through November

Sites: 200 sites with electrical hookups, 78 sites with no hookups, 25 equestrian sites with no hookups

Maximum RV length: 40

Facilities: Flush/vault toilets, showers, fire rings, grills, water, tables, picnic shelter, picnic area, dump station, boat launch, hiking/mountain biking/equestrian trails, beach, playground, fishing pier, concessionaire

Fee per night: $$-$$$$
Management: Michigan DNR
Contact: (269) 795-9081; www.michigandnr.com/parksandtrails
Finding the campground: From Hastings take MI 43 west for 2 miles but continue due west when MI 179 begins from where MI 43 takes a big turn south. Another 9 miles on MI 179 takes you to a left (south) on Briggs Road, where you'll continue 1 mile to turn right (west) on State Park Drive to arrive at the contact station and park office.
GPS coordinates: N 42 37.195' / W 85 30.790'
About the campground: Yankee Springs has both a modern campground and a rustic one, and they are nowhere near each other geographically or in atmosphere. The modern camp on the western side of the park at Gun Lake is big and busy, with campers relatively close to one another. Sites are shaded, but privacy is lacking. The beach area here gets busy with day users as well. The rustic Deep Lake sites are down a dusty road and spaced out nicely for tent campers; at best they are OK for pop-ups. Most are at least partly shaded, and there is a less-developed lake access. Twenty-five equestrian sites round out the options. The mountain biking here is the best in the area, and the entire park offers excellent hiking, including a crossing segment of the North Country National Scenic Trail. The geological feature called the Devil's Soup Bowl compels hikers to make the effort to get there. The park counts 9 lakes among its 5,200 acres.

72 Markin Glen County Park

Location: Just north of downtown Kalamazoo
Season: Late April through October
Sites: 38 sites with electrical hookups
Maximum RV length: 50
Facilities: Flush toilets, showers, fire rings, water, tables, picnic shelter, picnic area, dump station, multiuse paved trail, beach, playground, fishing pier, volleyball court, softball field, tennis courts
Fee per night: $$$$
Management: Kalamazoo County Parks
Contact: (269) 381-7570 or (269) 383-8778 for reservations; www.kalcounty.com/parks/markinglen
Finding the campground: Take Westnedge Avenue straight north from downtown Kalamazoo. US 131, MI 43, and MI 331 all intersect with Westnedge. The park is 1.5 miles north of US 131's intersection with Westnedge Avenue.
GPS coordinates: N 42 20.130' / W 85 35.394'
About the campground: This county park is situated next to a small swimmable and fishable pond. The sites are unshaded and not private at all. This is not a deep wilderness experience by any stretch of the imagination, but the 160 acres, simple trail, and wildflower field are a quick escape from the city and make a nice stop if you are visiting the area. Within the park is Kalamazoo's highest point, with a view of the town. Be aware that train tracks run nearby and could surprise you at night.

73 Fort Custer Recreation Area

Location: About 11 miles west of Battle Creek
Season: Year-round
Sites: 219 sites with electrical hookups, 3 rustic cabins
Maximum RV length: 60 feet
Facilities: Flush/vault toilets, showers, fire rings, grills, water, tables, picnic shelter, picnic area, dump station, boat launch, hiking/mountain biking/equestrian trails, beach, beach house, playground, fishing pier, disc golf, boat rental, concessionaire, camp store
Fee per night: $$$
Management: Michigan DNR
Contact: (269) 731-4200; www.michigandnr.com/parksandtrails
Finding the campground: From Battle Creek take MI 96 west to Fort Custer Drive and turn left (south), continuing 1.4 miles to find the park entrance on the left (south) side of the road.
GPS coordinates: N 42 19.404' / W 85 21.224'
About the campground: With the Kalamazoo River and 3 lakes, a disc golf course, plus over 25 miles of hiking, mountain biking, and equestrian trails through rolling meadows, wetlands, and mixed forest, there is much for the active camper to do in this 3,033-acre park. The campground is to the left (east) as you pass the contact station and is divided into 2 loops. Sites are spread out nicely, and many of them have good shade. Access to the water is not made via the campground. The modern restrooms are available from mid-April through mid-October. Over 90,000 troops passed through Camp Custer in 1917, and German POWs were held here during World War II. The Fort Custer Cemetery is open to visitors daily.

74 Cold Brook County Park

Location: About 15 miles east of Kalamazoo
Season: Late April through October
Sites: 29 sites with electrical hookups, 14 sites with no hookups
Maximum RV length: None
Facilities: Flush/vault toilets, showers, fire rings, grills, water, tables, picnic shelter, picnic area, dump station, boat launch, hiking trails, beach, beach house, playground, fishing pier, volleyball court, ball field, disc golf course, boat rental, concessionaire
Fee per night: $$–$$$
Management: Kalamazoo County Government
Contact: (269) 746-4270; www.kalcounty.com/parks/coldbrook/
Finding the campground: From I-94 take exit 88 and go south on 40th Street 2 miles to MN Avenue. Go left (east) and the park is 1 mile down the road on the left (north).
GPS coordinates: N 42 15.180' / W 85 21.248'
About the campground: Most of the 276 acres of this county park is water, including Blue, Long, and Portage Lakes plus some wetlands. Sites are spacious and spread out a bit but with no intervening brush. Trees provide a bit of shade. Accessible sites are available. The swimming beach is

Hall Lake at Yankee Springs Recreation Area

at Blue Lake, and nonmotorized boat rentals can be made. Along with the water attractions, there are 2.5 miles of hiking trails and a 24-hole championship disc golf course.

75 Cade Lake County Park and Campground

Location: About 2 miles east of Sturgis
Season: Year-round
Sites: 44 sites with electrical hookups, 18 sites with no hookups
Maximum RV length: None
Facilities: Flush/vault toilets, showers, fire rings, grills, water, tables, picnic shelter, picnic area, dump station, hiking trails, beach, playground, nature center, fishing pier and cleaning station, volleyball court, disc golf course, boat rental, camp store
Fee per night: $$$–$$$$
Management: St. Joseph County Parks
Contact: (269) 651-3330; www.stjosephcountymi.org/parks/parks_cadelake.php
Finding the campground: Go east on US 12 2 miles from Sturgis. Turn right (south) onto Plumb School Road and the park entrance is on the left (east) side of the road.
GPS coordinates: N 41 47.808' / W 85 22.176'

About the campground: This county park occupies 98 acres along the shores on a 32-acre lake that is otherwise undeveloped. The campground is divided into 2 halves, with sites 1–31 closer to the lake. There are sites with electric in both sections. A small man-made beach lies south of the camping area and is connected to the lakefront sites by a walking bridge. Nearby there is also a boardwalk into the water. This is a relatively young campground, so most of the sites lack any kind of tree cover. Accessible campsites are available. While you can rent rowboats, paddleboards, canoes, paddleboats, and kayaks here, there is no boat ramp. Park staff are on-site from May to October.

76 Shamrock Park

Location: About 14 miles southeast of St. Joseph
Season: Year-round
Sites: 59 sites with full hookups, 29 sites with water and electrical hookups, 13 sites with electrical hookups, 12 sites with no hookups
Maximum RV length: 50
Facilities: Flush toilets, showers, fire rings, grills, water, tables, picnic shelter, picnic area, dump station, boat launch, beach, playground, fish-cleaning station, boat rental, free Wi-Fi
Fee per night: $$$–$$$$
Management: Village of Berrien Springs
Contact: (269) 473-5691; www.shamrockpark.net
Finding the campground: From I-94 outside of St. Joseph, follow MI 139 southwest to Berrien Springs and it will take you all the way through town. On the east side cross the river and the park entrance is on the left (north) side of the road.
GPS coordinates: N 41 56.980' / W 86 19.920'
About the campground: A nice town park alongside the St. Joseph River, Shamrock caters generally to the RV crowd, with electrical and water hookups and some pull-through sites. However, the loveliest sites in the camp are those in the southwest corner of the park, sitting in the shade right along the bank of the river; these are the primitive sites. Some sites with electric only are right across the lane from them as well. The restrooms and fish-cleaning station are actually heated in winter. Anglers will find salmon, walleye, and steelhead, and if you don't have a boat, there are several rental agencies operating in the park. The area has a lot of farmers' markets, wineries, and pick-your-own farms, and there is hiking nearby.

77 Warren Dunes State Park

Location: About 19 miles south of Benton Harbor
Season: Early April through October
Sites: 182 sites with electrical hookups, 37 sites with no hookups
Maximum RV length: 40
Facilities: Flush/vault toilets, showers, fire rings, grills, water, tables, picnic shelter, picnic area, dump station, hiking trails, beach, beach house, playground, concessionaire

The dunes at Warren Dunes State Park

Fee per night: $$$–$$$$
Management: Michigan DNR
Contact: (269) 426-4013; www.michigandnr.com/parksandtrails
Finding the campground: From I-94 south of Benton Harbor take exit 16 for Bridgman. Take Old US 12/Red Arrow Highway south 2.3 miles and the park entrance is on the right (west) side of the road.
GPS coordinates: N 41 54.088' / W 86 35.693'
About the campground: The 260-foot sand dunes along this park's 3 miles of Lake Michigan shoreline are not to be missed. The campgrounds are to the west of the dunes, sheltered from the lake. The first 2 loops at the camp are the modern sites. Just beyond this, on a gravel road, is a loop of primitive sites. The sites are mostly shaded, and in the primitive circle there is some amount of privacy. A hiking trail passes along the camp, heading north into dune climbs or south over the sand to the swimming beach area.

78 Weko Beach Campground

Location: About 19 miles south of Benton Harbor
Season: Late April through mid-October
Sites: 40 sites with water and electrical hookups, 21 sites with electrical hookups, 7 cabins
Maximum RV length: 40

A view from the beach toward Lake Michigan at Warren Dunes State Park

Facilities: Flush toilets, showers, fire rings, grills, water, tables, picnic shelter, picnic area, dump station, beach, beach house, playground, cabins

Fee per night: $$$$

Management: City of Bridgman

Contact: (269) 465-3406; www.bridgman.org/165/Parks

Finding the campground: From I-94 south of Benton Harbor take exit 16 for Bridgman. Take Old US 12/Red Arrow Highway north 1 mile, then turn left (west) on Lake Street and follow it to the park just before you run into Lake Michigan.

GPS coordinates: N 41 56.490' / W 86 34.860'

About the campground: Just north of Warren Dunes State Park, this town-managed park lacks the big dunes but has nice beach access. Two loops to the north offer the more modern electrical sites and a modest bit of shade in many sites. The primitive loop to the south of the park road is exposed. Neither side offers water views. A few rental cabins are interspersed with the campsites.

79 Van Buren State Park

Location: About 5 miles south of South Haven

Season: March 30 to November 30

Sites: 220 sites with electrical hookups

Maximum RV length: 40

Facilities: Flush/vault toilets, showers, fire rings, grills, water, tables, picnic shelter, picnic area, dump station, hiking/biking trails, beach, playground

Fee per night: $$$

Management: Michigan DNR

Contact: (269) 637-2788; www.michigandnr.com/parksandtrails

Finding the campground: From the center of South Haven, take I-196 south to Blue Star Highway/CR A2. Turn right (west) and drive 4 miles to the park entrance on the right (east) side of the road.

GPS coordinates: N 42 20.020' / W 86 18.289'

About the campground: Welcome to a mile of sandy beach and dune formations. Though the park is situated right along the shores of Lake Michigan, none of the campsites have a water view. Campers can follow a short walkway to the beach and day-use area. The sites are laid out in 5 parallel loops, each one a bit farther from the beach. Shade is only partial at best in most sites, and the distance between campers is a bit tight. Because of the Big Lake, this park tends to fill up fast for summer weekends and more. Showers may not meet ADA standards. If boating is your thing, a nearby marina has outfitters. The park is just minutes from South Haven and city conveniences.

Northeast Michigan

For the Lower Peninsula, this northeastern portion of the state is arguably the most remote. Once famous for its lumber production, the attractions for travelers are uninterrupted shoreline along Lake Huron, a national forest, good paddling opportunities, and good wildlife viewing.

From Cheboygan just east of where the Mackinac Bridge connects the Upper Peninsula to the Lower, the shores of Huron make the long curve down to Saginaw Bay, showing a lot of shoreline beauty opportunities, including the Cape Cod of the Midwest, Tawas Point.

In Oscoda, find the trailhead of the 220-mile Shore-to-Shore Trail, accommodating horseback riders and hikers alike. You can get all the way to Lake Michigan via this route if you are ambitious about it.

Between Grayling and Oscoda lies Huron National Park, with 438,538 acres. In the nineteenth century much of this land was completely clear-cut. That's hard to imagine now, but the park was founded in 1909, and now you can see what a difference a century makes. Birders take note: The threatened Kirtland's warbler nests in these woods. Tours to go find them can be found on the Internet. This is often referred to as the Huron-Manistee National Forests; though the two are separate forests, they have shared the same administration since 1945.

Speaking of the lumber industry, check out Monument State Park, which celebrates lumbermen with a museum and a bronze statue. The Au Sable River, once a transportation highway for logs on their way to the sawmills, is now a National Wild and Scenic River. Paddlers and anglers come ride its current, but drivers take note of the 22-mile River Road National Scenic Byway that runs along its south side.

Pigeon River Country State Forest and the surrounding land are home to the largest free-roaming elk herd east of the Mississippi River. The nearly 100,000-acre state forest contains native hardwoods and pines that are interspersed with fields and forest openings. Viewing areas are designated throughout by the Department of Natural Resources to increase your chances of seeing these majestic creatures. Tuttle Marsh Wildlife Area offers wetland wildlife viewing and is especially hot for birds.

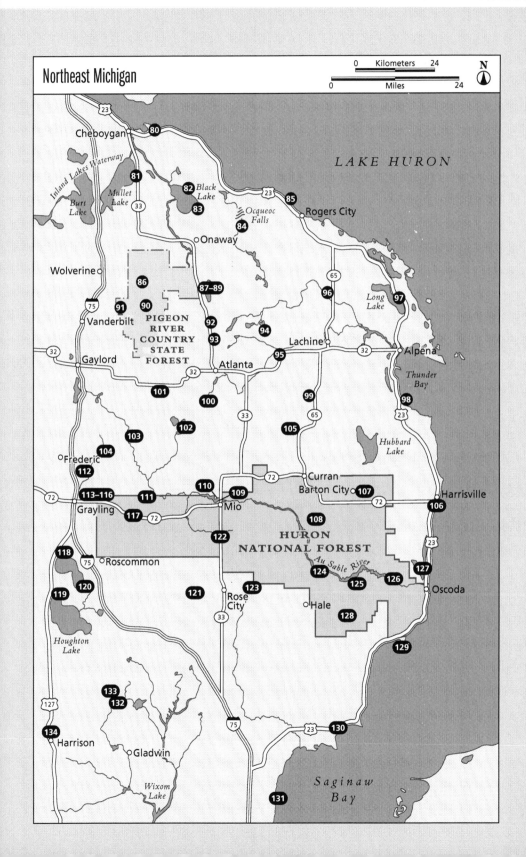

A bald eagle comes to camp in northwest Michigan.

Up in the northwesternmost corner of the region laid out in this section of the book is the Inland Lakes Waterway. A chain of lakes and rivers, it starts in Cheboygan and makes its way into the Northwest Michigan section in this book. A navigable waterway that connects Lake Huron to Lake Michigan right through this piece of the state, it includes Round Lake, Iduna Creek, Crooked Lake, Crooked River, Burt Lake, Indian River, Mullett Lake, and the Cheboygan River.

Anglers might want to check out Onaway, the Sturgeon Capital of Michigan. The state park of the same name located on the shores of Black Lake is close to a variety of good natural attractions, perhaps the most notable being one of the Lower Peninsula's only two waterfalls: Ocqueoc Falls.

Cheboygan to Presque Area

	Hookup Sites	Total Sites	Max RV Length	Hookups	Toilets	Showers	Drinking Water	Dump Station	Recreation	Fee	Reservations
80 Cheboygan State Park	76	76	50	E	F	Y	Y	Y	HSFBL	$$$	Y
81 Aloha State Park	283	283	45	E	F	Y	Y	Y	HFSBL	$$$	Y
82 Black Lake State Forest Campground	0	52	30	N/A	NF	N	Y	N	HFBLO	$$	Y
83 Onaway State Park	82	82	40	E	F	Y	Y	Y	HSFBL	$$	Y
84 Ocqueoc Falls State Forest Campground	0	15	40	N/A	NF	N	Y	N	FHC	$$	N
85 P. H. Hoeft State Park	126	126	40	E	F	Y	Y	Y	HSFBC	$$$$	Y
86 Pine Grove State Forest Campground	0	6	25	N/A	NF	N	Y	N	HFLO	$$	N
87 Shoepac Lake State Forest Campground	0	25	30	N/A	NF	N	Y	N	HFLO	$$	N
88 Tomahawk Lake State Forest Campground	0	25	25	N/A	NF	N	Y	N	HFLO	$$	N
89 Tomahawk Creek Flooding State Forest Campground	0	47	35	N/A	NF	N	Y	N	HFLO	$$	N
90 Pigeon River State Forest Campground	0	14	25	N/A	NF	N	Y	N	HFL	$$	N
91 Pickerel Lake State Forest Campground (Otsego)	0	39	35	N/A	NF	N	Y	N	HFL	$$	N
92 Clear Lake State Park	178	178	40	E	F	Y	Y	Y	HSFBLO	$$$	Y
93 Jackson Lake State Forest Campground	0	18	40	N/A	NF	N	Y	N	HFLO	$$	N
94 Ess Lake State Forest Campground	0	27	35	N/A	NF	N	Y	N	FL	$$	N
95 Emerick Park	34	38	50	WES	F	Y	Y	Y	F	$$	Y
96 Sunken Lake Campground and County Park	59	59	40	WE	F	Y	Y	Y	HSFL	$$$-$$$$	Y
97 Long Lake Campground and County Park	81	104	40	WE	F	Y	Y	Y	HSFBL	$$-$$$$	Y
98 Ossineke State Forest Campground	0	42	30	N/A	NF	N	Y	N	HFL	$$	N
99 Beaver Lake Campground and County Park	51	56	40	WE	F	Y	Y	Y	HSFBL	$$$-$$$$	Y
100 Avery Lake State Forest Campground	0	16	40	N/A	NF	N	Y	N	HFLO	$$	N

	Hookup Sites	Total Sites	Max RV Length	Hookups	Toilets	Showers	Drinking Water	Dump Station	Recreation	Fee	Reservations
101 Big Bear Lake and Big Bear Point State Forest Campgrounds	0	44	30–40	N/A	NF	N	Y	N	HFLOC	$$	N
102 Little Wolf Lake State Forest Campground	0	24	40	N/A	NF	N	Y	N	HF	$$	N
103 Shupac Lake State Forest Campground	0	30	25	N/A	NF	N	Y	N	HFL	$$	N
104 Jones Lake State Forest Campground	0	42	20	N/A	NF	N	Y	N	HFLO	$$	N
105 McCollum Lake State Forest Campground	0	20	40	N/A	NF	N	Y	N	FLO	$$	N
106 Harrisville State Park	195	195	50	E	F	Y	Y	Y	HSFBL	$$$–$$$$	Y
107 Jewell Lake Campground	0	32	25	N/A	NF	N	Y	N	HSFB	$$	N
108 Horseshoe Lake Campground–Huron National Forest	0	9	25	N/A	NF	N	Y	N	FLB	$$	N

See Amenities Charts Key on page xiii.

80   Cheboygan State Park

Location: About 3 miles east of Cheboygan
Season: Year-round
Sites: 76 sites with electrical hookups
Maximum RV length: 50
Facilities: Flush toilets, showers, firepits, grills, water, tables, picnic shelter, picnic area, dump station, boat launch, hiking/mountain biking trails, beach, beach house, playground, tepee rental
Fee per night: $$$
Management: Michigan DNR
Contact: (231) 627-2811; www.michigandnr.com/parksandtrails
Finding the campground: From Cheboygan follow US 23 east about 3 miles and the park entrance is on the left (north).
GPS coordinates: N 45 38.591' / W 84 23.989'
About the campground: The popular state park lies right on the Lake Huron coast, curling around Duncan Bay, and offers a wealth of activities. The swimming beach is sheltered in the bay, but a walk along the north beach shows the open lake. Color-coded hiking/mountain biking trails are well marked and give nice lake vistas, but none is longer than 2 miles. See the remains of the Cheboygan Point Light. The campsites are generally open to the sky above, though with shade

trees alongside. The loop lies close to the edge of the lake, separated from the sand by a thin band of forest. There are also some cabins for rent.

81 Aloha State Park

Location: About 9 miles south of Cheboygan
Season: Mid-April to mid-October
Sites: 283 sites with electrical hookups
Maximum RV length: 45
Facilities: Flush/vault toilets, showers, fire rings, grills, water, tables, picnic shelter, picnic area, dump station, boat launch, beach, playground, fishing pier, fish-cleaning station, ball field, basketball and volleyball courts, horseshoe pits
Fee per night: $$$
Management: Michigan DNR
Contact: (231) 625-2522; www.michigandnr.com/parksandtrails
Finding the campground: From Cheboygan take MI 33 south to MI 212/Center Street and go right (west). After 0.7 mile turn left (south) on 2nd Street and it will take you 300 feet to the park road.
GPS coordinates: N 45 31.574' / W 84 27.964'
About the campground: Mullett Lake, the location of this state park, lies at the center of the Inland Lakes Waterway, Michigan's longest chain of rivers and lakes. The area seems like a nicely manicured city park, with a lot of grass and scattered trees for at least some partial shade for sites more toward the southern end of the campground. The park has a boat launch close to the campsites, and the swimming area has a sandy bottom. The multiuse North Eastern State Trail runs right past the park. The park's pricing refers to semimodern sites. While all sites always have electricity, at the very beginning and end of the season the water is shut off, and only pit toilets are available at that time.

82 Black Lake State Forest Campground

Location: About 12 miles north of Onaway
Season: Year-round
Sites: 52 sites with no hookups
Maximum RV length: 30
Facilities: Vault toilets, fire rings, water, tables, boat launch, hiking/off-road vehicle trails
Fee per night: $$
Management: Michigan DNR
Contact: (231) 627-2811; www.michigandnr.com/parksandtrails
Finding the campground: From Onaway head north 5.2 miles on MI 211. Turn right (east) on Bonz Beach Highway for 0.2 mile, then go left (north) on CR 489 for 2.5 miles. At a fork, stay left on Black Mountain Road for 3.2 miles. Then turn left (west) on Doriva Beach Road, go 0.9 mile and turn left (south) on Eisen Trail, following it 0.4 mile into the campground.

GPS coordinates: N 45 29.378' / W 84 15.725'

About the campground: Mostly off-road enthusiasts know of this place, but the hiking and lake opportunities shouldn't be overlooked. The partly shaded sites are divided into Upper and Lower Units. The Upper Unit has 35 sites but is designated for off-road vehicle campers. Other campers have 17 sites in the Lower Unit, which are very close to the lake and are priced cheaper. The boat launch is in the Lower Unit. Hikers and bikers have 30 miles to explore on the paved and partly accessible Black Mountain Pathway. The trailhead is 2 miles east.

83 Onaway State Park

Location: About 5 miles north of Onaway
Season: April 6 to November 29
Sites: 82 sites with electrical hookups
Maximum RV length: 40
Facilities: Flush toilets, showers, firepits, grills, water, tables, picnic area, pavilion, dump station, boat launch, hiking trails, beach, playground, concessionaire, boat rentals
Fee per night: $$
Management: Michigan DNR
Contact: (989) 733-8279; www.michigandnr.com/parksandtrails
Finding the campground: From Onaway take MI 211 north and the road ends right at the park entrance.
GPS coordinates: N 45 25.933' / W 84 13.742'

About the campground: You might say Onaway is "on the way" to a bunch of sites. The park is a destination in its own right, with a sand and cobblestone beach on the beautiful 10,130-acre Black Lake, a 3-mile nature trail, rock formations, and stands of virgin white pine. But just short drives away are Ocqueoc Falls, Shoepac Lake, Black Mountain Forest Recreation Area with 30 miles of hiking, and the Sturgeon Capital of Michigan: Onaway. The sites are adequately spaced, separated by grassy areas, and nicely shaded. The lower campground offers sites closer to the lake.

84 Ocqueoc Falls State Forest Campground

Location: About 12 miles west of Rogers City
Season: Year-round
Sites: 15 sites with no hookups
Maximum RV length: 40
Facilities: Vault toilet, firepits, water, tables, hiking/mountain biking trails
Fee per night: $$
Management: Michigan DNR
Contact: (989) 734-2543; www.michigandnr.com/parksandtrails

Ocquoec Falls is one of two waterfalls in the Lower Peninsula. Matt Forster

Finding the campground: From Rogers City head west on MI 68 for almost 12 miles and turn right (west) onto Ocqueoc Falls Highway and go 0.5 mile to find the park entrance on the left (south) side of the road.

GPS coordinates: N 45 23.726' / W 84 03.379'

About the campground: The Upper Peninsula is famous for its abundance of fast water and waterfalls, while the Lower Peninsula has only 2 waterfalls. Ocqueoc is the easier one to get to and, as such, the most popular. The river also runs south to north, another rarity in the L.P. The park's Bicentennial Pathway is scenic and accommodates both hikers and mountain bikers. The campground is across the road from the south of the falls parking area. Campers have a partly shaded loop with some angler access to the river's brown trout and steelhead.

85 P. H. Hoeft State Park

Location: About 5 miles northeast of Rogers City
Season: Year-round
Sites: 126 sites with electrical hookups
Maximum RV length: 40

Facilities: Flush toilets, showers, firepits, grills, water, tables, picnic shelter, picnic area, dump station, hiking/biking trails, beach, playground

Fee per night: $$$$

Management: Michigan DNR

Contact: (989) 734-2543; www.michigandnr.com/parksandtrails

Finding the campground: From Rogers City go north on US 23 and the park entrance will be on the right.

GPS coordinates: N 45 27.818' / W 83 53.013'

About the campground: The drive along the Lake Huron coastline is quite scenic, and this state park makes a good stopping point on that journey. The core of the 300-acre park, one of Michigan's original 14 state parks, came from a man whose fortune was made cutting down trees. Lumber baron Paul H. Hoeft gave the land to Michigan in 1922. The picnic shelter we see today was built by the Civilian Conservation Corps in the 1930s. Today the park offers a mile of sandy lakeshore that draws day-trippers and campers. The sites are nicely shaded, and a small network of trails keeps hikers busy. The Huron Sunrise Trail, which connects Rogers City to the world's largest open-pit limestone mine, runs right past the park. This means bikers can make the 4-mile trip into town. An actual 1929 Sears and Roebuck mail-order cabin is on-site and can be rented.

86 Pine Grove State Forest Campground

Location: About 12 miles east and south of Wolverine

Season: Year-round

Sites: 6 sites with no hookups

Maximum RV length: 25

Facilities: Vault toilets, firepits, water, tables, boat launch, hiking/mountain biking/off-road vehicle trails

Fee per night: $$

Management: Michigan DNR

Contact: (989) 732-5485; www.michigandnr.com/parksandtrails

Finding the campground: From Wolverine head east out of town on Wolverine Road (which becomes Webb Road) for 8.2 miles. Turn right (south) on Clute Road, go 0.6 mile and make the slight right onto Campsite Road. Follow it, even as it turns right, for 1.9 miles to arrive at the end right in the campground.

GPS coordinates: N 45 14.677' / W 84 26.778'

About the campground: This is a remote, simple spot to get away from it all and have access to some paddling or trout fishing in the Pigeon River. The 80-mile High Country Trail connects this campground with 8 others throughout Pigeon River Country State Forest, famous for its large free-roaming elk herd. This isn't a bad home base for some hiking or paddling, and backcountry hikers/campers may choose it. But there's nothing here but the basics under a fine canopy of trees.

87 Shoepac Lake State Forest Campground

Location: About 13 miles south of Onaway
Season: Year-round
Sites: 25 sites with no hookups
Maximum RV length: 30
Facilities: Vault toilets, firepits, water, tables, boat launch, hiking/off-road vehicle trails
Fee per night: $$
Management: Michigan DNR
Contact: (989) 733-8279; www.michigandnr.com/parksandtrails
Finding the campground: From Onaway head south on MI 33 for 9.9 miles and turn left (northeast) on Tomahawk Lake Highway. Go 2.2 miles and turn left (northwest) on Shoepac Lake Road and drive 0.5 mile. The campground is on the left.
GPS coordinates: N 45 14.389' / W 84 10.227'
About the campground: The geology in this area is rather curious. Natural limestone dissolved over the years and formed sinkholes, making the landscape interesting and challenging to hikers and mountain bikers. The campground is connected to 8 other state forest campgrounds by the 80-mile High Country Trail. This is one of the larger campgrounds. The Sinkhole Trail is 2.5 miles long and passes through the karst topography of its namesake. The campsites are not right on the lake, and the ramp is up the road a bit, giving anglers access to catch bass, trout, and panfish. The Atlanta ATV trail is 1 mile south from here. Don't confuse this with Shupac Lake.

88 Tomahawk Lake State Forest Campground

Location: About 12 miles south of Onaway
Season: Year-round
Sites: 25 sites with no hookups
Maximum RV length: 25
Facilities: Vault toilets, fire rings, water, tables, boat launch, hiking/off-road vehicle trails
Fee per night: $$
Management: Michigan DNR
Contact: (989) 733-8279; www.michigandnr.com/parksandtrails
Finding the campground: From Onaway take MI 33 south almost 10 miles and turn left (east) on Tomahawk Lake Highway. Go 2.2 miles and the park road is on the right (southeast) side of the road.
GPS coordinates: N 45 14.012' / W 84 10.027'
About the campground: The High Country Trail offers 80 miles of pathway going from one state forest campground to another, for a total of 9 campgrounds, including this one. The park lies on the northern end of Tomahawk Lake (not to be confused with Tomahawk Creek Flooding just southwest of here). The on-site boat ramp gets anglers access to the lake's perch, bass, and bluegill. The campsites are under decent shade from some mixed forest and especially pine, and some of the sites back right up on the bank overlooking the water. The whole area consists of small fishing lakes with boat ramps but no high-speed boating.

89 Tomahawk Creek Flooding State Forest Campground

Location: About 17 miles north of Atlanta
Season: Year-round
Sites: 47 sites with no hookups
Maximum RV length: 35
Facilities: Vault toilets, fire rings, water, tables, boat launch, hiking/off-road vehicle trails
Fee per night: $$
Management: Michigan DNR
Contact: (989) 733-8279; www.michigandnr.com/parksandtrails
Finding the campground: From Atlanta take MI 33 north about 15 miles and turn right (east) on Tomahawk Lake Highway. Go 1.4 miles and turn right (east) on Spring Lake Road to go 0.6 mile to the park entrance.
GPS coordinates: N 45 13.247' / W 84 10.390'
About the campground: Directions are to the West Unit. The East Unit is just a short drive farther east on Spring Lake Road. Sites include shade trees but still get some sunlight. Boat ramps serve both units, which are separated by a swampy area at the north end of the impoundment. The 80-mile High Country Trail passes through the park, connecting 8 other state forest campgrounds. Check the Sinkhole Trail 1 mile north too. Anglers will find bass, bluegill, and pike here. See nesting loons in June and likely a bald eagle or osprey.

90 Pigeon River State Forest Campground

Location: About 13 miles east of Vanderbilt
Season: Year-round
Sites: 14 sites with no hookups
Maximum RV length: 25
Facilities: Vault toilets, firepits, water, tables, boat launch, hiking/mountain biking trails
Fee per night: $$
Management: Michigan DNR
Contact: (989) 732-5485; www.michigandnr.com/parksandtrails
Finding the campground: From Vanderbilt take Sturgeon Valley Road east for about 11.5 miles and take a slight left before a full left (north) on Witness Tree Road. Take this 1.3 miles north to the campground, which is on the left (west) side of the road.
GPS coordinates: N 45 10.601' / W 84 25.667'
About the campground: Welcome to elk country. The region around Pigeon River is home to the largest elk herd (not in captivity) east of the Mississippi. There are viewing points throughout the area from the roadside in places known to show elk. This campground and the elk area are named for the river that runs right through it. Paddlers have carry-in access, and anglers may catch 3 varieties of trout. Hikers will enjoy this spot, as it has a trailhead for the Shingle Mill Pathway, 5 loops through varying terrain adding up to 14 miles. A half mile west lies the High Country Trail with over 80 miles of trail connecting 8 other state forest campgrounds here in Pigeon River Country.

91 Pickerel Lake State Forest Campground (Otsego)

Location: About 10 miles east and north from Vanderbilt
Season: Year-round
Sites: 39 sites with no hookups
Maximum RV length: 35
Facilities: Vault toilets, firepits, water, tables, boat launch, hiking/mountain biking trails, beach
Fee per night: $$
Management: Michigan DNR
Contact: (989) 732-5485; www.michigandnr.com/parksandtrails
Finding the campground: From Vanderbilt go east on Sturgeon Valley Road for just over 7 miles and turn left (north) on Pickerel Lake Road. Go 1.8 miles farther and you'll find the park.
GPS coordinates: N 45 10.571' / W 84 31.022'
About the campground: The campground is part of Pigeon River Country State Forest, where the big elk herd of Michigan makes its home. Not likely you'll see them at camp, but anglers may launch from a gravel ramp here and find rainbow trout, bass, and bluegill. Otherwise, head east a few miles to Pigeon River for more trout fishing. The sites with gravel pads are distributed evenly along the park roads for optimal privacy and space. The forest, a mix of pine and hardwood, provides ample shade.

92 Clear Lake State Park

Location: About 9 miles north of Atlanta
Season: Year-round
Sites: 178 sites with electrical hookups
Maximum RV length: 40
Facilities: Flush/vault toilets, showers, firepits, grills, water, tables, picnic shelter, picnic area, dump station, boat launch, hiking/mountain biking/off-road vehicle trails, beach, playground, volleyball court, horseshoe pits, boat rentals
Fee per night: $$$
Management: Michigan DNR
Contact: (989) 785-4388; www.michigandnr.com/parksandtrails
Finding the campground: From Atlanta take MI 33 north 9.5 miles and the park entrance is on the left (west).
GPS coordinates: N 45 08.042' / W 84 10.619'
About the campground: One way to keep a lake less developed is to wrap it with state park land. The 290-acre state park, within Mackinaw State Forest, has two-thirds of this 133-acre, spring-fed lake's shoreline. The swimming area is sandy and shallow, making it nice for children. The loops and the sites themselves are moderately spacious and shaded, and the park has a reputation for being a quiet, peaceful place. A spur trail takes ORV riders to the Atlanta ORV route, and mountain bikers share 4.5 miles of a loop within the park with hikers. A 48-mile scenic drive, marked by yellow-topped signposts, explores areas outside the park. This is elk country, and if you are lucky you may hear or even see one.

93 Jackson Lake State Forest Campground

Location: About 6 miles north of Atlanta
Season: Year-round
Sites: 18 sites with no hookups
Maximum RV length: 40
Facilities: Vault toilets, firepits, water, tables, boat launch, hiking/biking/off-road vehicle trails
Fee per night: $$
Management: Michigan DNR
Contact: (989) 785-4388; www.michigandnr.com/parksandtrails
Finding the campground: From Atlanta head north on MI 33 for 6.3 miles, turn right (east) on Forest Campground Road, and it goes right into the park.
GPS coordinates: N 45 05.335' / W 84 09.647'
About the campground: This state forest campground is a shaded couple of loops in deciduous forest with a sprinkling of pine throughout. The carry-in boat launch gives access to the small and quiet lake and its smallmouth bass and panfish. Rush and Clear Lakes are nearby for the same catch. While there are hiking and ORV opportunities in the area, this campground has little to recommend it over campgrounds that actually have trails or spur trails to the network. Still, the sites are spacious and generally available, and 15 of them can handle a bigger RV.

94 Ess Lake State Forest Campground

Location: About 17 miles north and east of Atlanta
Season: Year-round
Sites: 27 sites with no hookups
Maximum RV length: 35
Facilities: Vault toilets, fire rings, water, tables, picnic area, boat launch, beach
Fee per night: $$
Management: Michigan DNR
Contact: (989) 785-4388; www.michigandnr.com/parksandtrails
Finding the campground: From Atlanta follow MI 33 north about 7 miles and go right (east) on CR 624 for 9 miles. Turn left (north) on Shore Drive and follow it 1.3 miles to the camp.
GPS coordinates: N 45 06.506' / W 83 58.913'
About the campground: Ess Lake is a quiet place with cottages and cabins dotting much of its shoreline. The campsites, located along the southern shore, are 2 loops in the woods with a boat ramp nearby. Anglers will prefer this place, as will campers who just want to get away from it all. The lake offers bass, trout, and panfish, while both Long Lake and Grass Lake are only 0.5 mile and 5 miles away, respectively, for more fishing options. This is Pigeon River Country, where Michigan's elk herd may be spotted.

95 Emerick Park

Location: About 24 miles west of Alpena
Season: Year-round
Sites: 12 sites with full hookups, 22 sites with water and electrical hookups, 4 sites with no hookups
Maximum RV length: 50
Facilities: Flush toilets, showers, firepits, grills, water, tables, dump station, boat ramp, playground, pavilion
Fee per night: $$
Management: Village of Hillman
Contact: (989) 733-0613; (989) 742-4751; www.hillmanmichigan.org
Finding the campground: From Alpena take MI 32 west for 23 miles and turn right (north) onto State Street in Hillman. About 0.5 mile north turn left (west) on Maple Street and go right into the park.
GPS coordinates: N 45 03.607' / W 83 54.052'
About the campground: A lovely village park, Emerick is situated on the banks of an impoundment on the Thunder Bay River. Other than fishing, there isn't so much to do at camp, but the area offers other opportunities. Campers are within walking distance of all the amenities of the village of Hillman, including stores and a library. While there is a boat launch, fishing from shore is also possible, and trout and several other species have been caught here. The park is grassy and offers good shade trees.

96 Sunken Lake Campground and County Park

Location: About 25 miles west and north of Alpena
Season: May 15 to September 15
Sites: 59 sites with water and electrical hookups
Maximum RV length: 40
Facilities: Flush toilets, showers, grills, water, tables, picnic area, pavilion, dump station, boat launch, hiking trails, playground, fish-cleaning station, ball diamond, game room, concessionaire
Fee per night: $$$-$$$$
Management: Alpena County
Contact: (989) 379-3055; www.alpenacounty.org/parks-recreation
Finding the campground: From Alpena take MI 32 west for about 14 miles, turn right (north) on MI 65 and continue 8.5 miles. Turn left (west) on Maple Road, go 1 mile, and go right (north) on Leer Road. Follow this 0.8 mile north to the park entrance.
GPS coordinates: N 45 12.531' / W 83 43.311'
About the campground: Limestone underlies the land in this area, and over time dissolving minerals create formations or collapsing sinkholes known as karst topography. Sinkholes can be viewed in the area, especially in this park. In fact, the lake level is controlled by sinkholes. The campground has partial shade and modern facilities but also sites of a rustic sort. The

easternmost sites of the campground loop have the lake right behind them. The 160-acre park is nicely wooded, and the lake offers good fishing.

97 Long Lake Campground and County Park

Location: About 10 miles north of Alpena
Season: May 15 to October 1
Sites: 81 sites with hookups, 23 sites with no hookups
Maximum RV length: 40
Facilities: Flush toilets, showers, fire rings, water, tables, picnic area, pavilions, boat launch, beach, playground
Fee per night: $$$–$$$$
Management: Alpena County
Contact: (989) 595-2401; www.alpenacounty.org/parks-recreation
Finding the campground: From Alpena head north on US 23 for about 10 miles and turn left (west) on Long Lake Park Road. Continue for 0.3 mile and the park road is on the left.
GPS coordinates: N 45 11.790' / W 83 26.727'
About the campground: This popular county park might have plenty to do on-site, but it is also in a good location for daytime activities up the road. Lake Huron and its lighthouses north of here are a short drive away, as is the beautiful Besser Natural Area. As for staying around camp, the beaches are quite nice, and fishing has gotten more popular since the lake was stocked with walleye. Nearly all the sites have at least partial shade and are a short walk from the lake.

98 Ossineke State Forest Campground

Location: About 12 miles south of Alpena
Season: Year-round
Sites: 42 sites with no hookups
Maximum RV length: 30
Facilities: Vault toilets, fire rings, grills, water, tables, day use area, boat launch, hiking/mountain biking trails, beach
Fee per night: $$
Management: Michigan DNR
Contact: (989) 724-5126; www.michigandnr.com/parksandtrails
Finding the campground: From Alpena drive south on US 23 about 10 miles and turn left (east) on Ossineke Road. Go 0.9 miles and turn left (east) on State Street, go to the end and turn left (north) on Adams Street. Follow that to the end and turn right (southeast) on Griffin Street to find the park entrance.
GPS coordinates: N 44 55.289' / W 83 24.893'
About the campground: This is a nice collection of rustic sites strung out with ample space among them under the shade of oak and white pine along the sandy shore of Lake Huron. Hikers and bikers have a mile of trail in the park as well as a boardwalk out to the lake. Get out on Lake

Huron for walleye, salmon, trout, and bass fishing using a boat launch 0.5 mile south of the campground. The camp faces the sunset over Thunder Bay and offers a quiet, relaxing environment.

99 Beaver Lake Campground and County Park

Location: About 13 miles south of Lachine
Season: May 15 to October 1
Sites: 48 sites with water and electrical hookups, 3 sites with electrical hookups, 5 sites with no hookups
Maximum RV length: 40
Facilities: Flush toilets, showers, grills, tables, picnic area, pavilions, dump station, boat launch, beach, playground, fishing dock, fish-cleaning station, volleyball court, ball field, horseshoe pits, concessionaire
Fee per night: $$$-$$$$
Management: Alpena County Parks
Contact: (989) 379-4462; www.alpenacounty.org/parks-recreation
Finding the campground: From Lachine head south on MI 65 about 9 miles and turn right (west) on Beaver Lake Par Road. Go 1.3 miles to the park.
GPS coordinates: N 44 55.773' / W 83 47.575'
About the campground: Beaver Lake is spring-fed and actually one of the deepest lakes in the state. The lake, which shows development around most of its shoreline, is good for fishing. Some of the sites have moderate shade, while most of them are exposed. The park also has a teen activity center, wide grassy areas for sports, a swimming area, and a camp store, making this a good destination for families who want something more than Mother Nature to entertain the kids.

100 Avery Lake State Forest Campground

Location: About 7 miles south of Atlanta
Season: Year-round
Sites: 16 sites with no hookups
Maximum RV length: 40
Facilities: Vault toilets, fire rings, water, tables, hiking/ATV trails, boat launch
Fee per night: $$
Management: Michigan DNR
Contact: (989) 785-4388; www.michigandnr.com/parksandtrails
Finding the campground: From Atlanta follow Main Street south out of town and it becomes CR 487. Continue following its bends and turns for 5.4 miles until you turn right (west) on Avery Lake Road. From there go 2.7 miles to a fork; keep right (west) to stay on Avery Lake Road and the campground is 0.4 mile farther on your right.
GPS coordinates: N 44 55.924' / W 84 11.203'

About the campground: This little lake-in-the-woods campground is as secluded as they come. Sixteen rustic sites are set up on 2 little loops in the woods, but 10 of them can fit a 40-foot RV. Three sites are walk-in. Boats have ramp access to Avery Lake just south of the camping area, and also Crooked Lake 5 miles north. Both the lakes and Thunder Bay River are good for fishing perch, bass, pike, walleye, and bluegill. All sites are first come, first served, and there is a self-pay tube for fees.

101 Big Bear Lake and Big Bear Point State Forest Campgrounds

Location: About 19 miles east of Gaylord
Season: Year-round
Sites: 44 sites with no hookups
Maximum RV length: 30–40
Facilities: Vault toilets, firepits, water, tables, boat launch, hiking/biking/off-road vehicle trails
Fee per night: $$
Management: Michigan DNR
Contact: (989) 732-5485; www.michigandnr.com/parksandtrails
Finding the campground: From Gaylord head east on MI 32 for about 18 miles. Turn right (south) on CR 495/Meridian Line Road and continue 1.4 miles and turn right (west) on Bear Lake Road. The camp is 0.6 mile on the left (south).
GPS coordinates: N 44 56.722' / W 84 22.804'
About the campground: These are 2 nice campgrounds on the north end of a partly developed lake. Big Bear Lake, with 30 sites, has a long, sandy swimming beach, while Big Bear Point, with 14 sites, is out on a sandy point just a bit west of the other park. The lake is home to muskie, pike, and panfish. A trailhead for the Big Bear Lake Trail, a 2.2-mile double loop for hikers and mountain bikers, is inside the lake campground. The trail passes marshy areas where you may spot beavers in action. Buttles Road Pathway is also nearby for more mileage for bikers. While this campground is generally recommended for tents and small trailers, there are 11 sites at Big Bear Lake Campground that can take in a 40-foot vehicle. The bulk of the sites have some tree cover and line up parallel to the shore and are just a few steps off the beach.

102 Little Wolf Lake State Forest Campground

Location: About 3 miles south of Lewiston
Season: Year-round
Sites: 24 sites with no hookups
Maximum RV length: 40
Facilities: Vault toilets, firepits, water, tables, hiking/mountain biking
Fee per night: $$
Management: Michigan DNR

Contact: (989) 732-5485; www.michigandnr.com/parksandtrails

Finding the campground: From CR 612 through Lewiston, head east out of town and turn right (south) on Bear Lake Road/CR 489. Go 1.5 miles and turn left (east) on Wolf Lake Road, go 0.9 mile and turn right (west) on State Park Road, and follow that 0.3 mile to the site.

GPS coordinates: N 44 51.304' / W 84 16.969'

About the campground: Located at the narrowest and shallowest point of Little Wolf Lake (which could be 2 lakes if water levels dropped), this quiet little out-of-the-way campground has spacious sites ample enough in size to park a big rig. Sites are shaded by mixed hardwood forest. Fishing on the lake is only for panfish, and there is no proper boat landing. The closest hiking or biking trail is Buttles Road Pathway, located 6 miles to the northwest.

103 Shupac Lake State Forest Campground

Location: About 23 miles northeast of Grayling

Season: Year-round

Sites: 30 sites with no hookups

Maximum RV length: 25

Facilities: Vault toilets, firepits, water, tables, boat launch

Fee per night: $$

Management: Michigan DNR

Contact: (989) 348-7068; www.michigandnr.com/parksandtrails

Finding the campground: From Grayling take MI 93 northeast 10.5 miles, turn right (east), and go 9.1 miles on CR 612. Turn left (north) on Twin Bridge Road, go 2 miles, and turn right (east) on Campground Trail. The park is 0.8 mile on the right.

GPS coordinates: N 44 49.425' / W 84 28.771'

About the campground: Shupac Lake is OK for fishing for panfish, but boat motors are restricted. If you're looking for trout, the Au Sable River is a half mile west. The campground claims there's hiking, but the closest trail is about 15 miles away at Big Bear Lake, a 2.2-mile loop. The campsites are short and shaded and strung out in a long line, the eastern side just some paces from the lakeside behind them. Hartwick Pines State Park is more developed, but this is a good place for a simple, quiet escape. Don't confuse this with Shoepac Lake.

104 Jones Lake State Forest Campground

Location: About 9 miles east of Frederic

Season: Year-round

Sites: 42 sites with no hookups

Maximum RV length: 20

Facilities: Vault toilets, grills, water, tables, boat launch, hiking/off-road trails

Fee per night: $$

Management: Michigan DNR

Contact: (989) 348-7068; www.michigandnr.com/parksandtrails

Finding the campground: From Frederic head east on CR 612. Turn right (south) on Jones Lake Road and at 0.2 mile the entrance to the camping area is on the right (west) side of the road.

GPS coordinates: N 44 46.959' / W 84 35.247'

About the campground: These sites are arranged in branching lollipop loops in the woods on the east side of Jones Lake. The boat ramp makes this ideal for anglers looking to catch some of the resident walleye, pike, bass, and panfish, but that is the end of on-site activities. The closest hiking is 16 miles southeast on the 11.5 miles of rolling terrain at the Mason Tract. The North Branch of the Au Sable River is 10 miles away as well.

105 McCollum Lake State Forest Campground

Location: About 10 miles north and west of Curran

Season: May to October

Sites: 20 sites with no hookups, 4 walk-in sites (out of a total 20 sites)

Maximum RV length: 11 sites will accommodate larger 40-foot vehicle trailers

Facilities: Vault toilets, firepits, water, tables, picnic area, boat launch, off-road vehicle trails

Fee per night: $$

Management: Clinton Township

Contact: (989) 848-8545; www.michigandnr.com/parksandtrails

Finding the campground: From Curran follow MI 72 north and then stay on it when it turns west for 3.7 more miles. Turn right (north) on McCollum Lake Road and go 2.7 miles and the park entrance is on the right (east).

GPS coordinates: N 44 46.244' / W 83 54.124'

About the campground: This is a simple state forest campground that has a loyal following. When the state was planning to close this campground due to budget cuts, the Township of Clinton rallied to get permission to manage it and keep it open. Some of the sites get full sun, but there is a nice scattering of shade trees. Four sites are walk-in sites for a backcountry experience without the long trek. A trailhead across the road from the camp connects into 25 miles of ATV trails. Paddlers and anglers have lake access, and the fishing turns up pike, bass, walleye, and panfish. An alternative is Au Sable River at Lost Creek just 13 miles away.

106 Harrisville State Park

Location: About 16 miles north of Oscoda

Season: Year-round

Sites: 195 sites with electrical hookups, 15 pull-through sites

Maximum RV length: 50

Facilities: Flush/vault toilets, showers, fire rings, grills, water, tables, picnic shelter, picnic area, dump station, hiking trails, beach, playground, bike rental, telephone

Fee per night: $$$-$$$$

Management: Michigan DNR

Contact: (989) 724-5126; www.michigandnr.com/parksandtrails

Finding the campground: From Oscoda head north on US 23 for 16 miles and the park is on the right just south of Harrisville.

GPS coordinates: N 44 38.876' / W 83 18.121'

About the campground: This small but nicely wooded park is one of the oldest state parks, dating back to 1921, but it has expanded from its original 6 acres to include 107 sitting right on the shore of Lake Huron facing east. The beach is sandy and wide, and a nature trail runs 2 miles through a forest of pine and cedar. While there is a put-in spot for watercraft here, it is really for cartop-sized boats only. The campsites are spacious and separated by grassy areas. All are shaded by tall hardwoods spread evenly throughout. The Sturgeon Point Lighthouse is near the park, and a paved trail connects to the village of Harrisville.

107 Jewell Lake Campground

Location: Just outside Barton City

Season: May 15 to September 10

Sites: 32 sites with no hookups

Maximum RV length: 25

Facilities: Vault toilets, grills, water, tables, boat ramp, hiking trails, beach, dunes

Fee per night: $$

Management: Camp Management Service—Fischer/USDA Forest Service

Contact: (989) 739-0728; www.fs.usda.gov/recarea/hmnf/recreation/wateractivities/recarea/?recid=18830&actid=82

Finding the campground: From MI 72 just south of Barton City, go north on Sanborn Road and follow the curve left (west) as it becomes Richardson Road. The sign for the park is on the right, but the park road is on the left (south).

GPS coordinates: N 44 40.650' / W 83 35.827'

About the campground: With 193 acres, Jewell Lake is a quaint fishing spot at the edge of a very small town. The campground lies on the east side of the lake in good tree cover, and while the sites are not right on the water, it is a short walk and there is a boat launch. There's even a tiny beach. Anglers may catch sunfish, bass, pike, and walleye. Also on-site is a half-mile interpretive trail. This might make a good "roughing it" spot for someone going that route for the first time.

108 Horseshoe Lake Campground– Huron National Forest

Location: About 38 miles west of Harrisville

Season: April 28 to October 4

Sites: 9 sites with no hookups

Maximum RV length: 25

Facilities: Vault toilets, fire rings, water, tables, boat launch

Fee per night: $

Management: Camp Management Service—Fischer/USDA Forest Service

Contact: (989) 739-0728; www.fs.usda.gov/recarea/hmnf/recreation/wateractivities/recarea/?recid=18822&actid=78

Finding the campground: From Harrisville travel west on MI 72 for 22 miles. Turn left (south) on MI 65 for 3 miles. Then turn right (west) on FR 4124 for 1 mile.

GPS coordinates: N 44 36.061' / W 83 45.956'

About the campground: If you are looking for solitude, this lightly used campground in the middle of the Huron National Forest may satisfy your needs. All sites are first come, first served, but this little lake is often overlooked. Anglers have a boat ramp and can catch sunfish, trout, and bass. There is no development on this lake. The park roads are dirt and gravel with low clearance, and the sites are spaced out nicely under shade trees.

Grayling to Mio (North of MI 72)

	Hookup Sites	Total Sites	Max RV Length	Hookups	Toilets	Showers	Drinking Water	Dump Station	Recreation	Fee	Reservations
109 Oscoda County Park	65	153	45	E	F	Y	Y	Y	HSFB	$$-$$$	Y
110 Mio Pond State Forest Campground	0	24	20	N/A	NF	N	Y	N	FLO	$$	N
111 Rainbow Bend State Forest Campground and Canoe Camp	0	7	20	N/A	NF	N	Y	N	HFO	$$	N
112 Hartwick Pines State Park	100	100	50	WES	F	Y	Y	Y	FH	$$$$	Y
113 Au Sable River Canoe Camp	0	13	20	N/A	NF	N	Y	N	HFO	$$	N
114 Keystone Landing State Forest Campground	0	18	30	N/A	NF	N	Y	N	HFO	$$	N
115 Burton's Landing State Forest Campground	0	12	25	N/A	NF	N	Y	N	HFO	$$	N
116 Kneff Lake Campground	0	27	25	N/A	NF	N	Y	N	SFB	$$	N
117 Canoe Harbor State Forest Campground and Canoe Camp	0	45	20	N/A	NF	N	Y	N	HFO	$$	N

See Amenities Charts Key on page xiii.

109 Oscoda County Park

Location: On the north side of Mio south of Mio Dam Pond
Season: April 15 to December 1
Sites: 65 sites with electrical hookups, 88 sites with no hookups
Maximum RV length: 45
Facilities: Flush toilets, showers, fire rings, water, tables, pavilion area, dump station, off-road vehicle trails, beach, playground, volleyball court, basketball court, tetherball court, horseshoe pits, free Wi-Fi
Fee per night: $$-$$$
Management: Oscoda County
Contact: (989) 826-5114; www.oscodacountymi.com/county-park
Finding the campground: Coming into Mio from the west on MI 72, turn left (north) on Jay Smith Drive and follow it 0.4 mile; the park entrance is on the left.
GPS coordinates: N 44 39.408' / W 84 08.355'

About the campground: Though this is right at the edge of town, the park does a nice job of giving a wilderness feeling with its prime location along the edge of this dammed section of the Au Sable River. The sites are divided into a central modern section and 2 rustic sections on either side. The West Rustic sites have 2 loops, and the East Rustic sites have 1. Stairways lead from each section down to the lakeside. Showers are coin-operated, and wood and ice are sold on-site. For something more rustic, try Mio Pond State Forest Campground across the pond.

110 Mio Pond State Forest Campground

Location: About 1.5 miles north and west of Mio, north of Mio Dam Pond
Season: Year-round
Sites: 24 sites with no hookups, 10 walk-in/canoe-in group sites
Maximum RV length: 20
Facilities: Vault toilets, firepits, water, tables, boat launch, off-road vehicle trails
Fee per night: $$
Management: Michigan DNR
Contact: (989) 473-2258; www.michigandnr.com/parksandtrails
Finding the campground: From the center of Mio head north on MI 33/MI 72/Morenci Avenue for 0.7 mile and turn left (west) on Pond Drive. After 0.4 mile, go right on Gerber Road (west) for 0.6 mile and the park entrance is on the left.
GPS coordinates: N 44 39.919' / W 84 08.807'
About the campground: This campground is a rustic and well-wooded alternative to the larger Oscoda County Park across the waters of the Mio Pond to the south. Paddlers will find a livery in Mio and will enjoy some on-site access to the water. Anglers look for trout, walleye, pike, and bass. There are also 10 walk-in sites and areas for groups of paddlers traveling the Au Sable River to set up for the night. The sites are nicely separated from each other and get good coverage from the tree canopy.

111 Rainbow Bend State Forest Campground and Canoe Camp

Location: About 22 miles east of Grayling
Season: Year-round
Sites: 7 sites with no hookups
Maximum RV length: 20
Facilities: Vault toilets, water, fire rings
Fee per night: $$
Management: Michigan DNR
Contact: (989) 348-7068; www.michigandnr.com/parksandtrails

Finding the campground: From Grayling take MI 72 east 15 miles and turn left (north) on McMasters Bridge Road. After the bend turn left (north) on Conners Flat Road and take the third left onto White Eagle Road. The camp is on the left (south) side of the road.

GPS coordinates: N 44 40.183' / W 84 25.077'

About the campground: Situated along the Au Sable River, the small campground is accessible by canoe and popular with paddlers. The river is home to 3 trout species and attracts a variety of wildlife, most notably bald eagles. Sites are nicely shaded and offer some privacy. Water can be taken from a hand-pump well. All sites are first come, first served. The park office is actually back in Grayling.

112 Hartwick Pines State Park

Location: About 6 miles northeast of Grayling

Season: Year-round

Sites: 36 sites with full hookups, 64 sites with electrical hookups

Maximum RV length: 50

Facilities: Flush toilets, showers, grills, water, tables, picnic shelter, picnic area, dump station, hiking/mountain biking trails, playground, fishing pier, pay phone, amphitheater

Fee per night: $$$$

Management: Michigan DNR

Contact: (989) 348-7068; www.michigandnr.com/parksandtrails

Finding the campground: From I-75 just north of Grayling, take MI 93 northeast 2 miles and the park entrance is on the left (north) side of the road.

GPS coordinates: N 44 44.125' / W 84 40.183'

About the campground: Prior to the rise of the logging industry, old-growth trees dominated this state. These days there are very few examples left, but this park takes its name from 49 acres of old-growth pine that were part of an 8,000-acre donation to the state from Karen Hartwick, daughter of a logging company founder. The lumber museum on-site, built by a CCC work crew, was her request. Despite all the trees, just under half the campsites actually have only a small amount of shade. The other half of the sites are in thicker tree cover. Trails total over 15 miles.

113 Au Sable River Canoe Camp

Location: About 6 miles north and east of Grayling

Season: Year-round

Sites: 8 sites with no hookups, 5 rustic walk-in/canoe-in sites

Maximum RV length: 20

Facilities: Vault toilets, fire rings, water, tables, hiking/off-road vehicle trails

Fee per night: $$

Management: Michigan DNR

Contact: (989) 348-7068; www.michigandnr.com/parksandtrails

Old-growth pines have been preserved in Hartwick Pines State Forest. MATT FORSTER

Finding the campground: From Business I-75/MI 93 passing through Grayling, go east on North Down River Road just over 4 miles and take Headquarters Road right (south) about 1.2 miles and the park is on the right.

GPS coordinates: N 44 40.046' / W 84 38.856'

About the campground: The Au Sable is a gorgeous river, and it attracts paddlers and anglers along its length as it flows east to Lake Huron. There are various spots along the way for canoe-camping, but also a few places where drive-up camping is allowed and campers can fish or paddle all day and return to camp. This is a small collection of wooded sites that serve the river, and just a few are reserved strictly for paddlers. Trout are the prized catch in the river. An alternative to this site is Burton's Landing State Forest Campground, just across the river and a bit farther east from here.

114 Keystone Landing State Forest Campground

Location: About 4 miles east of Grayling
Season: Year-round
Sites: 18 sites with no hookups
Maximum RV length: 30
Facilities: Vault toilets, fire rings, water, tables, hiking/off-road vehicle trails
Fee per night: $$
Management: Michigan DNR

Contact: (989) 348-7068; www.michigandnr.com/parksandtrails
Finding the campground: From Grayling follow MI 72 east for 4 miles and turn left (north) on Keystone Landing Road. The park entrance is 0.5 mile north on the right.
GPS coordinates: N 44 39.801' / W 84 37.641'
About the campground: Located on the south side of the Au Sable River, this campground caters to paddlers but not exclusively. Access to the river is on-site for both paddlers putting in and anglers in search of brown, brook, or rainbow trout. The sites are laid out in a series of loops, making them spacious and private. The tree cover is good, but sites are not without a bit of sunshine. Site pads are best suited for tent campers or short trailers.

115 Burton's Landing State Forest Campground

Location: About 3 miles east of Grayling
Season: Year-round
Sites: 12 sites with no hookups
Maximum RV length: 25
Facilities: Vault toilets, fire rings, water, tables, hiking/off-road vehicle trails
Fee per night: $$
Management: Michigan DNR
Contact: (989) 348-7068; www.michigandnr.com/parksandtrails
Finding the campground: From Grayling follow MI 72 east for 3 miles and turn left (north) on Burton's Landing Drive.
GPS coordinates: N 44 39.751' / W 84 38.859'
About the campground: The Au Sable River is a beauty, and while this small collection of rustic sites sits along its edge, it doesn't have much in the way of shade for the sites. An alternative that is rather close is Au Sable River Canoe Camp. Paddlers do, however, have carry-in access to the river, and the closest rentals are in Grayling. Anglers hit the river for trout.

116 Kneff Lake Campground

Location: About 8 miles east and south of Grayling
Season: May 19 to November 11
Sites: 27 sites with no hookups
Maximum RV length: 25
Facilities: Vault toilets, grills, water, tables, beach
Fee per night: $$
Management: Camp Management Service—Fischer/USDA Forest Service
Contact: (989) 826-3252; www.fs.usda.gov/recarea/hmnf/recarea/?recid=18832
Finding the campground: From Grayling travel east on MI 72 for 6.5 miles. Turn right (south) on Stephan Bridge Road and go 1 mile. Turn left (east) on FR 4003 and drive about 1 mile.
GPS coordinates: N 44 38.309' / W 84 34.324'

About the campground: The 20-acre lake has some private holdings along the shore, so this doesn't have the deep-woods feel to it, but the waters are stocked with rainbow trout each year, making it attractive to anglers. There is also a beach and swimming area. Sites are arranged in a couple loops set back from the gravel boat ramp. It's first come, first served but generally doesn't fill up. Most come for day-use fishing.

117 Canoe Harbor State Forest Campground and Canoe Camp

Location: About 13 miles east of Grayling
Season: Year-round
Sites: 41 sites with no hookups, 4 canoe campsites
Maximum RV length: 20
Facilities: Vault toilets, fire rings, water, tables, hiking/off-road vehicle trails
Fee per night: $$
Management: Michigan DNR
Contact: (989) 821-6125; www.michigandnr.com/parksandtrails
Finding the campground: From Grayling go east on MI 72 for 12.5 miles and turn right (south) on Canoe Harbor Road. The park entrance is 0.8 mile south on the left side of the road.
GPS coordinates: N 44 36.451' / W 84 28.284'
About the campground: The South Branch of the Au Sable flows north to connect with the rest of the river flowing east. While this campground is accessible from the water and favored by paddlers, there are abundant sites for those who just prefer to stay in one place and enjoy the scenic river either with day paddle excursions or for fishing and hiking along its length. The sites are on dirt/gravel pads and best for smaller trailers. The trees afford some shade, but most sites still get some sun. The Mason Tract next to the camp has over 11 miles of hiking on rolling terrain.

	Hookup Sites	Total Sites	Max RV Length	Hookups	Toilets	Showers	Drinking Water	Dump Station	Recreation	Fee	Reservations
118 North Higgins Lake State Park	174	174	50	E	F	Y	Y	Y	HSFBL	$$$$	Y
119 Houghton Lake State Forest Campground	0	50	40	N/A	F	N	Y	N	F	$$	N
120 South Higgins Lake State Park	400	400	50	WES	F	Y	Y	Y	HFSL	$$$$	Y
121 Ambrose Lake State Forest Campground	0	25	40	N/A	NF	N	Y	N	HFLO	$$	N
122 Wagner Lake Campground	0	12	50	N/A	NF	N	Y	N	SFB	$$	N
123 Rifle River Recreation Area	75	174	50	E	F	Y	Y	Y	HSFL	$$-$$$	Y
124 Rollways Campground	0	19	50	N/A	NF	N	Y	N	FB	$$	Y
125 Monument Campground–Huron National Forest	0	19	50	N/A	NF	N	Y	N	HFBLO	$$	Y
126 Old Orchard Campground	280	335	45	WE	F	Y	Y	Y	F	$$$	Y
127 Van Etten Lake State Forest Campground	0	49	40	N/A	NF	N	Y	N	FLO	$$	N
128 Round Lake Campground and Day Use Area	0	33	25	N/A	NF	N	Y	N	SFB	$$	N
129 Tawas Point State Park	193	193	40	E	F	Y	Y	Y	HSFBLC	$$$$	Y
130 Au Gres Riverfront Campground	109	109	40	WES	F	Y	Y	Y	FL	$$$$	Y
131 Pinconning Park Campground	62	62	50	WE	F	Y	Y	Y	F	$$$$	Y
132 Trout Lake State Forest Campground	0	35	40	N/A	NF	N	Y	N	HFLC	$$	N
133 House Lake State Forest Campground	0	41	40	N/A	NF	N	Y	N	HFL	$$	N
134 Wilson State Park	158	158	45	E	F	Y	Y	Y	SFB	$$$	Y

See Amenities Charts Key on page xiii.

118 North Higgins Lake State Park

Location: About 8 miles west of Roscommon
Season: Year-round
Sites: 174 sites with electrical hookups
Maximum RV length: 50
Facilities: Flush toilets, showers, grills, water, tables, picnic shelter, picnic area, dump station, boat launch, hiking trails, beach, playground, volleyball court, horseshoe pits
Fee per night: $$$$
Management: Michigan DNR
Contact: (989) 821-6125; www.michigandnr.com/parksandtrails
Finding the campground: From I-75 just west of Roscommon, take Higgins Lake Drive west about 2 miles and the park entrance is on the left (south) side of the road.
GPS coordinates: N 44 30.893' / W 84 45.567'
About the campground: At one time this park was the world's largest seedling nursery, and it remains a great place for seeing birds and other wildlife. The campground is split into 2 very separate loops, with 82 sites in the east loop and 92 in the west loop. A boat launch and sandy beach let visitors enjoy the lake. Almost 12 miles of hiking trails lie to the north in the park across Higgins Lake Drive, where you will also find the fascinating museum dedicated to the Civilian Conservation Corps and the Depression-era work over 100,000 men accomplished in Michigan's forests.

119 Houghton Lake State Forest Campground

Location: About 20 miles south of Grayling
Season: Mid-April to mid-September
Sites: 50 sites with no hookups
Maximum RV length: 40
Facilities: Flush toilets, fire rings, water, tables
Fee per night: $$
Management: Michigan DNR
Contact: (989) 821-6125; www.michigandnr.com/parksandtrails
Finding the campground: From Grayling head south on I-75 and take the slight right on US 127. Take exit 201 to Higgins Lake Road. Turn left (east) on Pine Road/CR 104 and at 0.6 mile turn right (south) on Harrison Road. Go 2.1 miles and turn left (east) on Bradford Drive/CR 300 and left on Houghton Lake Drive. It is 0.5 mile to the camp entrance on the right.
GPS coordinates: N 44 24.061' / W 84 46.493'
About the campground: Lake Houghton is big for fishing and boating and shows a lot of residential and cabin development around its shores considering this is a state forest campground. The camp is located on North Bay, which is an area that is somewhat sheltered from the rest of the lake. The sites are mostly shaded, and a few of them will take the bigger rigs. Fishing is for pike, bass, walleye, and panfish. Half of these sites can be reserved. The closest ATV trail is West Higgins, 4 miles north.

120 South Higgins Lake State Park

Location: About 9 miles southwest of Roscommon
Season: Year-round
Sites: 12 pull-through sites, 41 full hookups, 347 sites with electrical hookups
Maximum RV length: 50
Facilities: Flush toilets, showers, firepits, grills, water, tables, picnic shelter, picnic area, dump station, boat launch, hiking trails, beach, beach house, playground, boat rental, concessionaire
Fee per night: $$$$
Management: Michigan DNR
Contact: (989) 821-6374; www.michigandnr.com/parksandtrails
Finding the campground: From Roscommon head south on MI 18 and cross under I-75. Turn right (northwest) on CR 103/Robinson Lake Road and travel 3.2 miles. Turn left (south) on Higgins Lake Drive/CR 100 and go 3.1 miles to find the park entrance on the right (west) side of the road.
GPS coordinates: N 44 25.387' / W 84 40.692'
About the campground: South Higgins Lake State Park is in a nice position for 2 lakes—not just the large, spring-fed Higgins Lake but also the small Marl Lake just to the south and its 700 acres of hardwood and pine forest. Marl lacks the development along Higgins Lake. The nicely shaded campground is the second largest in a state park, and reservations go fast each year. But multiple toilet/shower facilities serve the abundant number of campers. Fishing in Higgins is for perch and trout, while Marl turns up perch, smallmouth bass, and northern pike.

121 Ambrose Lake State Forest Campground

Location: About 7 miles west of Rose City
Season: Year-round
Sites: 25 sites with no hookups
Maximum RV length: 40
Facilities: Vault toilets, grills, water, tables, boat launch, hiking/off-road vehicle trails
Fee per night: $$
Management: Michigan DNR
Contact: (989) 473-2258; www.michigandnr.com/parksandtrails
Finding the campground: From Rose City head west on Rose City Road for 5.1 miles. Turn left (south) on CR 15/Fairview Road and drive 1 mile to CR 20/Houghton Creek Road. Turn right (west) and follow it just over a mile to the camp.
GPS coordinates: N 44 24.428' / W 84 15.142'
About the campground: Situated on the eastern shore of Ambrose Lake, the campground has a boat ramp. The best sites, of course, are the ones located right along the lake, roughly a third of the total sites. Some sites are on a back loop deeper in the forest and offer more privacy. All of them have decent shade. Anglers will find panfish and bass. Nine miles of ATV trail have a trailhead on-site and connect to the Michigan Cross Country Cycle Trail. Ogemaw Hills and Rose City offer other off-road opportunities.

122 Wagner Lake Campground

Location: About 10 miles north of Rose City
Season: May 19 to November 15
Sites: 12 sites with no hookups
Maximum RV length: 50
Facilities: Vault toilets, fire rings, water, tables, boat ramp, dumpster
Fee per night: $$
Management: Camp Management Service—Fischer/USDA Forest Service
Contact: (989) 826-3252; www.fs.usda.gov/recarea/hmnf/recreation/wateractivities/recarea/?recid=18846&actid=82
Finding the campground: From Rose City head north on MI 33 for 9.2 miles and turn left (west) on Wagner Lake Road and follow that 1.1 miles to the campground.
GPS coordinates: N 44 33.248' / W 84 08.841'
About the campground: Within the Huron National Forest, the campground is simple and nice, just a dirt/gravel loop in a hardwood forest next to a shallow lake. Sites are mostly shaded and the area is quite quiet. The small lake is OK for a bit of limited paddling and fishing. All sites are first come, first served. While long vehicles can get in here, be aware that the clearance is low.

123 Rifle River Recreation Area

Location: About 4 miles east of Rose City
Season: Year-round
Sites: 75 sites with electrical hookups, 99 sites with no hookups
Maximum RV length: 50
Facilities: Flush/vault toilets, showers, firepits, grills, water, tables, dump station, picnic shelter, picnic area, boat launch, hiking/mountain biking trails, beach, playground
Fee per night: $$–$$$
Management: Michigan DNR
Contact: (989) 473-2258; www.michigandnr.com/parksandtrails
Finding the campground: From Rose City go east on Main Street and it becomes Rose City Road/CR 28. Follow this just over 4 miles east and turn right (south) on Ridge Road to enter the park.
GPS coordinates: N 44 25.293' / W 84 01.325'
About the campground: Formerly the private hunting retreat of an auto manufacturer, the Department of Conservation purchased it and turned it into a field research laboratory before passing it on to the Parks Division in 1963. Rifle River offers a wonderful collection of lakes, navigable rivers, and wilderness. Modern sites are located in Grousehaven campground, while 3 other campgrounds in the park offer a rustic experience. The multiuse trail offers 14 miles for hikers and mountain bikers. Canoe launches lie on several points along Rifle River. Fishing is good in the 10 lakes and many miles of streams. The Au Sable River Road Scenic Byway is 20 miles east of here.

Wild turkeys roam the forest in northwest Michigan.

124 Rollways Campground

Location: About 7 miles north of Hale
Season: May 15 to October 11
Sites: 19 sites with no hookups
Maximum RV length: 50
Facilities: Vault toilets, grills, water, tables
Fee per night: $$
Management: Camp Management Service—Fischer/USDA Forest Service
Contact: (989) 739-0728; www.fs.usda.gov/recarea/hmnf/recreation/wateractivities/recarea/?recid=18998&actid=79
Finding the campground: From Hale head north on MI 65 for 6.7 miles and turn left (north) on Rollway Road. The park is 0.2 mile on the right side.
GPS coordinates: N 44 27.562' / W 83 46.410'
About the campground: This single loop in the forest near the Au Sable River is ideal for campers looking for a nice, quiet nature experience. On-site is an observation area as well as a log-built shelter. The spacious sites are shaded by hardwood and pine forest and offer privacy. Despite the river's proximity, however, there is no canoe launch here, nor do the sites have a view of the river. There are launches nearby and liveries. Despite the rustic nature, pull-through RVs can still get in here.

125 Monument Campground–Huron National Forest

Location: About 15 miles west of Oscoda
Season: Memorial Day Weekend through Labor Day
Sites: 19 sites with no hookups
Maximum RV length: 50
Facilities: Vault toilets, grills, water, tables, lantern posts
Fee per night: $$
Management: USDA Forest Service
Contact: (989) 739-0728; www.fs.usda.gov/recarea/hmnf/recarea/?recid=18836
Finding the campground: From Oscoda head west on River Road for 15.4 miles and turn right on Monument Road; the park entrance is on the right at 0.2 mile.
GPS coordinates: N 44 26.055' / W 83 37.197'
About the campground: This single-loop Huron National Forest campground has a bit of history and thus the monument for which it is named. The 14-foot bronze Lumberman's monument on-site remembers the clearing out of the trees around here. The Civilian Conservation Corps was responsible for bringing back the forest in 1938. As you might imagine, the sites are well shaded by pine. The camp is on the River Road Scenic Byway and just off the Au Sable River. Of the 19 sites, 10 are reservable and 2 are double-sized.

126 Old Orchard Campground

Location: About 8 miles west of Oscoda
Season: March to November
Sites: 280 sites with water and electrical hookups, 55 sites with no hookups
Maximum RV length: 45
Facilities: Flush toilets, showers, water, tables, pavilion, dump station, boat ramps, hiking trails, beach, playground, fishing pier, volleyball court, concessionaire
Fee per night: $$$
Management: Township of Oscoda
Contact: (989) 739-7814; www.oscodatwp.com/1/322/old_orchard_campground.asp
Finding the campground: Head east 8 miles on River Road and the park entrance is on the right (north) side of the road.
GPS coordinates: N 44 26.601' / W 83 28.980'
About the campground: Situated along the River Road Scenic Byway as you head west from Oscoda and Lake Huron, this campground is actually one of the largest in the state. Measuring 4 miles in length, it has shoreline on Foote Pond, which was created when the Foote Dam was built on the Au Sable River in 1906. Shore fishing is popular, and there is an accessible fishing pier. Plentiful park equipment and easy hiking trails make this popular with families. Sites are partly shaded, but on a busy weekend you can expect over 1,000 people in the park. Thirty-one premium waterfront sites, including 10 pull-through sites, are reservable for dates after May 1.

127 Van Etten Lake State Forest Campground

Location: About 4 miles northwest of Oscoda
Season: Year-round
Sites: 49 sites with no hookups
Maximum RV length: 40
Facilities: Vault toilets, grills, water, tables, boat launch
Fee per night: $$
Management: Michigan DNR
Contact: (989) 362-5041; www.michigandnr.com/parksandtrails
Finding the campground: From US 23 in Oscoda, go west on CR F41 for 3.5 miles and the park entrance is on the right (north).
GPS coordinates: N 44 28.198' / W 83 22.489'
About the campground: The former Wurtsmith Air Force Base lies just south of this park. During the Cold War B-52 bombers were kept here. Now it's a local airport with no scheduled flights that might disturb (or fascinate) campers. Van Etten Lake's campground offers easy access and a boat launch to get on the water, but be aware that much of the shoreline outside the park is developed. The campsites offer good shade in mixed forest and are spacious. Only half of the sites can be reserved, and just a few sites remain open through winter. South of here about 20 minutes is the Tuttle Marsh Wildlife Area, an impressive 5,000-acre wetlands reserve that is a major draw for wildlife viewing, especially birds and especially during spring migration.

128 Round Lake Campground and Day Use Area

Location: About 10 miles east and south of Hale
Season: May 10 to September 12
Sites: 33 sites with no hookups
Maximum RV length: 25
Facilities: Vault toilets, firepits, water, tables, picnic area, boat ramp, beach, lantern posts
Fee per night: $$
Management: Krumm Management Team/USDA Forest Service
Contact: (989) 739-0728 or (877) 444-6777 for reservations; www.fs.usda.gov/recarea/hmnf/recarea/?recid=18840
Finding the campground: From Hale head east out of town on Main Street, which becomes Esmond Road, then Vaughn Road, and finally Indian Lake Road as you pass north of Sand Lake. Turn left on Latham Street and go 0.7 mile to find the park road on the right.
GPS coordinates: N 44 20.601' / W 83 39.709'
About the campground: Round Lake is 1 of 7 in a cluster of lakes that are surrounded mostly by private land. This campground is the only public access to the lake and is quiet and difficult to find. The sites are well shaded by mixed forest. While the sites are spaced out for privacy, clearance is low and anything larger than a small trailer will have trouble negotiating the campsites. Probably best suited for anglers, the lake is cold but shallow, and the best catches are sunfish,

bass, and maybe some pike. Most sites are first come, first served, but the first 13 require advance reservations.

129 Tawas Point State Park

Location: About 3 miles east and south of East Tawas
Season: May to November
Sites: 193 sites with electrical hookups
Maximum RV length: 40
Facilities: Flush toilets, showers, grills, water, tables, picnic shelter, picnic area, dump station, hiking/biking trails, beach, beach house, playground, concessionaire, lighthouse
Fee per night: $$$$
Management: Michigan DNR
Contact: (989) 362-5041; www.michigandnr.com/parksandtrails
Finding the campground: From East Tawas take US 23 north 1 mile to Tawas Beach Road. Turn right (east) and go 2.5 miles to the park entrance on the right side of the road.
GPS coordinates: N 44 15.498' / W 83 26.534'
About the campground: Some may call Tawas Point the Cape Cod of the Midwest. The park is halfway out on a point that includes a Victorian-style lighthouse and an interpretive trail that runs the length of the peninsula with beaches on both sides. The campsites are laid out in 3 parallel loops, and all have a good mix of shade and exposure. The waters of Tawas Bay are a bit warmer than the usual Lake Huron experience, making it good for a swim, and the fishing is quite good as well. Birders can expect a lot of migratory species in the spring. Cabins are available year-round.

130 Au Gres Riverfront Campground

Location: In downtown Au Gres
Season: Year-round
Sites: 26 sites with full hookups, 83 sites with water and electrical hookups
Maximum RV length: 40
Facilities: Flush toilets, showers, grills, water, tables, picnic area, dump station, boat launch, playground, fish-cleaning station, volleyball court, tennis court, baseball fields, basketball courts, horseshoe pits, gazebo
Fee per night: $$$$
Management: City of Au Gres
Contact: (989) 876-8310; www.cityofaugresmi.com/city-augres-campground
Finding the campground: From US 23 through Au Gres, go north 1 block on Main Street and the park is on the left (west) side of the road.
GPS coordinates: N 44 02.990' / W 83 41.158'
About the campground: This city park gets quite busy because of its convenient location. While the camp is situated on the Au Gres River, the boat launch there connects watercraft to Saginaw Bay and Lake Huron. Fishing is one of the main attractions, though the park's many facilities play

to families. The sites in the loop along the river have shade trees, while the sites closer to the road are right out in the open. Thirty-three of the sites are along the riverfront. Reservations for holiday weekends require a 3-night minimum and advance payment.

131 Pinconning Park Campground

Location: About 2 miles east of Pinconning
Season: Year-round
Sites: 42 sites with water and electrical hookups, 20 sites with electrical hookups
Maximum RV length: 50
Facilities: Flush toilets, showers, fire rings, grills, water, tables, picnic area, pavilion, gazebo, dump station, boat launch, playground, basketball court, horseshoe pits, Wi-Fi
Fee per night: $$$$
Management: Bay County Recreation Division
Contact: (989) 879-5050; www.baycounty-mi.gov/PinconningPark
Finding the campground: From MI 13 through Pinconning, head east on 5th Street and it becomes Pinconning Road just east of town. Follow this to the end and the campground entrance is on the left (north) side.
GPS coordinates: N 43 51.191' / W 83 55.528'
About the campground: The park nestles up against Saginaw Bay a short drive from I-75. Abundant walleye (and other species) draw anglers, and the day-use area offers a boat launch. The sites are laid out in one long arm heading north, parallel to the lake but separated from it by forest. Other than 10 sites with concrete pads, sites have gravel pads, and most of them are only partly shaded. A few big oaks offer better protection but may be a hassle for bigger rigs. The park has 4 nature trails passing through forest and marshlands, as well as along the lake. During migration season the park is especially popular with birders.

132 Trout Lake State Forest Campground

Location: About 18 miles north of Gladwin
Season: Year-round
Sites: 35 sites with no hookups
Maximum RV length: 40
Facilities: Vault toilets, grills, water, tables, boat launch, hiking/mountain biking trails
Fee per night: $$
Management: Michigan DNR
Contact: (989) 539-3021; www.michigandnr.com/parksandtrails
Finding the campground: From Gladwin head north on MI 18 for 16 miles and turn right (east) on Sugar River Road. At 2.1 miles the road comes to the campground.
GPS coordinates: N 44 08.046' / W 84 33.912'

About the campground: Trout Lake is quite similar to House Lake State Forest Campground, and the two are actually connected by a 2.7-mile hiking trail. The sites here are smaller and more private, however, and only 10 of them can take in a big rig of 40 feet. Fishing on this lake, as well as on House and Hoister Lakes, is only for panfish.

133 House Lake State Forest Campground

Location: About 19 miles north of Gladwin
Season: Year-round
Sites: 41 sites with no hookups
Maximum RV length: 40
Facilities: Vault toilets, grills, water, tables, boat launch, hiking/mountain biking trails
Fee per night: $$
Management: Michigan DNR
Contact: (989) 539-3021; www.michigandnr.com/parksandtrails
Finding the campground: From Gladwin head north on MI 18 for 16 miles and turn right (east) on Sugar River Road. At 1.5 miles turn left (north) on Joy Drive to continue for another 0.5 mile and follow Joy Road to the right (east). At the fork go left (north) and take the immediate right (east) and follow that to find the park road on the left (north) at about 0.2 mile.
GPS coordinates: N 44 08.424' / W 84 34.177'
About the campground: House Lake is part of a threesome of accessible lakes. Though rustic, most of these sites will accommodate a 40-foot vehicle/trailer combo. Hikers have 2.7 miles of gently rolling trails around Trout Lake. Anglers can either carry in with canoes here or use a boat launch at Trout Lake or Hoister Lake. But the only fish to catch are panfish.

134 Wilson State Park

Location: On the north side of Harrison
Season: Year-round
Sites: 158 sites with electrical hookups
Maximum RV length: 45
Facilities: Flush/vault toilets, showers, firepits, grills, water, tables, picnic shelter, picnic area, dump station, beach, beach house, playground, ball field, basketball court, tepee rental
Fee per night: $$$
Management: Michigan DNR
Contact: (989) 539-3021; www.michigandnr.com/parksandtrails
Finding the campground: From where MI 60 and Business US 127 meet in the center of Harrison, go north 0.7 mile on Business US 127 and the park entrance is on the right.
GPS coordinates: N 44 01.730' / W 84 48.332'
About the campground: Donated to the state of Michigan by a lumber company that operated on-site in the late 1800s, these 36 acres of woods include a sandy swimming beach along the

northwest end of Budd Lake. Anglers may find muskie, bass, panfish, perch, and walleye, and there's a boat launch outside the park at the southern end of the lake. This is a common place to camp for attendees of the many summer events at Clare County Fairgrounds right across the street. Other area activities include mini golf, go-karts, and paddling on the Muskegon River.

Northwest Michigan

Thanks to the Leelanau and Old Mission Peninsulas, the northwest region of Michigan has a tremendous amount of shoreline on Lake Michigan. Directly to the north of it all is Grand Traverse Bay, a bay divided into west and east arms by the Old Mission Peninsula. The particular climate conditions formed here are ideal for cherries and vineyards, so one can expect an abundance of wineries (especially on the peninsula) and local cherry products.

Petoskey to the north on the eastern side of Grand Traverse shares its name with the Michigan state stone, pebbles that visitors spend hours searching for on the lakeshore. They contain ancient coral fossils and only reveal themselves to patient eyes. Just offshore on this side of the bay are several islands, including the one-time kingdom of a Mormon preacher, Beaver Island. Now known as America's Emerald Isle, it requires a ferry ride to get your camper or gear there but is rewarding in its beauty and isolation.

From the east the Inland Lakes Waterway enters this region with its navigable chain of lakes and rivers that connect the two Great Lakes Michigan and Huron. Also entering from the Northeast Michigan region is the Shore-to-Shore Trail, which crosses from Empire inside Sleeping Bear Dunes National Lakeshore all the way east to Oscoda on Lake Huron, offering hikers and horseback riders 220 miles of dedicated pathway.

Coming into the Northwest region along Lake Michigan from the south, you'll come to Ludington. The SS *Badger* car ferry connects the city to Manitowoc, Wisconsin. North of here is the Nordhouse Dunes Wilderness Area, which showcases some ancient sand dunes rising up to about 140 feet above the lake.

But even farther north along Lake Michigan lies the Leelanau Peninsula, home to Sleeping Bear Dunes National Lakeshore, the impressive sloping sandy wonder that has often been referred to as one of our nation's most impressive natural sights. Visitors flock here in summer to climb down the massive dunes to the lakeside, or to get sweeping vistas of them and the islands off shore. While camping on North and South Manitou Islands is strictly for backcountry campers, there are two campgrounds on the mainland and others outside but still near to the park.

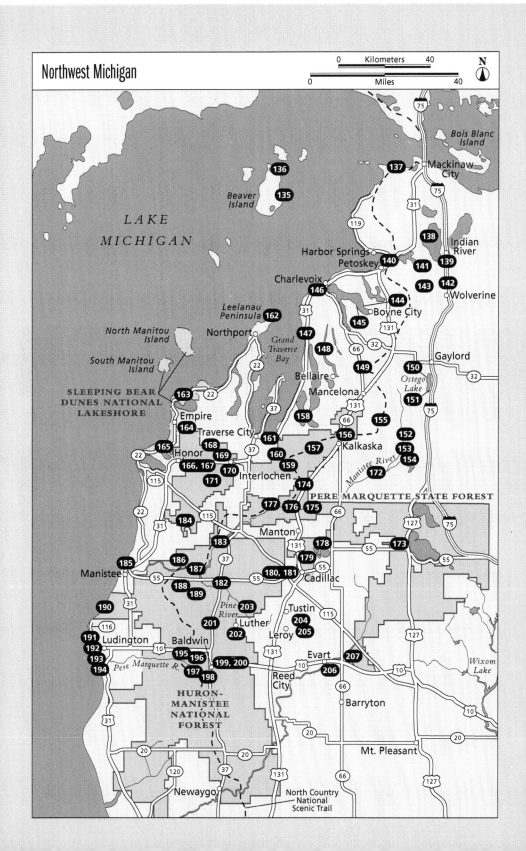

A loon on a lake in Michigan

But there's more than just lakeshore. Huron-Manistee National Forests offers an abundance of fishing lakes and deep-woods camping. The Pere Marquette River is one of three National Wild and Scenic Rivers in this region. Its waters form one of the best trout streams in the Midwest. The lower Manistee River runs slow and wide, and anglers can catch salmon while paddlers take a lazy ride. Finally there's the Pine River with fine scenery and rapid current for canoes and small boats.

Petoskey Area

	Hookup Sites	Total Sites	Max. RV Length	Hookups	Toilets	Showers	Drinking Water	Dump Station	Recreation	Fee	Can Reserve
135 Bill Wagner Peaine Township Campground	0	22	40	N/A	NF	N	Y	N	S	$	N
136 St. James Township Campground	0	12	40	N/A	NF	N	Y	N	H	$	N
137 Wilderness State Park	250	250	50	E	F	Y	Y	Y	HSFBL	$$$-$$$$	Y
138 Maple Bay State Forest Campground	0	35	25	N/A	NF	N	Y	N	HFLO	$$	N
139 Burt Lake State Park	306	306	50	E	F	Y	Y	Y	HSFBL	$$$$	Y
140 Petoskey State Park	180	180	40	E	F	Y	Y	Y	HS	$$$$	Y
141 Camp Petosega	90	90	40	WES	F	Y	Y	Y	HS	$$$$	Y
142 Haakwood State Forest Campground	0	18	40	N/A	NF	N	Y	N	HFO	$$	N
143 Weber Lake State Forest Campground	0	18	25	N/A	NF	N	Y	N	HFOC	$$	N
144 Young State Park	240	240	50	E	F	Y	Y	Y	HSFBL	$$$$	Y
145 Whiting County Park	13	56	40	E	F	Y	Y	N	HSL	$$-$$$	Y
146 Fisherman's Island State Park	0	81	50	N/A	NF	N	Y	N	HSF	$$	Y
147 Barnes Park	67	80	40	E	F	Y	Y	Y	HS	$$$$	Y
148 Thurston Park	40	40	50	WES	F	Y	Y	Y	SFL	$$$	Y
149 Graves Crossing State Forest Campground	0	10	20	N/A	NF	N	Y	N	HFO	$$	N
150 Otsego Lake County Park	80	80	45	E	F	Y	Y	N	SL	$$$	Y
151 Otsego Lake State Park	155	155	50	E	F	Y	Y	Y	HSFBL	$$$	Y

See Amenities Charts Key on page xiii.

135 Bill Wagner Peaine Township Campground

Location: About 7 miles south of St. James Harbor
Season: April 1 to November 30
Sites: 22 sites with no hookups
Maximum RV length: 40
Facilities: Vault toilets, water, tables

Fee per night: $

Management: St. James Township

Contact: (231) 448-2505; www.beaverisland.org/camping

Finding the campground: From the ferry head southwest on Main Street and turn right on Forest Avenue. Take the next left on King's Highway and travel 6 miles south, turn left on Hannigan, and continue another 1.4 miles to East Side Drive. Turn right here and the camp is on the left.

GPS coordinates: N 45 39.341' / W 85 29.806'

About the campground: Beaver Island is known as America's Emerald Isle, partly because so many Irish settled here—from Donegal, thus the name Donegal Bay—but also because of its abundant greenery. In 1850 it was ruled by a monarch, James Jesse Strang, a Mormon leader who declared himself king of his followers, who had settled there in 1848 after the death of Joseph Smith. This campground is rustic and set along the beach facing the mainland. Contact the Beaver Island Boat Company at (888) 446-4095 or visit bibco.com.

136 St. James Township Campground

Location: About 1 mile west of St. James Harbor

Season: April 1 to November 30

Sites: 12 sites with no hookups

Maximum RV length: 40

Facilities: Vault toilets, water, tables

Fee per night: $

Management: St. James Township

Contact: (231) 448-2505; www.beaverisland.org/camping

Finding the campground: From the ferry turn left (south) on Main Street and then right (west) on Donegal Bay Road. Drive about 1 mile and the camp entrance is on the right.

GPS coordinates: N 45 44.935' / W 85 32.293'

About the campground: Beaver Island is Lake Michigan's largest island. Visitors can see 2 lighthouses, hike in Jordan River State Forest, or explore the coastline by land or by sea kayak. Of the island's 2 campgrounds, this is the easier to get to from the ferry, but it is also halfway into town. Four of the sites have lake views, and all offer some good shade. Getting here requires a 2-hour ferry ride and quite a fee to bring a vehicle. Contact the Beaver Island Boat Company at (888) 446-4095 or visit bibco.com.

137 Wilderness State Park

Location: About 11 miles west of Mackinaw City

Season: Year-round

Sites: 250 sites with electrical hookups, 2 hike-in rustic sites, 9 cabins

Maximum RV length: 50

Facilities: Flush toilets, grills, water, showers, tables, picnic area, dump station, boat launch, hiking/mountain biking trails, beach, playground
Fee per night: $$$$
Management: Michigan DNR
Contact: (231) 436-5381; www.michigandnr.com/parksandtrails
Finding the campground: From downtown Mackinaw City take Central Avenue west to its end and turn left (south) on Wilderness Park Drive. This goes all the way to the park entrance with a couple of turns to follow along the way.
GPS coordinates: N 45 44.745' / W 84 53.999'
About the campground: With 26 miles of lakeshore, visitors can find a bit of Lake Michigan for themselves. But there are also 10,000 acres of wilderness and over 20 miles of hiking trails to explore it. The campsites are arranged in 2 loops: the Lakeshore section along the shore of Big Stone Bay on Lake Michigan, and the Pines, another loop set back and across the park road south from those. Many of them offer at least partial shade. The first 75 sites of the lakeshore received an upgrade in 2020. Two rustic sites are set apart for hike-in camping. There are also 6 cabins and 3 rustic bunkhouses for rent.

138 Maple Bay State Forest Campground

Location: About 18 miles northeast of Petoskey
Season: Year-round
Sites: 35 sites with no hookups
Maximum RV length: 25
Facilities: Vault toilets, grills, water, tables, boat launch, hiking/mountain biking/off-road vehicle trails
Fee per night: $$
Management: Michigan DNR
Contact: (231) 238-9392; www.michigandnr.com/parksandtrails
Finding the campground: From Petoskey head north on US 31 for 14.3 miles and turn right (east) on Brutus Road. Go 3.6 miles and turn right (south) on Maple Bay Road and the park is 0.3 mile south on the right side.
GPS coordinates: N 45 29.329' / W 84 42.407'
About the campground: This campground is right on the shore of a bay on the west side of Burt Lake, named for a 19th-century surveyor of the area. Burt Lake is 10 miles, north to south, and 5 miles at its widest point. Boat access here is great, and the sandy beach makes for good swimming. But the larger story is that Burt Lake is part of the Inland Lakes Waterway, a series of lakes and rivers that connects Lake Michigan and Lake Huron right across the northern reaches of the state. Anglers will be interested in the resident lake sturgeon. Hikers should check out nearby Chaboiganing Nature Preserve. The sites are shaded in 2 loops extending from the lake. The sites at the end overlook the water.

139 Burt Lake State Park

Location: At the southern edge of the town of Indian River
Season: May through October
Sites: 306 sites with electrical hookups
Maximum RV length: 50
Facilities: Flush toilets, grills, water, tables, picnic shelter, picnic area, dump station, boat launch, hiking trails, beach, playground, volleyball beach, horseshoe pits, ball diamond, concessionaire
Fee per night: $$$$
Management: Michigan DNR
Contact: (231) 238-9392; www.michigandnr.com/parksandtrails
Finding the campground: Follow MI 68 south where it leaves Indian Trail. The park road is on the right (west) side.
GPS coordinates: N 45 24.086' / W 84 37.167'
About the campground: This is the heart of Michigan's Inland Lakes Waterway, a 38-mile chain of lakes and rivers popular with boaters. The sites are arranged more or less as contiguous long loops lying parallel to the lake. Abundant trees shade the majority of them, but the row closest to the lake has a lot of sunshine. The beach offers swimming or fishing on Burt Lake, and hiking is limited to 1 mile of trail. Though there are a very large number of sites, facilities also include 4 toilet and shower buildings to serve all those campers.

140 Petoskey State Park

Location: About 5 miles east and south of Harbor Springs
Season: Year-round
Sites: 180 sites with electrical hookups
Maximum RV length: 40
Facilities: Flush toilets, grills, water, tables, picnic area, dump station, hiking/biking trails, beach, beach house, playground
Fee per night: $$$$
Management: Michigan DNR
Contact: (231) 347-2311; www.michigandnr.com/parksandtrails
Finding the campground: From Harbor Springs head east on Main Street/MI 119 for 5.5 miles and the park entrance is on the right (west) side of the road.
GPS coordinates: N 45 24.478' / W 84 54.136'
About the campground: Located at the eastern end of Little Traverse Bay, the park surprisingly has no boat launches. Not to worry, however, as both Harbor Springs and Petoskey in either direction have public launches to get out on the water. The park has 2 campgrounds: Dunes and Tannery Creek. Dunes has 80 sites that are mostly shaded and separated from the lake by a narrow band of trees and the dunes. This is closer to the day-use area. Tannery Creek, which lies farther south, away from the day traffic, has 98 sites laid out in 4 loops extending perpendicular to the lake. The

Petoskey stones COURTESY TRAVERSE CITY CONVENTION & VISITORS BUREAU

southernmost loop offers the most sunshine; otherwise most are shaded. About 3 miles of hiking trails are on-site, and the beach is sandy.

141 Camp Petosega

Location: About 12 miles east of Petoskey
Season: Year-round
Sites: 90 sites with water and electrical hookups, 10 universally accessible sites, 5 sites with full hookups
Maximum RV length: 40
Facilities: Flush toilets, showers, grills, water, tables, picnic area, dump station, boat launch, hiking trails, beach, playground, volleyball court, tennis court, basketball court, pavilion
Fee per night: $$$$
Management: Emmet County
Contact: (231) 347-6536; www.emmetcounty.org/parks-recreation/camp-petosega; www.camp-petosega.org
Finding the campground: From Petoskey take Mitchell Road east almost 9 miles and turn left (north) on Ellsworth Road, following it 1.6 miles to turn right (east) on Pickerel Lake Road. Follow this 1.2 miles and it curves north as Botsford Road. Stay on this another mile and it runs right into the park.
GPS coordinates: N 45 23.397' / W 84 44.427'

About the campground: This county park occupies 300 acres on Pickerel Lake. The sites, however, are set back into the woods and are arranged in loops A through D. They are generally open to the sky, but trees are plentiful and will give you at least some partial shade. The sites are also nicely spaced, with some intervening trees or brush making them more private. Reservations are a good idea. The park hosts events for campers throughout the summer season.

142 Haakwood State Forest Campground

Location: About 2 miles north of Wolverine
Season: Year-round
Sites: 18 sites with no hookups
Maximum RV length: 40
Facilities: Vault toilets, fire rings, water, tables, hiking/off-road vehicle trails
Fee per night: $$
Management: Michigan DNR
Contact: (231) 238-9392; www.michigandnr.com/parksandtrails
Finding the campground: From I-75 get off at the Wolverine exit and follow Main Street west into town. Turn right (north) on Straits Highway and go 2.1 miles north to the park entrance on the right (east).
GPS coordinates: N 45 18.140' / W 84 37.033'
About the campground: The Sturgeon River is the Lower Peninsula's fastest-flowing river, and it makes its serpentine way through this state forest campground. The sites are close to the water, making it attractive to paddlers, and anglers can find brown and rainbow trout here. The 62-mile North Central State Trail (formerly the Gaylord to Mackinaw City Trail) shared by hikers and bikers is a converted rail bed with crushed limestone that runs right past the park. The campsites vary in tree coverage from wide open and grassy to quite shaded, but they are spread out nicely to give some privacy.

143 Weber Lake State Forest Campground

Location: About 7 miles west of Wolverine
Season: Year-round
Sites: 18 sites with no hookups
Maximum RV length: 25
Facilities: Vault toilets, fire rings, water, tables, hiking/biking/off-road vehicle trails
Fee per night: $$
Management: Michigan DNR
Contact: (231) 238-9392; www.michigandnr.com/parksandtrails
Finding the campground: From Wolverine head west on Wolverine Road for 5.1 miles. Turn left on Peru Road and go 0.5 mile to the park entrance on the right.
GPS coordinates: N 45 17.785' / W 84 43.296'

About the campground: For campers who also enjoy a bit of hiking, this state forest camp offers a nice combo. Lost Tamarack Trail is a double loop with 4.75 miles of pathway suitable for both trekkers and mountain bikers. It leaves from the north end of the site but is not always clearly marked. Fishing in Weber Lake might get you some brown or rainbow trout, perch, or largemouth bass. The sites are arranged in a series of loops running north to south along the east side of the lake. The woods are thick here for a bit of privacy and shade, although a couple sites may offer some sunshine at midday. The sites are not quite on the water, and there is no proper boat launch in the campground.

144 Young State Park

Location: About 2 miles northwest of Boyne City
Season: Year-round
Sites: 240 sites with electrical hookups
Maximum RV length: 50
Facilities: Flush toilets, grills, water, tables, picnic area, dump station, boat launch, hiking trails, beach, beach house, playground, concessionaire
Fee per night: $$$$
Management: Michigan DNR
Contact: (231) 582-7523; www.michigandnr.com/parksandtrails
Finding the campground: Drive north from Boyne City on Lake Street. Turn left (west) on Michigan Avenue, which becomes Charlevoix Road at the curve. The park road is on the left (west) side of the road.
GPS coordinates: N 45 14.153' / W 85 02.525'
About the campground: Situated on the eastern reaches of the 17,260-acre Lake Charlevoix, this state park has 3 campgrounds: Oak, Spruce, and Terrace. The park offers nearly 5 miles of hiking trails. The lake is stocked with rainbow, brown, and lake trout, but Mirror Pond lets the kids fish for rock bass and sunfish. Terrace Campground has 41 sites and has a boat launch within its loops. Oak Campground has the same number of sites and is also close to the lake. Spruce is the largest campground and has 158 sites in 4 loops, the western ends of each loop being closest to the lake. Most of the sites within the park have partial shade, with trees scattered throughout.

145 Whiting County Park

Location: About 5 miles north of Boyne City
Season: May 4 to October 14
Sites: 13 sites with electrical hookups, 43 sites with no hookups
Maximum RV length: 40
Facilities: Flush toilets, showers, grills, water, tables, boat launch, hiking trails, beach, playground, pavilions
Fee per night: $$-$$$
Management: Charlevoix County

Contact: (231) 582-7040; www.charlevoixcounty.org/whitingpark/index.php
Finding the campground: From Boyne City go north on Lake Shore Drive for 3.8 miles and the park is on the right (east) side of the road.
GPS coordinates: N 45 14.251' / W 85 05.417'
About the campground: This family campground has a nice setting, with a half mile of beach on Lake Charlevoix. Many sites are situated right on the lake, but those that are not are quite near anyway. Sites are partly shaded generally but are side by side and lack privacy. Fourteen of the sites are universally accessible. The sandy beach is very nice for swimming, with a designated boat-free area.

146 Fisherman's Island State Park

Location: About 4 miles west of Charlevoix
Season: Year-round
Sites: 81 sites with no hookups
Maximum RV length: 50
Facilities: Vault toilets, grills, water, tables, picnic area, hiking trails, beach
Fee per night: $$
Management: Michigan DNR
Contact: (231) 547-6641; www.michigandnr.com/parksandtrails
Finding the campground: From Charlevoix head west on US 31 for 2.3 miles and then turn right (north, curving west) on Bells Bay Road. Follow this 1.2 miles to the park's entrance on the left (south).
GPS coordinates: N 45 18.480' / W 85 18.622'
About the campground: The name of the park isn't entirely accurate anymore. What was an island has now become a sandy peninsula due to years of low water levels on Lake Michigan. The state park's campsites are divided into 2 campgrounds along the shore, offering sites among the sand dunes and a hiking trail that connects both areas. The beach, along Lake Michigan, faces the sunset and is good for swimming. The terrain is lovely, with rolling dunes overgrown with aspen, birch, and maple forest and interspersed by cedar and black spruce bogs. The entry road is from the north end of the park.

147 Barnes Park

Location: About 15 miles northwest of Bellaire
Season: May 11 to October 22
Sites: 67 sites with electrical hookups, 6 sites with no hookups, 7 walk-in sites
Maximum RV length: 40
Facilities: Flush toilets, showers, firepits, grills, tables, pavilions, picnic area, dump station, hiking/biking trails, beach, playground, volleyball area, baseball fields, basketball courts, horseshoe pits, Wi-Fi
Fee per night: $$$$

Management: Antrim County
Contact: (231) 599-2712; www.antrimcounty.org/barnespark.asp
Finding the campground: From Bellaire follow MI 88 north 14.1 miles to where it crosses US 31. Go straight across (west) and continue on Barnes Park Road for 0.5 mile and this will lead right into the park.
GPS coordinates: N 45 06.659' / W 85 21.641'
About the campground: This county park has some nice real estate. Set right along Grand Traverse Bay and facing west for sunset, there are 1,200 feet of sandy beach. The sites are set back from the sand in a modestly wooded loop. Sites are spacious.

148 Thurston Park

Location: Inside the Village of Central Lake
Season: Year-round
Sites: 11 sites with full hookups, 3 sites with water and electrical hookups, 26 sites with electrical hookups
Maximum RV length: 50
Facilities: Flush toilets, showers, grills, water, tables, picnic area, dump station, boat launch, beach, bathhouse, playground
Fee per night: $$$
Management: Village of Central Lake
Contact: (231) 544-6483; https://centrallakemi.org/?page_id=23
Finding the campground: From Main Street/MI 88 in the center of town, go east on State Street for 2 blocks and take a left (south) on Lake Street. The park is on the left (east) side of the road.
GPS coordinates: N 45 04.132' / W 85 15.580'
About the campground: Thurston Park sits on the northern end of Intermediate Lake, one of the Chain of Lakes, and is within the village limits. Waterfront sites cost a few dollars more per night than those set back a little from the lake. All sites are mostly sunny. The modern conveniences of the town are right at hand. Long-term discounts are available.

149 Graves Crossing State Forest Campground

Location: About 7 miles north of Mancelona
Season: Year-round
Sites: 10 sites with no hookups
Maximum RV length: 20
Facilities: Vault toilets, grills, water, tables, hiking/off-road trails
Fee per night: $$
Management: Michigan DNR
Contact: (231) 582-7523; www.michigandnr.com/parksandtrails
Finding the campground: From Mancelona head north on MI 66 for 6.7 miles and the park entrance is on the right (east) side of the road.

Wildflowers along the North Country National Scenic Trail in Graves Crossing

GPS coordinates: N 45 00.361' / W 85 03.782'

About the campground: The Jordan River was Michigan's first to be designated a Wild and Scenic River, and it runs right past this campground. Paddlers have carry-in access and can head downriver from here, while upriver only allows anglers without boats. The sites are wooded. Hikers enjoy 18 miles of trekking along the Jordan Valley Pathway, which includes some North Country National Scenic Trail. Anglers may catch brown and rainbow trout, steelhead, and salmon. Intermediate Lake and Lake Charlevoix are also short drives away.

150 Otsego Lake County Park

Location: About 5 miles south of Gaylord
Season: May to October
Sites: 80 sites with electrical hookups
Maximum RV length: 45
Facilities: Flush toilets, showers, firepits, tables, picnic area, pavilions, boat launch, beach, playground, volleyball court, basketball court, horseshoe pits, boat rental, concessionaire, Wi-Fi
Fee per night: $$$
Management: Otsego County

Contact: (989) 731-6448; http://otsegocountyparksrec.com

Finding the campground: From MI 32 in Gaylord head south on Business I-75 for 1.7 miles and turn right (west) on McCoy Road; go 0.5 mile and take Dickerson to the left (south) for another mile. Then turn right (west) on Otsego Lake Drive and go 2.2 miles to turn left (east) on County Park Road.

GPS coordinates: N 44 57.984' / W 84 42.149'

About the campground: Otsego Lake runs north to south, and this county park is about midway down on the west side of this popular fishing lake. The park is well taken care of. Abundant pine and some deciduous trees shelter the sites separated by maintained grass. Lakeside sites are truly right at the edge of the lake. The beach is a narrow strip of sand at the lakeside, facing a swimming area marked with buoys. This isn't wilderness camping; you are basically still inside town, but it is a nice place to spend a night. Compare to the state park of the same name.

151 Otsego Lake State Park

Location: About 7 miles south of Gaylord

Season: April 27 to October 28

Sites: 155 sites with electrical hookups

Maximum RV length: 50

Facilities: Flush/vault toilets, showers, firepits, grills, water, tables, picnic shelter, picnic area, dump station, boat launch, hiking trails, beach, beach house, playground, fishing pier, fish-cleaning station, concessionaire

Fee per night: $$$

Management: Michigan DNR

Contact: (989) 732-5485; www.michigandnr.com/parksandtrails

Finding the campground: From Main Street/MI 32 in Gaylord, take Business I-75 south and continue, passing under I-75, onto what becomes Old 27. The park entrance is on the right (west) side about 4 miles from I-75.

GPS coordinates: N 44 55.697' / W 84 41.323'

About the campground: Much larger than its county counterpart, Otsego Lake State Park is on the southeast side of the lake and has more hustle and bustle, plus modern conveniences and facilities. In the north loop, campsites sit on higher ground, are quite spacious, and have shade from a mix of maple, oak, and pine; 21 have lake views. The sites in the southern loop are not quite as roomy, but 12 have lake views, and the whole loop is closer to lake level. The beach and swimming area are nice. For a bit more peace and quiet and closer lake perches, consider Otsego Lake County Park.

Traverse City Area

	Hookup Sites	Total Sites	Max RV Length	Hookups	Toilets	Showers	Drinking Water	Dump Station	Recreation	Fee	Reservations
152 Goose Creek State Forest Campground	0	9	20	N/A	NF	N	Y	N	HF	$$	N
153 Manistee River Bridge State Forest Campground	0	23	25	N/A	NF	N	Y	N	FO	$$	N
154 Lake Margrethe State Forest Campground	0	37	25	N/A	NF	N	Y	N	HSFBLO	$$	Y
155 Pickerel Lake State Forest Campground (Kalkaska)	0	13	25	N/A	NF	N	Y	N	FLO	$$	N
156 Log Lake County Park and Campground	38	38	40	FE	F	N	Y	N	HSFL	$$$	Y
157 Guernsey Lake State Forest Campground	0	35	30	N/A	NF	N	Y	N	HFLO	$$	N
158 Whitewater Township Park	55	55	40	E	F	Y	Y	Y	HSFL	$$$	Y
159 Scheck's Place State Forest Campground	0	30	25	N/A	NF	N	Y	N	HFBLO	$$	N
160 Arbutus Lake State Forest Campground	0	25	25	N/A	NF	N	Y	N	HFL	$$	N
161 Keith J. Charters Travese City State Park	343	343	50	E	F	Y	Y	Y	HSFB	$$$$	Y
162 Leelanau State Park	0	52	40	N/A	NF	N	Y	Y	HS	$$	Y
163 D. H. Day Campground–Sleeping Bear Dunes National Lakeshore	0	88	40	N/A	NF	N	Y	Y	H	$$	Y
164 Empire Township Campground	9	60	40	E	F	Y	Y	Y	N/A	$$$	N
165 Platte River Campground–Sleeping Bear Dunes National Lakeshore	96	174	40	E	F/NF	Y	Y	Y	HF	$$$–$$$$	Y
166 Platte River State Forest Campground	0	26	25	N/A	NF	N	Y	N	HF	$$	N
167 Veterans Memorial State Forest Campground	0	24	25	N/A	NF	N	Y	N	HF	$$	N
168 Lake Ann State Forest Campground	0	30	25	N/A	NF	N	Y	N	HFBL	$$	N

	Hookup Sites	Total Sites	Max RV Length	Hookups	Toilets	Showers	Drinking Water	Dump Station	Recreation	Fee	Reservations
169 Lake Dubonnet State Forest Campground	0	50	25	N/A	NF	N	Y	N	HFL	$$	Y
170 Interlochen State Park	421	480	50	E	F/NF	Y	Y	Y	HSFBL	$$-$$$	Y
171 Grass Lake State Forest Campground	0	15	30	N/A	NF	N	Y	N	HFL	$$	N
172 CCC Bridge State Forest Campground	0	31	25	N/A	NF	N	Y	N	FO	$$	N

See Amenities Charts Key on page xiii.

152 Goose Creek State Forest Campground

Location: About 13 miles west and north of Grayling
Season: Year-round
Sites: 9 sites with no hookups
Maximum RV length: 20
Facilities: Vault toilets, grills, water, tables, hiking trails
Fee per night: $$
Management: Michigan DNR–Hartwick Pines State Park
Contact: (989) 348-7068; www.michigandnr.com/parksandtrails
Finding the campground: From Grayling head west on MI 72 for 6.9 miles and turn right (north) on Manistee River Road, driving 6 miles until Pine Bend Road. Turn left (west) and take the first left again, which leads another 0.2 mile to the sites.
GPS coordinates: N 44 45.663' / W 84 50.346'
About the campground: This simple campground is located along the Upper Manistee River. The sites are rather spacious, and some of them offer shade; nevertheless, these are best for tents or smaller trailers. This is close to the equestrian Goose Creek Trail Camp as well as the Shore-to-Shore Riding and Hiking Trail. All sites are first come, first served.

153 Manistee River Bridge State Forest Campground

Location: About 7 miles west of Grayling
Season: Year-round
Sites: 23 sites with no hookups
Maximum RV length: 25
Facilities: Vault toilets, fire rings, water, tables, off-road vehicle trails
Fee per night: $$

Management: Michigan DNR–Hartwick Pines State Park
Contact: (989) 348-7068; www.michigandnr.com/parksandtrails
Finding the campground: From Grayling head west on MI 72 for 7.3 miles and turn right on Campground Road to enter the campground.
GPS coordinates: N 44 41.595' / W 84 50.932'
About the campground: The Manistee River is excellent for canoes and kayaks, and this particular campground is located right across the river from a livery. As the camp is just off the highway, it is not as quiet as it might be, but the sites are spacious and offer moderate shade. Fishing here is for brown, rainbow, and brook trout, but Lake Margrethe and the Au Sable River aren't far off either. For less developed river land, go 7 miles north on the river to Deward Track.

154 Lake Margrethe State Forest Campground

Location: About 6 miles west of Grayling
Season: Year-round
Sites: 37 sites with no hookups, 9 walk-in sites
Maximum RV length: 25
Facilities: Vault toilets, fire rings, water, tables, boat launch, hiking/biking/off-road vehicle trails
Fee per night: $$
Management: Michigan DNR–Hartwick Pines State Park
Contact: (989) 348-7068; www.michigandnr.com/parksandtrails
Finding the campground: From Grayling take MI 72 west for about 5 miles and turn left (south) on McIntyre's Landing Road. Go 0.2 mile and take the first right (west) on Portage Heights Avenue. Turn left (south) on Euclid Avenue and go 0.8 mile to the campground.
GPS coordinates: N 44 39.481' / W 84 49.086'
About the campground: The campground is situated on the west shore of a developed portion of Lake Margrethe. In fact, much of the shoreline is privately owned, and an industrial park sits along the southernmost shore, but at least the camp is nicely wooded and is buffered from development to the south by state forest. Across the lake to the east is Hanson State Game Area, but this is separated from the water by a strip of cottages and homes. Anglers can find walleye, pike, perch, and smallmouth bass; both the Manistee and Au Sable Rivers are a short drive from here for good trout fishing and paddling.

155 Pickerel Lake State Forest Campground (Kalkaska)

Location: About 18 miles north of Kalkaska
Season: Year-round
Sites: 13 sites with no hookups
Maximum RV length: 25
Facilities: Vault toilets, grills, water, tables, boat launch, off-road vehicle trails
Fee per night: $$
Management: Michigan DNR–Hartwick Pines State Park

Contact: (989) 348-7068; www.michigandnr.com/parksandtrails

Finding the campground: From Kalkaska go east on MI 72 and turn left (north) on CR 571 (starting as Sigma Road) for 7 miles. Turn right (east) on CR 612, go 4.1 miles, and turn left (north) on Sunset Trail Road. The park entrance is 1.8 miles on the left.

GPS coordinates: N 44 47.798' / W 84 58.356'

About the campground: Pickerel Lake is known best for its panfishing, and while the campground has a boat ramp, there are also other nearby lakes worth fishing, including Manistee Lake. The sites are shaded and private but large enough only for a small trailer. The lakeshore is lightly developed. ORV enthusiasts have Kalkaska Trail to the south, and the Manistee River is 8 miles northeast, though paddlers should prefer sites right on the river.

156 Log Lake County Park and Campground

Location: About 2 miles northeast of Kalkaska

Season: May through October

Sites: 10 sites with full hookups, 28 sites with electrical hookups

Maximum RV length: 40

Facilities: Flush toilets, picnic area, pavilions, boat launch, hiking/mountain biking trails, beach, volleyball court, disc golf, baseball field, horseshoe pits

Fee per night: $$$

Management: Kalkaska County

Contact: (231) 258-2940; www.kalkaskacounty.net/departments/parks_and_recreation

Finding the campground: From US 131/MI 66 in Kalkaska, go east on CR 612/Nash Road for 1.1 miles. Turn left (north) on Log Lake Road and the camp is 0.5 mile on the right.

GPS coordinates: N 44 44.955' / W 85 09.078'

About the campground: This county park offers a full range for the varying levels of camper: rustic or modern sites, hikes in the woods or disc golf on a course, fishing and swimming in the lake, or golfing and casino gambling nearby. The sites are spacious and wooded. Hikers are within 2 miles of both the North Country National Scenic Trail and the Shore-to-Shore hiking/horse trail. Modern convenience is close in town, but the fairly modest development on the small lake still offers a nice forest experience.

157 Guernsey Lake State Forest Campground

Location: About 8 miles west of Kalkaska

Season: Year-round

Sites: 27 sites with no hookups, 8 walk-in sites

Maximum RV length: 30

Facilities: Vault toilets, grills, water, tables, boat launch, hiking/mountain biking/off-road vehicle trails

Fee per night: $$

Management: Michigan DNR

Contact: (231) 922-5270; www.michigandnr.com/parksandtrails

Finding the campground: From US 131/MI 66/MI 72 in Kalkaska, take 1st Street west and it becomes Island Lake Road. Stay on it 6.9 miles then turn left (south) on Guernsey Lake Road. The camp is 1 mile more on the right.

GPS coordinates: N 44 42.902' / W 85 19.219'

About the campground: If you are looking for wildlife, Sand Lakes Quiet Area is a good place to set up camp. The rolling hills of pine and oak forest and its 5 marl lakes are rich with critters. Trails for both hikers and bikers total over 10 miles here and connect right into the campground. Guernsey Lake itself offers bass, bluegill, and trout for anglers. But for the ORV enthusiast, the closest trail is the 66-mile Grand Traverse trail, 4 miles southwest of here.

158 Whitewater Township Park

Location: About 16 miles east and north of Traverse City

Season: Memorial Day through mid-October

Sites: 55 sites with electrical hookups

Maximum RV length: 40

Facilities: Flush toilets, fire rings, water, tables, showers, dump station, playground, hiking trails, boat launch, volleyball

Fee per night: $$$

Management: Whitewater Township

Contact: (231) 267-5091; www.whitewatertownshippark.org

Finding the campground: From Traverse City take MI 72 east about 10 miles and turn left (north) on Williamsburg Road/Elk Lake Road, then go 3 miles and turn right (east) on Park Road. Follow this 0.8 mile into the park.

GPS coordinates: N 44 48.973' / W 85 23.277'

About the campground: This campground is very popular with boaters who want to get on Elk Lake. The swimming area isn't the best, as there is a lot of boat traffic and the bottom is covered with sharp rocks. A dirt road runs past the sites, which are moderately spaced, and abundant pines provide shade as well as a fine carpet of needles. The camp is very well kept, but only a few sites have lake views.

159 Scheck's Place State Forest Campground

Location: About 15 miles south and east of Traverse City

Season: Year-round

Sites: 30 sites with no hookups

Maximum RV length: 25

Facilities: Vault toilets, grills, water, tables, boat launch, hiking/off-road vehicle trails

Fee per night: $$

Management: Michigan DNR

Contact: (231) 922-5270; www.michigandnr.com/parksandtrails

Finding the campground: From US 31 in Traverse City go south on Garfield Avenue 8.9 miles and turn left (east) on Arbutus Hill Road/Hobbs Highway and go 1.7 miles. Turn right (south) on Ranch Rudolf Road, go 3 miles, and turn right (west) on Brown Bridge Road. The park entrance is 0.7 mile on the left.

GPS coordinates: N 44 39.139' / W 85 27.318'

About the campground: The Boardman River originates in a swamp northeast of here but then flows north again out into Grand Traverse Bay. Anglers come to try and nab brown trout, and paddlers enjoy the easy river access. Hikers will delight that the venerable North Country National Scenic Trail actually passes through the site, and other trails are not far off. Sites are mostly shaded, with a few that get exposure at midday. Also nearby is the equestrian trail camp, which does allow all campers. A spur trail connects users to the 355-mile Shore-to-Shore Riding/Hiking Trail.

160 Arbutus Lake State Forest Campground

Location: About 10 miles southeast of Traverse City

Season: Year-round

Sites: 25 sites with no hookups (11 of them tent sites with stair access)

Maximum RV length: 25

Facilities: Vault toilets, firepits, water, tables, boat launch

Fee per night: $$

Management: Michigan DNR

Contact: (231) 922-5270; www.michigandnr.com/parksandtrails

Finding the campground: From Traverse City go east on US 31/MI 72 for 1.8 miles and turn right (south) on 3 Mile Road. Go 4.4 miles and turn left (east) on Potter Road, driving 1 mile to 4 Mile Road. Go right (south) and drive 0.5 mile, turn left (east) on Arbutus Lake Road, and the park is 0.7 mile on the right.

GPS coordinates: N 44 40.721' / W 85 31.347'

About the campground: Just 20 minutes from Traverse City and you can be in wilderness. This campground is just inside some hilly terrain of mostly hardwoods, especially oaks. Just to the north of Arbutus Lake #4, which is at the upper end of a small chain of lakes, the rustic camp has good shade and privacy but short sites for the trailer crowd. The boat launch is down a separate road from the campsites. Go farther east on Arbutus Lake Road to find it. The lake offers anglers bass, perch, pike, and bluegill. Hikers have nothing on-site, but Sand Lakes Quiet Area 10 miles northeast has hiking and mountain biking, while Vasa Trail 4 miles northeast runs 16.7 miles.

161 Keith J. Charters Traverse City State Park

Location: About 2 miles from downtown Traverse City

Season: Year-round

Sites: 343 sites with electrical hookups

Maximum RV length: 50

A view of Grand Traverse Bay from Old Mission Peninsula near Traverse City State Park

Facilities: Flush toilets, grills, water, tables, showers, picnic area, dump station, hiking/biking trails, beach, beach house, playground, boat rental, concessionaire

Fee per night: $$$$

Management: Michigan DNR

Contact: (231) 922-5270; www.michigandnr.com/parksandtrails

Finding the campground: From the center of Traverse City, head east on US 31/MI 72 just past 3 Mile Road and the camp is on the right (south) side of the road opposite the bay.

GPS coordinates: N 44 44.878' / W 85 33.225'

About the campground: This popular urban park brings camping to town and offers a quarter-mile beach on Grand Traverse Bay as well. A pedestrian walkway allows campers to cross the busy highway to get to the beach area easily and safely. The park has plenty of tree cover, but the place can feel rather crowded when full. The 22-mile, multiuse paved TART Trail goes right through the park, allowing campers to explore the area by bike. The location is ideal for taking advantage of the stores, restaurants, and bars of Traverse City and the wineries of Old Mission Peninsula. The Sleeping Bear Dunes are just about 30 miles from here.

162 Leelanau State Park

Location: About 7 miles northeast of Northport
Season: Year-round
Sites: 52 sites with no hookups

Maximum RV length: 40

Facilities: Vault toilets, firepits, grills, water, tables, dump station, picnic shelter, picnic area, hiking trails, beach, lighthouse, playground, gift shop

Fee per night: $$

Management: Michigan DNR

Contact: (231) 386-5422; www.michigandnr.com/parksandtrails

Finding the campground: From MI 201 in Northport go right (east) on 6th Street and turn left (north) on Shore Drive. Follow this road about 1.7 miles and go right (east) on Woolsey Lake Road, then take the left in the next fork to stay on it. Go 2.8 miles and turn left (north) on Purkiss Road, driving 1.4 miles to turn left on Lighthouse Point Road. Another 1.4 miles takes you to the park road on the right.

GPS coordinates: N 45 12.593' / W 85 32.862'

About the campground: The Leelanau Peninsula is Michigan's "Little Finger," and right at the tip of this land, thrust into Lake Michigan on the west side of Grand Traverse Bay, lies a 1,300-acre park. The campsites are arranged in a loop along the shore east of the lighthouse, and though the sites are tucked into the woods for shade, the sandy shore is right at hand. The Grand Traverse Lighthouse Museum is in the park, and hikers have 8.5 miles to explore. Be aware that no pets are ever allowed on the shoreline here, to protect rare nesting piping plover. Visitors may still look for Petoskey stones here though. The peninsula is also home to several wineries.

163 D. H. Day Campground– Sleeping Bear Dunes National Lakeshore

Location: About 7 miles north of Empire

Season: First Friday in April through the last Sunday in November

Sites: 88 sites with no hookups

Maximum RV length: 40

Facilities: Vault toilets, grills, water, tables, dump station, hiking trails, beach, amphitheater, recycling station, public phone

Fee per night: $$

Management: Sleeping Bear Dunes National Park Service

Contact: (231) 326-4700 ext. 5035; www.nps.gov/slbe/planyourvisit/dhdaycamp.htm

Finding the campground: From Empire go north on MI 22 for 2 miles and turn left on MI 109. Continue for 5.3 miles and the entrance to the campground will be on your left.

GPS coordinates: N 44 53.769' / W 86 01.202'

About the campground: The massive 450-foot dunes, the long beaches, and the turquoise water of Lake Michigan have made Sleeping Bear Dunes one of America's favorite national parks. The campground is nicely shaded, and the sites are private. A trail leads out the north end of the campground to the beach. This is also close to the Dune Climb and Pierce Stocking Scenic Drive. Be aware that this fills fast and takes no reservations. Rangers lead evening programs in summer. For reservable sites, see the park's Platte River Campground. South and North Manitou Islands also offer camping, but it is backcountry style and reachable only by ferry.

A dune trail at Sleeping Bear Dunes National Lakeshore

164 Empire Township Campground

Location: About 5 miles east and south of Empire
Season: May 15 to September 15
Sites: 9 sites with electrical hookups, 51 sites with no hookups
Maximum RV length: 40
Facilities: Flush/vault toilets, fire rings, tables, showers, water, dump station
Fee per night: $$$
Management: Empire Township
Contact: (231) 326-5285; www.leelanau.cc/empiretwpcamp.asp
Finding the campground: From Empire head east on MI 72 for about 3 miles and turn right (south) on Benzonia Trail. Go 1.6 miles and turn right (west) on Osborn Road. Go 0.2 mile and the campground entrance is on the right.
GPS coordinates: N 44 47.153' / W 86 00.123'
About the campground: Sleeping Bear Dunes National Lakeshore is highly popular all summer, and if you don't have a campsite, a place like this is a welcome backup plan. The sites are divided into Pines and Hardwood sections, and all of them are quite spacious and private with good shade. There is one shower building with coin-op showers and a single flush toilet, and there are several vault toilets throughout the campground. A small airstrip is just east of the camp.

165 Platte River Campground– Sleeping Bear Dunes National Lakeshore

Location: About 10 miles south of Empire
Season: Year-round
Sites: 96 sites with electrical hookups, 53 sites with no hookups, 25 walk-in sites
Maximum RV length: 40
Facilities: Flush toilets, showers, grills, water, tables, picnic area, dump station, canoe launch, hiking trails, beach, fish-cleaning station, amphitheater, public phone
Fee per night: $$$-$$$$
Management: Sleeping Bear Dunes National Park Service
Contact: (231) 326-5134; campground number (231) 326-4700 ext 5029; www.nps.gov/slbe/planyourvisit/platterivercamp.htm
Finding the campground: From Empire head south on MI 22 about 10 miles and the campground entrance is on the right at Lake Michigan Road.
GPS coordinates: N 44 42.706' / W 86 07.040'
About the campground: Another of the magnificent Sleeping Bear Dunes campgrounds, this is surely its most popular, filling throughout the summer every night. But it is better suited for those planning ahead than the first-come, first-served D. H. Day Campground. Reservations went so fast on a limited number of sites that the park expanded reservable campsites to two-thirds of the total sites. Reservations can be made up to 6 months in advance for the period from the first

Friday in May until October 1. The rustic sites are excellent, and a few hike-in sites give a back-country experience without the effort of getting to the Manitou Islands.

166 Platte River State Forest Campground

Location: About 2.5 miles southeast of Honor
Season: Year-round
Sites: 26 sites with no hookups
Maximum RV length: 25
Facilities: Vault toilets, grills, water, tables, hiking/mountain biking trails
Fee per night: $$
Management: Michigan DNR
Contact: (231) 276-9511; www.michigandnr.com/parksandtrails
Finding the campground: From Honor go east on US 31 just under a mile and turn right (south) on Goose Road. The park is 1.7 miles along on the right.
GPS coordinates: N 44 38.767' / W 85 58.704'
About the campground: The Platte River runs over 29 miles from Lake Dubonett through Pere Marquette State Forest and empties into Lake Michigan at Sleeping Bear Dunes National Lakeshore. Healthy wetlands keep its waters clear, and the cooler temperature is ideal for trout. The river is popular with paddlers, and this campground gives access to the river just 3 miles from where it widens into Platte Lake. Hikers also have an interpretive trail on-site. Sites are shaded and arranged in a square loop, with the southwestern corner being closest to the water. This is 11 miles west of Sleeping Bear Dunes.

167 Veterans Memorial State Forest Campground

Location: About 4 miles east of Honor
Season: Year-round
Sites: 24 sites with no hookups
Maximum RV length: 25
Facilities: Vault toilets, grills, water, tables, hiking trails
Fee per night: $$
Management: Michigan DNR
Contact: (231) 276-9511; www.michigandnr.com/parksandtrails
Finding the campground: From Honor go east on US 31 for 3.7 miles and the park entrance is on the right (south) side of the highway.
GPS coordinates: N 44 39.566' / W 85 56.672'
About the campground: The clear-water Platte River runs right past this campground, which is located just off the highway. The sites are in the woods but with abundant open spaces above for sunlight. Paddlers can get here from the water, and anglers will enjoy the trout fishing. This campground is similar to Platte River State Forest Campground but is closer to the main road and lacks

the on-site nature trail. The river runs right to the Sleeping Bear Dunes, which are just about 11 miles west of here.

168 Lake Ann State Forest Campground

Location: About 15 miles west of Traverse City
Season: Year-round
Sites: 30 sites with no hookups
Maximum RV length: 25
Facilities: Vault toilets, grills, water, tables, boat launch, hiking/mountain biking trails
Fee per night: $$
Management: Michigan DNR
Contact: (231) 276-9511; www.michigandnr.com/parksandtrails
Finding the campground: From Traverse City take CR 610/Long Lake Road west about 14 miles (it becomes Maple Street in Lake Ann) and turn left (south) on Reynolds Road. The park entrance is 1 mile south on the left.
GPS coordinates: N 44 42.683' / W 85 51.785'
About the campground: The campground is far more rustic than its counterpart at Interlochen State Park. Spread out under deciduous tree cover in 3 arms ending in small loops, the campground is a quiet retreat most amenable to anglers and boaters. Pike, bass, and panfish may be caught here, and Platte River and Sweet Lake are just a few minutes' drive away. The Lake Ann Pathway runs 5.8 miles, offering a moderate challenge to hikers and mountain bikers. The boat launch is down a separate entrance from the road in. Sleeping Bear Dunes National Lakeshore is 12 miles west of here.

169 Lake Dubonnet State Forest Campground

Location: About 4 miles north of Interlochen
Season: Year-round
Sites: 50 sites with no hookups
Maximum RV length: 25
Facilities: Vault toilets, grills, water, tables, boat launch, hiking/mountain biking trails
Fee per night: $$
Management: Michigan DNR
Contact: (231) 276-9511; www.michigandnr.com/parksandtrails
Finding the campground: From Interlochen go north on MI 137 and turn left (west) on US 31. Go 1.5 miles and turn right (north) on Gonder Road. The campground is 1.6 miles north.
GPS coordinates: N 44 40.909' / W 85 47.911'
About the campground: Tucked into some mixed forest cover just to the southwest of Lake Dubonnet, this camp is best for hikers and anglers. Lost Lake Trail offers 6.3 miles of easy pathway for both hikers and mountain bikers, and a spur trail connects the park to the 355-mile

Shore-to-Shore Trail. Also nearby is the Lake Dubonnet Trail camp, which caters to equestrian campers, especially those on the Shore-to-Shore, but it is also open for other campers.

170 Interlochen State Park

Location: About 15 miles southwest of Traverse City
Season: Year-round
Sites: 421 sites with electrical hookups, 59 sites with no hookups
Maximum RV length: 50
Facilities: Flush/vault toilets, firepits, grills, water, tables, picnic shelter, picnic area, dump station, boat launch, hiking trails, beach, playground, volleyball court, ball field, basketball court, concessionaire
Fee per night: $$–$$$
Management: Michigan DNR
Contact: (231) 276-9511; www.michigandnr.com/parksandtrails
Finding the campground: From Traverse City take US 31 south and then follow it west a total of about 12 miles, then turn left (south) on MI 137. Go 2.1 miles to the park entrances on either side of the road.
GPS coordinates: N 44 37.685' / W 85 45.943'
About the campground: Back in 1917, Interlochen became Michigan's first state park, preserving 200 acres that included some of the last virgin pine left after the logging era. Now it is one of the largest state park campgrounds. As the name suggests, the park is located between lakes: Duck Lake and Green Lake, which have a modern and a rustic campground, respectively. Each camp has boat access to its respective lake. A nature trail has 1 mile for hikers to explore. To the north and south of the park, as well as around both lakes, is residential development.

171 Grass Lake State Forest Campground

Location: About 22 miles southwest of Traverse City
Season: Year-round
Sites: 15 sites with no hookups
Maximum RV length: 30
Facilities: Vault toilets, water, grills, tables, boat launch, hiking trails
Fee per night: $$
Management: Colfax Township
Contact: (231) 631-9227; www.michigandnr.com/parksandtrails
Finding the campground: From Traverse City follow US 31 south about 16 miles and turn left (south) on Reynolds Road. Go 2 miles, turn right (west) on Cinder Road/CR 608, and take the first left (south) to get back on Reynolds Road for another 2.9 miles. Then turn left (east) on Grass Lake Dam Road to get into the camp.
GPS coordinates: N 44 35.527' / W 85 51.098'

About the campground: The campground lies to the north side of Betsie River and right where a dam meters its flow to create an impoundment. A simple gravel ramp offers boat access above the dam, and a carry-in access serves paddlers going for the river beneath the dam. The sites are sheltered by a mix of hardwoods and some pine, and most of them are too short for larger vehicles/trailers. There are bass, perch, and bluegill above the dam and trout below. This is about a 20-mile drive from Sleeping Bear Dunes.

172 CCC Bridge State Forest Campground

Location: About 18 miles east and south of Kalkaska
Season: Year-round
Sites: 31 sites with no hookups
Maximum RV length: 25
Facilities: Vault toilets, grills, water, tables, off-road vehicle trails
Fee per night: $$
Management: Michigan DNR
Contact: (231) 922-5270; www.michigandnr.com/parksandtrails
Finding the campground: From Kalkaska go east on MI 66/MI 72 for about 8 miles and turn right (south) on Sigma Road. Go 5 miles and turn left (east) on Mecum Road, continue 2.4 miles and turn right (south) on Sunset Trail Road. Continue 2.8 miles and the park entrance is on the right.
GPS coordinates: N 44 36.846' / W 84 59.435'
About the campground: Paddlers and trout fishers may enjoy this camp best. Straddling the Manistee River, the campground has steps down to the water for canoe access near the historical bridge. The river is highly scenic and passes through long undeveloped stretches just north of this point. The campsites are spread out on either side of the river and offer some intervening understory for privacy as well as good shade. In summer the place can be busy on both sides. Very small sites are designated for tents only.

Cadillac Area

	Hookup Sites	Total Sites	Max RV Length	Hookups	Toilets	Showers	Drinking Water	Dump Station	Recreation	Fee	Reservations
173 Reedsburg Dam State Forest Campground	0	47	40	N/A	NF	N	Y	N	FLO	$$	N
174 Spring Lake State Forest Campground	0	30	20	N/A	NF	N	Y	N	HFLO	$$	N
175 Hopkins Creek State Forest Campground	0	7	40	N/A	NF	N	Y	N	HF	$$	N
176 Old US-131 State Forest Campground	0	25	40	N/A	NF	N	Y	N	HFLO	$$	N
177 Baxter Bridge State Forest Campground	0	25	40	N/A	NF	N	Y	N	HFLO	$$	N
178 Long Lake State Forest Campground (Missaukee)	0	11	20	N/A	NF	N	Y	N	HFLO	$$	N
179 Long Lake State Forest Campground (Wexford)	0	12	20	N/A	NF	N	Y	N	HFLOC	$$	N
180 William Mitchell State Park	221	221	40	E	F	Y	Y	Y	HSFBL	$$$$	Y
181 Hemlock Campground– Huron-Manistee National Forests	0	19	25	N/A	NF	N	Y	N	FBL	$$	N

See Amenities Charts Key on page xiii.

173 Reedsburg Dam State Forest Campground

Location: About 8 miles northwest of Houghton Lake
Season: Year-round
Sites: 47 sites with no hookups
Maximum RV length: 40
Facilities: Vault toilets, fire rings, water, tables, boat launch
Fee per night: $$
Management: Michigan DNR–North Higgins Lake State Park
Contact: (989) 821-6125; www.michigandnr.com/parksandtrails
Finding the campground: From US 127 just west of Houghton Lake, take the exit for MI 55 and go west about 2 miles. Turn right (north) on County Line Road/Reedsburg Road and follow it 1.6 miles right to the park.
GPS coordinates: N 44 21.576' / W 84 51.288'

About the campground: A dam on the Muskegon River created the Dead Stream Flooding, one of the Lower Peninsula's biggest managed wetlands projects. Birders will find plenty of waterfowl in the marshy areas, and paddlers can get on the Muskegon River nearby. The sites are arranged along the west bank close to the dam, and 15 of them extend out from the camp road almost to the water. The trees are thinner toward the shoreline but still provide adequate shade.

174 Spring Lake State Forest Campground

Location: About 11 miles north of Manton
Season: Year-round
Sites: 30 sites with no hookups
Maximum RV length: 20
Facilities: Vault toilets, water, tables, boat launch, hiking/off-road trails
Fee per night: $$
Management: Michigan DNR–Mitchell State Park
Contact: (231) 775-7911; www.michigandnr.com/parksandtrails
Finding the campground: From Manton head north on US 131 for 7.2 miles and watch for an unmarked dirt road on the right (east) side of the road right before a railroad viaduct over the highway. This is the park entrance.
GPS coordinates: N 44 33.804' / W 85 22.009'
About the campground: Nicely spread out in a couple loops through the woods with good shade trees, these sites are private and only useful to tent campers and small trailers. The camp has boat access to undeveloped Spring Lake, and a canal connects that to the much larger and more residentially developed Fife Lake. Anglers can expect bass, walleye, pike, bluegill, and sunfish.

175 Hopkins Creek State Forest Campground

Location: About 8 miles northeast of Manton
Season: Year-round
Sites: 7 sites with no hookups
Maximum RV length: 40
Facilities: Vault toilets, water, trails
Fee per night: $$
Management: Michigan DNR
Contact: (231) 775-7911; www.michigandnr.com/parksandtrails
Finding the campground: From US 131 east of Manton take MI 42 east for 5.1 miles and turn left (north) on Lucas Road, going 5.5 miles to Moorestown Road. Go left (west) for 1.5 miles.
GPS coordinates: N 44 28.919' / W 85 19.288'
About the campground: Situated along Hopkins Creek, this is primarily an equestrian camp, but tents and campers are welcome. Equestrian campers have direct access to a segment of the 355-mile Shore-to-Shore Riding/Hiking Trail. Anglers have access to the Manistee River, where they can

Paddling on the Manistee River

fish for walleye and brown/rainbow trout. The North Country National Scenic Trail is 3 miles north of here for hikers.

176 Old US-131 State Forest Campground

Location: About 7 miles north of Manton
Season: Year-round
Sites: 20 sites with no hookups, 5 walk-in sites
Maximum RV length: 40
Facilities: Vault toilets, water, tables, boat launch, hiking/mountain biking/off-road trails, snowmobile riding
Fee per night: $$
Management: Michigan DNR
Contact: (231) 775-7911; www.michigandnr.com/parksandtrails
Finding the campground: From Manton head north on US 131 about 2 miles and turn left (west) on No. 4 Road. Go 0.5 mile and turn left (south) on Old US Highway 131 and the entrance is 0.2 mile on the right.
GPS coordinates: N 44 29.494' / W 85 24.999'
About the campground: This wooded loop is situated on the Manistee River, and as such it is best for paddling and trout fishing. However, the camp also connects to the North Country National Scenic Trail via a 1-mile spur trail for some good hiking and mountain biking. Any sort of off-road

vehicle trails are nearby but not on-site. The sites are private and well shaded, the walk-in sites for tents being the best for privacy. The boat launch is carry-in. Canoe rentals can be made back in Manton. Fishing is for trout, bass, and walleye.

177 Baxter Bridge State Forest Campground

Location: About 12 miles northwest of Manton
Season: Year-round
Sites: 25 sites with no hookups
Maximum RV length: 40
Facilities: Vault toilets, water, boat launch, hiking/off-road vehicle trails
Fee per night: $$
Management: Michigan DNR
Contact: (231) 775-7911; www.michigandnr.com/parksandtrails
Finding the campground: From Manton go west on MI 42 for 5.5 miles and head right (north) on 31 Road; 1.9 miles later it curves left (west) and then right (north) again as 29 Road. The entry to the campground is on the right before you cross the river.
GPS coordinates: N 44 29.513' / W 85 31.624'
About the campground: Located on the Manistee River, the campground attracts anglers, paddlers, and nature lovers. Sites are best for tents and small trailers. The 40-foot maximum is only available on 3 sites. The North Country National Scenic Trail is 1 mile north of here, and the North Missaukee Trail is an ATV trail 10 miles to the east. Anglers come for brown and rainbow trout in the river, as well as walleye and bass. Paddlers can carry in from the camp or use the launch across the road.

178 Long Lake State Forest Campground (Missaukee)

Location: About 18 miles north and east of Cadillac
Season: Year-round
Sites: 11 sites with no hookups
Maximum RV length: 20
Facilities: Vault toilets, water, boat launch, hiking/mountain biking pathways, off-road vehicle trails
Fee per night: $$
Management: Michigan DNR
Contact: (231) 775-7911; www.michigandnr.com/parksandtrails
Finding the campground: From Cadillac take MI 55 east about 6 miles and turn left (north) on MI 55/MI 66 going north 5.5 miles. Turn left (west) on Randall Road and 0.5 mile later turn right (north) on Al Moses Road. Take the second left (west) on Goose Lake Road, go 0.4 mile, and take the slight right onto Green Road and another slight left 0.5 mile later to be on Goose Lake Park Road. The third left, 0.6 mile from there, is Long Lake Park, and the campground is 0.6 mile down on the right.
GPS coordinates: N 44 21.214' / W 85 15.217'

About the campground: Don't get confused, but there is more than one Long Lake in Michigan, and in fact, this one is just over the county line from the Wexford Long Lake (also in this book). Set on Long Lake and just a quarter mile from Goose Lake behind it, this campground and its shallow waters are attractive for anglers. The road is gravel and the sites are tight, though they are private and shaded. There is ramp access here as well as on Goose Lake and Lake Missaukee nearby.

179 Long Lake State Forest Campground (Wexford)

Location: About 9 miles north of Cadillac
Season: Year-round
Sites: 12 sites with no hookups
Maximum RV length: 20
Facilities: Vault toilets, water, boat launch, hiking/mountain biking/off-road vehicle trails
Fee per night: $$
Management: Michigan DNR
Contact: (231) 775-7911; www.michigandnr.com/parksandtrails
Finding the campground: Get on Business US 131 in Cadillac and it becomes Mitchell Street inside town. Take this road north out of town and it becomes 41½ Road. Just over 4 miles north of Cadillac, go right on 24¾ Road for 2.5 miles and the road curves around Long Lake to take you to the camp entrance, which is on the right (west) side of the road.
GPS coordinates: N 44 19.992' / W 85 22.520'
About the campground: Don't get confused, but there is more than one Long Lake in Michigan, and in fact, this one is just over the county line from the Missaukee Long Lake (also in this book). The camp has a boat ramp, so it is popular for anglers looking for time on Long Lake. The road is rustic, and the sites and clearance are OK, but sites are too small for much more than a small trailer. Six miles to the north is the North Country National Scenic Trail, but frankly hikers have better options.

180 William Mitchell State Park

Location: About 4 miles west of Cadillac
Season: Year-round
Sites: 22 sites with 50-amp electrical hookups, 199 with electrical hookups
Maximum RV length: 40
Facilities: Flush/vault toilets, showers, grills, water, tables, picnic shelter, picnic area, dump station, boat launch, hiking trails, beach, beach house, playground, fishing pier, volleyball court, horseshoe pits, observation platform
Fee per night: $$$$
Management: Michigan DNR
Contact: (231) 775-7911; www.michigandnr.com/parksandtrails

Finding the campground: From its juncture with US 131 just south of Cadillac, head northwest on MI 55/MI 115. Where MI 115 leaves MI 55 and continues north, go another 0.2 mile and the camp entrance is on the right (west) side of the road before the boat channel.

GPS coordinates: N 44 14.299' / W 85 27.297'

About the campground: The state park lies between Lake Cadillac to the east and Lake Mitchell to the west, and the northern edge of the campground borders the boat channel that connects the two. A few sites along the channel are completely sunny, but the rest of the camp enjoys good shade trees. The lakes are notable for walleye and can be accessed by boat as well as some canal-side fishing. Beaches and boat launches are both at the campground and across the highway to the west. The Carl T. Johnson Hunting and Fishing Center offers information and educational displays. The northern portion of the state park has good nature observation from trails, a platform, and a shelter.

181 Hemlock Campground– Huron-Manistee National Forests

Location: About 6 miles west of Cadillac

Season: Mid-May through mid-September

Sites: 19 sites with no hookups

Maximum RV length: 25

Facilities: Vault toilets, fire rings, water

Fee per night: $$

Management: Cadillac/Manistee Ranger District

Contact: (231) 577-8902; www.fs.usda.gov/recarea/hmnf/null/recarea?recid=18860&actid=31

Finding the campground: From Cadillac head west on MI 55/Lake Mitchell Drive. Watch for where Lake Mitchell Drive splits right from MI 55 (it is also 44½ Road here). The camp entrance is 1.4 miles from this break from the highway and on the right (north) side of the road.

GPS coordinates: N 44 13.820' / W 85 30.202'

About the campground: The camp is located on a sheltered bay and marshy area at the west end of Lake Mitchell, a 1,600-acre lake surrounded by residential properties. Swimming is not recommended here, but a boat launch is on-site. While the clearance can be low and the sites can't fit anything larger than 25 feet, the pads are at least asphalt. This is best for anglers, and traffic here is light for a reason.

Manistee Area

	Hookup Sites	Total Sites	Max RV Length	Hookups	Toilets	Showers	Drinking Water	Dump Station	Recreation	Fee	Reservations
182 Peterson Bridge South Campground—Huron-Manistee National Forests	0	30	25	N/A	F/NF	N	Y	N	FBL	$-$$$	Y
183 Seaton Creek Campground—Huron-Manistee National Forests	0	17	25	N/A	NF	N	Y	N	H	$$	N
184 Healy Lake State Forest Campground	0	24	25	N/A	NF	N	Y	N	HFL	$$	N
185 Orchard Beach State Park	166	166	45	E	F	Y	Y	Y	HSF	$$$$	Y
186 Bear Track Campground—Huron-Manistee National Forests	0	16	25	N/A	NF	N	Y	N	HF	$$	N
187 Tippy Dam Recreation Area Campground	0	40	35	N/A	NF	N	Y	N	HFL	$$	N
188 Pine Lake Campground—Huron-Manistee National Forests	0	12	25	N/A	NF	N	Y	N	SFB	$$	N
189 Sand Lake Campground—Huron-Manistee National Forests	0	45	50	N/A	F/NF	Y	Y	N	HSFB	$$$	Y
190 Lake Michigan Recreation Area Campground—Huron-Manistee National Forests	0	99	50	N/A	F/NF	N	Y	N	HS	$$$	N

See Amenities Charts Key on page xiii.

182 Peterson Bridge South Campground– Huron-Manistee National Forests

Location: About 30 miles east of Manistee
Season: May to mid-September
Sites: 20 sites with no hookups, 10 walk-in sites

Maximum RV length: 25

Facilities: Flush/vault toilets, grills, water, tables, picnic area, boat launch, beach

Fee per night: $-$$$

Management: American Land and Leisure/Cadillac-Manistee Ranger Station

Contact: (231) 577-8902; www.fs.usda.gov/recarea/hmnf/recreation/fishing/recarea/?recid=18654&actid=43

Finding the campground: From just north of Manistee on US 31 turn right (east) on MI 55. Go 25.7 miles and turn right (south) on MI 37. Continue 1.5 miles and turn left (east) to enter the park.

GPS coordinates: N 44 12.124' / W 85 47.871'

About the campground: If your goal is to get on the National Scenic River, the Pine River, this is the only national forest campground that serves you. While 10 of these sites are slightly remote— either walk-in or paddle-up—there are still 20 standard sites. In addition to the paddling and trout-fishing opportunities, this area of the river is also good for a swim and has a sandy beach along the bank. The proper boat launch is located on the north side of the river, across from most of the campsites. Take the highway north over the bridge to get to the entrance road.

183   Seaton Creek Campground– Huron-Manistee National Forests

Location: About 28 miles northwest of Cadillac

Season: Early May to mid-September

Sites: 17 sites with no hookups

Maximum RV length: 25

Facilities: Vault toilets, water, fire rings, tables, hiking trails

Fee per night: $$

Management: Cadillac/Manistee Ranger District

Contact: (231) 577-8902; www.fs.usda.gov/recarea/hmnf/recreation/hiking/recarea?recid=18880&actid=51

Finding the campground: Take MI 115 northwest from Cadillac 15.4 miles and turn left (south) on MI 37. At 4.2 miles turn right (west) on 22½ Road and go 1.4 miles to turn left (south) on 3¼ Road. Take the immediate first right (west) on Seaton Road and take Seaton Road to the left again at 0.4 mile. Turn right (northwest) on McClush Road and it heads right into the camp loop.

GPS coordinates: N 44 21.425' / W 85 48.621'

About the campground: The name suggests some water use, but really the creek is too shallow for much of anything. Sites are all first come, first served. Enjoy the shade and the shelter of pine trees here, and if you are a hiker, try the connector trail to the Manistee River Trail. Connectors between that trail and the North Country National Scenic Trail offer a 23-mile loop. A suspension bridge crosses the Manistee River to connect to the national trail segment.

184 Healy Lake State Forest Campground

Location: About 25 miles north and east of Manistee
Season: Year-round
Sites: 24 sites with no hookups
Maximum RV length: 25
Facilities: Vault toilets, grills, water, tables, boat launch, hiking trails
Fee per night: $$
Management: Springdale Township
Contact: (231) 864-2531; www.michigandnr.com/parksandtrails
Finding the campground: From Manistee head north on US 31 about 17 miles and turn right (east) on 13 Mile Road. Go 6.7 miles and turn left (north) on Hendrickson Road. The camp is 0.6 mile on the left.
GPS coordinates: N 44 26.293' / W 85 59.598'
About the campground: In 2010 Springdale Township took over the management of this state forest campground to keep it open as budget cuts were forcing the Department of Natural Resources to close some small, lesser-used sites. The lake is quiet and undeveloped, drawing anglers and their boats for its good panfishing. The sites are private and nicely shaded in deciduous forest. Betsie River offers the closest hiking at about 5 miles northeast.

185 Orchard Beach State Park

Location: About 3 miles north of Manistee
Season: Year-round
Sites: 166 sites with electrical hookups
Maximum RV length: 45
Facilities: Flush toilets, grills, water, tables, showers, picnic shelter, picnic area, fish-cleaning station, dump station, hiking trails, beach, playground
Fee per night: $$$$
Management: Michigan DNR
Contact: (231) 723-7422; www.michigandnr.com/parksandtrails
Finding the campground: Take US 31 north from Manistee about 1 mile and turn left (northwest) on Lakeshore Road/MI 110. Continue 1.4 miles and the park entrance is on the left.
GPS coordinates: N 44 17.024' / W 86 18.812'
About the campground: For a grand view of Lake Michigan and a popular swimming beach, you can't go wrong here. The campground looks over the water from a high bluff, and campers must take the steps down to the beach. There are 3 miles of trails across Lakeshore Road to the east, including a 0.5-mile self-guided interpretive trail. Fishing is possible from piers in nearby Manistee or by taking out a boat on the big lake or Manistee Lake.

186　Bear Track Campground–
Huron-Manistee National Forests

Location: About 21 miles east and south of Manistee
Season: Year-round
Sites: 16 sites with no hookups
Maximum RV length: 25
Facilities: Vault toilets, fire rings, tables, hiking trails
Fee per night: $$
Management: American Land and Leisure/Cadillac-Manistee Ranger Station
Contact: (231) 577-8902; www.fs.usda.gov/recarea/hmnf/recarea/?recid=18674
Finding the campground: From US 31 just north of Manistee, take MI 55 east 14 miles and turn right (south) on Udell Hills Road for 5.5 miles. Turn left (south) on Skocelas Road for 0.5 mile, then left (east) on Little River Road for 4 miles and the entrance is on the left.
GPS coordinates: N 44 17.504' / W 86 01.841'
About the campground: The park's name came from a bear print found on-site when it was being set up years ago, a story that suggests what a struggle it is to name the incredibly numerous camps in the woods here in Michigan. The camp is situated in a forested area along the south side of the Manistee River. Stairs lead down to the river for a paddler's carry-in. A 1.5-mile spur trail connects hikers to the North Country National Scenic Trail. Anglers can come for salmon, trout, and steelhead.

187　Tippy Dam Recreation Area Campground

Location: About 30 miles east of Manistee
Season: Year-round
Sites: 40 sites with no hookups
Maximum RV length: 35
Facilities: Vault toilets, grills, tables, boat launch, hiking trails
Fee per night: $$
Management: Michigan DNR
Contact: (231) 848-4880; www.michigandnr.com/parksandtrails
Finding the campground: From just north of Manistee on US 31, go east on MI 55/Caberfae Highway for 23 miles. Go left (north) on Warfield Road for 5.1 miles and turn left (west) on Brethren Highway. Go 2.1 miles, turn left on River Road, and stay on it through turns for 4.8 miles. Take the slight left on Dilling Road and the camp is on the right.
GPS coordinates: N 44 15.682' / W 85 56.442'
About the campground: Overlooking both the Manistee River to the south and west and Tippy Dam Pond to the east, the campground has water on three sides. The dam is right there on-site. The boat launches, above and below the dam, are the only ones that also offer overnight camping here. Paddlers can get on the Big Manistee, and hikers are only about 1.5 miles south of the North Country National Scenic Trail.

188 Pine Lake Campground– Huron-Manistee National Forests

Location: About 18 miles east of Manistee
Season: Year-round
Sites: 12 sites with no hookups
Maximum RV length: 25
Facilities: Vault toilets, grills, water, tables, picnic area, boat ramp
Fee per night: $$
Management: American Land and Leisure/Cadillac-Manistee Ranger Station
Contact: (231) 577-8902; www.fs.usda.gov/recarea/hmnf/recarea/?recid=18876
Finding the campground: From Manistee head east on MI 55 for 17 miles, turn right (south) on Bosschem Road/CR F669 for 1 mile, turn right (west) on Pine Lake Road. Follow it left at about 3 miles (don't take West Pine Lake Road) and the road should go right into the campground.
GPS coordinates: N 44 11.742' / W 86 00.620'
About the campground: The swampy area to the west of the lake is a good place to spot eagles while you're out fishing this little lake in the woods for trout and panfish. To the east side the shore is lined with private cabins. The campground is lightly used and offers a gravel boat ramp as well as a shallow swimming area with a gravel bottom. After September 16 there are no fees to camp here.

189 Sand Lake Campground– Huron-Manistee National Forests

Location: About 28 miles north of Baldwin
Season: May to mid-September
Sites: 45 sites with no hookups
Maximum RV length: 50
Facilities: Flush/vault toilets, showers, water, tables, picnic area, hiking trails, beach
Fee per night: $$$
Management: Cadillac-Manistee Ranger District
Contact: (231) 577-8902; www.fs.usda.gov/recarea/hmnf/recarea/?recid=18906
Finding the campground: From Baldwin take MI 37 north for about 20 miles and turn left (west) on 48½ Road and go 1 mile. Turn left (south) on Hoxeyville Road and follow that for 5.9 miles. Turn left (south) on Seaman Road and go 0.5 mile to turn right on Sand Lake Road.
GPS coordinates: N 44 09.994' / W 85 56.029'
About the campground: This is the only public access on shallow Sand Lake. The sites are surrounded by woods but open to the sky above. The boat access is carry-in only, making this best suited for canoes or kayaks. Unlike many national forest camps, this one does accept reservations, though 22 sites still are first come, first served, and it actually has showers. For all those

conveniences the place itself is mostly for fishing or just a peaceful stay. The beach is sandy and shallow but becomes a muddy bottom not far out.

190 Lake Michigan Recreation Area Campground– Huron-Manistee National Forests

Location: About 14 miles south of Manistee
Season: Year-round (managed May 15 to October 8)
Sites: 99 sites with no hookups
Maximum RV length: 50
Facilities: Flush/vault toilets, grills, water, tables, picnic area, hiking/biking trails, beach, playground, amphitheater
Fee per night: $$$
Management: American Land and Leisure/Cadillac-Manistee Ranger Station
Contact: (231) 577-8902; www.fs.usda.gov/recarea/hmnf/recarea/?recid=18902
Finding the campground: From Manistee head south on US 31 about 5 miles and turn right (west) on County Line Road. Go 1.2 miles and turn left (south) on Quarterline Road. At 3.2 miles turn right (west) on Forest Trail Road (FR 5629) and follow it 5.1 miles to the camp entrance on the left.
GPS coordinates: N 44 06.995' / W 86 25.421'
About the campground: This campground is quite close to Lake Michigan, with trails leading out to the beach, and just north of Nordhouse Dunes Wilderness Area and its trail system. The interpretive trails tell of history and the ecology of the dunes. The sites are arranged in multiple small loops in the forest: Violet, Oak, Orchid, and Hemlock. Violet and Hemlock have running water. Violet and Oak are fee-free after October 8, and Hemlock and Orchid loops close September 15. Vehicle clearance is low, but the roads are paved. The sites are nicely shaded.

Ludington Area

	Hookup Sites	Total Sites	Max RV Length	Hookups	Toilets	Showers	Drinking Water	Dump Station	Station Recreation	Fee	Reservations
191 Ludington State Park	352	362	40	E	F/NF	Y	Y	Y	HSFBL	$$-$$$$	Y
192 Cartier Park Campground	79	160	35	WES	F	Y	Y	Y	HFLC	$$$-$$$$	Y
193 Buttersville Campground	48	48	40	E	F	Y	Y	Y	S	$$$-$$$$	N
194 Mason County Campground	56	56	45	WES	F	Y	Y	Y	H	$$$	Y
195 Timber Creek Campground–Huron-Manistee National Forests	0	9	50	N/A	NF	N	Y	N	H	$	N
196 Sulak Campground–Huron-Manistee National Forests	0	12	25	N/A	NF	N	N	N	HF	No fee	N
197 Bowman Bridge Campground–Huron-Manistee National Forests	0	20	50	N/A	NF	N	Y	N	H F	$$	Y
198 Claybanks Campground–Huron-Manistee National Forests	0	9	25	N/A	NF	N	N	N	F	$	N
199 Leverentz Lake State Forest Campground	0	25	25	N/A	NF	N	Y	N	HFLO	$$	N
200 Bray Creek State Forest Campground	0	9	25	N/A	NF	N	Y	N	HFLO	$$	N
201 Old Grade Campground–Huron-Manistee National Forests	0	20	40	N/A	NF	N	Y	N	H	$$	N
202 Carrieville State Forest Campground	0	31	40	N/A	NF	N	Y	N	HFO	$$	N
203 Silver Creek State Forest Campground	0	26	25	N/A	NF	N	Y	N	HFO	$$	N
204 Rose Lake Park	148	160	40	WE	F	Y	Y	Y	S	$$-$$$	Y
205 Sunrise Lake State Forest Campground	0	17	25	N/A	NF	N	Y	N	HFLO	$$	N
206 Crittenden Park	9	19	40	WES	F	Y	Y	Y	SFL	$$-$$$	Y
207 Mud Lake State Forest Campground	0	8	20	N/A	NF	N	Y	N	HFO	$$	N

See Amenities Charts Key on page xiii.

191 Ludington State Park

Location: About 3 miles north of Ludington
Season: Year-round
Sites: 352 sites with electrical hookups, 10 hike-in sites with no hookups
Maximum RV length: 40
Facilities: Flush/vault toilets, showers, grills, water, tables, picnic shelter, picnic area, dump station, boat launch, hiking trails, beach, beach house, playground, nature center, boat rental, concessionaire, lighthouse, biking, paddling, Wi-Fi, amphitheater, Hamlin Dam
Fee per night: $$-$$$$
Management: Michigan DNR
Contact: (231) 843-2423; www.michigandnr.com/parksandtrails
Finding the campground: From Ludington go north 3 miles on MI 116/Lakeshore Drive and it goes right to the park entrance.
GPS coordinates: N 43 59.624' / W 86 28.131'
About the campground: This 5,300-acre state park lies between Lake Michigan and Hamlin Lake, offering beaches on both. Camping is divided into 3 sections: Pines with its 99 sites (closest to Lake Michigan), Cedars with 106 sites, and Beechwood with 147 sites (closest to Hamlin and Lost Lakes). Online maps indicate the sunny versus shady sites. All have mini cabins as well, plus there are hike-in sites north of the modern loops. Big Sable Point Lighthouse is within the park. Paddlers enjoy a "pathway" in Hamlin Lake, and hikers have over 21 miles of trails to explore the woods, marshlands, and dunes.

192 Cartier Park Campground

Location: Just a mile north of Ludington
Season: May 1 to October 15
Sites: 46 sites with full hookups, 33 sites with electrical hookups, 81 sites with no hookups
Maximum RV length: 35
Facilities: Flush toilets, showers, tables, dump station, boat launch, hiking trails, playground, volleyball court, basketball hoop, Wi-Fi, concessionaire, picnic gazebo
Fee per night: $$$-$$$$
Management: Owned by the City of Ludington
Contact: (231) 845-6237; www.cpcampground.com
Finding the campground: From Ludington take Lakeshore Drive north 1.5 miles and the park entrance is at Slagle Avenue on the right (east) side of the road right before Lincoln Lake.
GPS coordinates: N 43 58.611' / W 86 27.562'
About the campground: Located in an orchard next to Lincoln Lake, the campground is managed by the local community. Some lanes are too narrow for bigger vehicles. Activities are aimed at families with kids, and there is a bit of nature walking on-site. Be informed that the park has received some negative reviews regarding bathroom conditions and site sizes for RVs, though others enjoy the place for their kids. No alcohol or generators are allowed inside the park.

The lighthouse near Ludington State Park

193　Buttersville Campground

Location: About 6 miles south of Ludington
Season: Year-round, but vehicle gate is usually closed and there is no staff during winter
Sites: 48 sites with electrical hookups
Maximum RV length: 40
Facilities: Flush toilets, showers, fire rings, grills, water, tables, picnic shelter, picnic area, dump station, beach, playground
Fee per night: $$$-$$$$
Management: Pere Marquette Township Park Commission
Contact: (231) 843-2114; (231) 845-1277; http://pmtwp.org/residents/recreational_parks .php
Finding the campground: From US 10/Ludington Avenue in Ludington go south 2.1 miles on Marquette Road and turn right (west) on Iris Road. Go 1.5 miles and turn right (north) on Lakeshore Drive and the park is 1.2 miles north on the left (west) side of the road.
GPS coordinates: N 43 56.168' / W 86 27.017'
About the campground: The campground, south of the day-use section of the park of the same name, lies on an isthmus between Lake Michigan and Pere Marquette Lake. The sites are on the bigger lake's side of Lakeshore Drive and are well shaded by trees. There are no water views, as the dunes and their overgrowth separate the sites from the shore. Wooden stairs lead to the beach. Not all sites have grills.

194　Mason County Campground

Location: About 6 miles south of Ludington
Season: Memorial Day Weekend to October 1
Sites: 56 sites with electrical hookups
Maximum RV length: 45
Facilities: Flush toilets, showers, fire rings, grills, water, tables, picnic shelter, picnic area, dump station, hiking trails, playground, concessionaire, disc golf, Wi-Fi
Fee per night: $$$
Management: Mason County Parks
Contact: (231) 845-7609; www.masoncounty.net/departments/parks-recreation/campground .html
Finding the campground: From Ludington on Ludington Avenue, go south on Business US 31 for 2.1 miles and turn right (west) on Iris Road. Where the road splits take Inman Road to the left for another 1.3 miles and turn left (east) on Chauvez Road. The camp is on the left (north) side of the road.
GPS coordinates: N 43 54.438' / W 86 25.619'
About the campground: Tall hardwoods give nice shade to these campsites, and they are arranged around a loop. Sites 2–23 don't face other campers. Sites 28–31 are listed for tent campers. While the park is not on Lake Michigan, the day-use area of Buttersville Park is just over a mile away. The disc golf course offers 72 "holes," and a world-class course is nearby.

195 Timber Creek Campground– Huron-Manistee National Forests

Location: About 10 miles north and west of Baldwin
Season: Year-round
Sites: 9 sites with no hookups
Maximum RV length: 50
Facilities: Vault toilets, fire rings, water, tables
Fee per night: $
Management: Baldwin/White Cloud Ranger District
Contact: (231) 745-4631; www.fs.usda.gov/recarea/hmnf/recarea/?recid=18884
Finding the campground: From Baldwin head north on US 10/MI 37 for 2.8 miles and go left (west) on US 10 for 7.3 miles. The park entrance is on the right (north) side of the road.
GPS coordinates: N 43 56.787' / W 85 59.849'
About the campground: Typically parks like these aren't good for larger RVs, but this is an exception. Clearance, however, is still low, and the roads are rustic as well. Though water is nearby, this is not a good place for fishing. Occupancy is generally light even in the high season, but hikers take advantage of the Tank Creek trailhead of the North Country National Scenic Trail. This site is actually plowed in winter, making it useful to snowmobilers looking to get on the nearby Ward Hills Snowmobile Trail.

196 Sulak Campground– Huron-Manistee National Forests

Location: About 6 miles west and north of Baldwin
Season: Year-round
Sites: 12 sites with no hookups
Maximum RV length: 25
Facilities: Vault toilets, fire rings, hiking trails
Fee per night: No fee
Management: Baldwin/White Cloud Ranger District
Contact: (231) 745-4631; www.fs.usda.gov/recarea/hmnf/recarea/?recid=18640
Finding the campground: From Baldwin head north on US 10/MI 37 for 1.9 miles and turn left (west) on 32nd Street. At 3.4 miles turn left (south) on Nugent Drive and follow it 0.9 mile to the park entrance on the right (north) side of the road.
GPS coordinates: N 43 55.427' / W 85 55.979'
About the campground: This camp is close to the Pere Marquette National Scenic River, but access is via a quarter-mile hike through federal land. This is a primitive site, and not even water is available. Hunters and anglers are the most common campers. The river is home to salmon, brown and rainbow trout, and steelhead. Sites are best for tents, and the low clearance won't work for much more than a short trailer.

197 Bowman Bridge Campground– Huron-Manistee National Forests

Location: About 5 miles west of Baldwin
Season: Mid-May to mid-October
Sites: 16 sites with no hookups, 4 walk-in sites with no hookups
Maximum RV length: 50
Facilities: Vault toilets, water, tables, hiking trails, lantern posts, host
Fee per night: $$
Management: Baldwin/White Cloud Ranger District
Contact: (231) 745-4631; www.fs.usda.gov/recarea/hmnf/null/recarea?recid=18614&actid=43
Finding the campground: From Baldwin head west on Washington Street and take the third left (south) on Astor Road. Continue 0.5 mile and turn right (west) on 52nd Street. Go 2.4 miles and turn left (southwest) on 56th Street, continuing 1.6 miles before turning right (north) on FR 6087 near the camp entrance.
GPS coordinates: N 43 53.258' / W 85 56.389'
About the campground: This camp is popular for paddlers and anglers. Campers come here for the rich forest environment and for easy access to the Pere Marquette National Scenic River at the Bowman Bridge Boat Landing that is just down the hill. All sites are paved, and shade is limited due to damage to the surrounding tree cover from a 2005 tornado. Anglers catch trout, salmon, and steelhead. Hikers have access to the North Country National Scenic Trail via a connector trail. Reservations are needed mid-May to mid-September.

198 Claybanks Campground– Huron-Manistee National Forests

Location: About 3 miles southwest of Baldwin
Season: Year-round
Sites: 9 sites with no hookups
Maximum RV length: 25
Facilities: Vault toilets, lantern posts, stairs to the river
Fee per night: $
Management: Baldwin/White Cloud Ranger District
Contact: (231) 745-4631; www.fs.usda.gov/recarea/hmnf/null/recarea?recid=18616&actid=43
Finding the campground: From Baldwin head west on Washington Street and take the third left (south) on Astor Road. Continue 1 mile and turn right (west) on 56th Street. Go 0.3 mile, turn left (south) on Jigger Trail, and follow that into camp.
GPS coordinates: N 43 52.203' / W 85 52.999'
About the campground: Set in the woods along Pere Marquette National Scenic River, this camp is best for anglers. Fishing here is flies only, and a steep staircase grants access to the river. The

camp road and sites are packed dirt/gravel, and tree cover is good for shade; but there is no water, so bring your own. These sites are first come, first served.

199 Leverentz Lake State Forest Campground

Location: About 2.5 miles east and north of Baldwin
Season: Year-round
Sites: 18 sites on Big Leverentz Lake and 7 sites on Little Leverentz Lake with no hookups
Maximum RV length: 25 feet
Facilities: Vault toilets, water, boat launch, hiking/mountain biking/off-road vehicle trails, floating dock
Fee per night: $$
Management: Michigan DNR
Contact: (231) 745-9465; www.michigandnr.com/parksandtrails
Finding the campground: From Baldwin take US 10 east 1.7 miles, go left (north) on Forest Drive for 0.2 mile, and the camp entrance is on the left, leading 0.7 mile to the site.
GPS coordinates: N 43 54.535' / W 85 49.171'
About the campground: Take your pick of lakes here, as this campground offers sites on Big and Little Leverentz for tents and small trailers. Boat ramps serve both lakes, and Big Leverentz has a 50-foot floating dock, plus paths from the sites grant shore fishing access. Hikers and mountain bikers have the 4.5-mile Sheep Ranch Trail, and anglers will find perch and bluegill in the lakes. Sites offer good shade.

200 Bray Creek State Forest Campground

Location: About 2 miles northwest of downtown Baldwin
Season: Year-round
Sites: 9 sites with no hookups
Maximum RV length: 25
Facilities: Vault toilets, firepits, water, tables, boat launch, hiking/mountain biking/off-road vehicle trails
Fee per night: $$
Management: Michigan DNR
Contact: (231) 745-9465; www.michigandnr.com/parksandtrails
Finding the campground: From US 10/MI 37 just north of Baldwin, go east on North Avenue/44th Street for 0.8 mile. Take a slight left (northwest) on Merriville Road, continue 0.6 mile to take a right (east) on 40th Street, and the camp road is 0.3 mile on the right (south) side of the road.
GPS coordinates: N 43 54.910' / W 85 49.480'
About the campground: Situated along the Baldwin River, the camp often attracts anglers in search of trout. The sites are basic, shaded by forest, and set up on a gravel-road loop. There is

access to Pine Forest Pathway for hikers and bikers, which makes a long loop south and partly follows the river. In winter the water pump handle is removed and roads are not plowed.

201 Old Grade Campground– Huron-Manistee National Forests

Location: About 11 miles north of Baldwin
Season: End of April to late September
Sites: 20 sites with no hookups
Maximum RV length: 40
Facilities: Vault toilets, fire rings, water, lantern posts, hiking trail
Fee per night: $$
Management: American Land and Leisure/Baldwin-White Cloud Ranger District
Contact: (231) 745-4631; www.fs.usda.gov/recarea/hmnf/recarea?recid=18872
Finding the campground: From Baldwin go north 11.1 miles on MI 37. Turn left (west) on Old Grade Road and it goes right into the camp 0.3 mile later.
GPS coordinates: N 44 03.648' / W 85 50.945'
About the campground: Located in the national forest among wetlands, this campground is best for getting away from it all and seeing some wildlife. There's even a short interpretive trail through the forest. Sites are shaded by birch and hemlock forest. Although this is right on the Little Manistee River, it is a shallow stretch, so paddling is not recommended, and the only angler interest is likely to be some trout fishing.

202 Carrieville State Forest Campground

Location: About 18 miles northeast of Baldwin
Season: Year-round
Sites: 31 sites with no hookups
Maximum RV length: 40
Facilities: Vault toilets, water, hiking/off-road trails
Fee per night: $$
Management: Michigan DNR
Contact: (231) 745-9465; www.michigandnr.com/parksandtrails
Finding the campground: From Baldwin take MI 37 10.8 miles north and turn right (east) on Old MI 63. Take this 6.1 miles, turn right (south) on Kings Highway, and the park will be 1.6 miles south on the right.
GPS coordinates: N 44 02.242' / W 85 43.346'
About the campground: A rustic campground on a river, these sites are best for tents and small trailers, as only 1 site can take something as long as 40 feet. Most offer at least partial shade. ATVs have direct access to Little Manistee Trail. Paddlers can put into the Little Manistee River right inside the campground, and the river is good for fishing brown and rainbow trout. Hiking trails

nearby include Pine Valley 5 miles to the northwest with 8.2 miles, and Silver Creek 8 miles to the southeast with 4 miles.

203 Silver Creek State Forest Campground

Location: About 5 miles north of Luther
Season: Year-round
Sites: 26 sites with no hookups
Maximum RV length: 25
Facilities: Vault toilets, fire rings, water, tables, hiking/mountain biking/off-road trails
Fee per night: $$
Management: Michigan DNR
Contact: (231) 745-9465; www.michigandnr.com/parksandtrails
Finding the campground: From Luther take State Road due north 5.1 miles and the camp entrance is on the left (west) side.
GPS coordinates: N 44 06.872' / W 85 41.003'
About the campground: Giving access to both Pine River and Silver Creek, this campground is best for anglers in search of trout. Paddling is possible on the Pine, and a carry-in access point is on-site. Hikers and mountain bikers can take the Silver Creek Trail, which runs 4 miles over rolling terrain to Lincoln Bridge State Forest Campground. Sites are nicely spread out and mostly shaded. Some are rather close to the water.

204 Rose Lake Park

Location: About 6 miles east and south of Tustin
Season: Mid-May through September
Sites: 148 sites with water and electrical hookups, 12 sites with no hookups
Maximum RV length: 40
Facilities: Flush toilets, showers, grills, water, tables, picnic shelter, picnic area, dump station, boat launch, beach, playground, basketball court, baseball, concessionaire, minigolf, shuffleboard
Fee per night: $$–$$$
Management: Osceola County Parks
Contact: (231) 768-4923; www.osceola-county.org/residents/county_departments/parks/index .php
Finding the campground: From Tustin just east of US 131, head east through town on 20 Mile Road (Church Street/Marion Road in town) and continue to 180th Avenue. Go right (south) 2 miles and turn left (east) on 18 Mile Road/Rose Lake Road, continuing 3 miles to turn right (south) on Youth Drive, which heads right to the park entrance.
GPS coordinates: N 44 04.278' / W 85 22.959'
About the campground: Rose Lake is surrounded by residential property, but this county park lies on the western shore. Sites here are mostly shaded by pine and hardwood trees but for a few toward the open center of the park. The beach is a short walk away and offers 1,300 feet of sandy

lakeshore. There are 12 options for tent campers who want to rough it a bit more, otherwise all sites have electric or even water hookups. The abundant activities make this nice for kids.

205 Sunrise Lake State Forest Campground

Location: About 6 miles east of Leroy
Season: Year-round
Sites: 15 sites with no hookups, 2 walk-in sites
Maximum RV length: 25
Facilities: Vault toilets, fire rings, water, tables, boat launch, hiking/mountain biking/off-road trails
Fee per night: $$
Management: Michigan DNR–Wilson State Park
Contact: (989) 539-3021; www.michigandnr.com/parksandtrails
Finding the campground: From just south of Leroy, go east on 15 Mile Road/Sunrise Lake Road for 6.1 miles where the road curves southeast. The park entrance is on the left side of the road.
GPS coordinates: N 44 01.725' / W 85 19.981'
About the campground: Set along the western shore of Sunrise Lake, this small, rustic camp has sites spread through the woods along the lake. Hiking trails are limited to a half-mile stroll on-site. There is a boat launch for anglers hoping to catch some of the resident trout, and another ramp is available at Rose Lake County Park as well. One mile south, off-road enthusiasts can run a 23-mile looping motorcycle trail. Sites are small but shaded, and all are first come, first served.

206 Crittenden Park

Location: About 19 miles east of Reed City
Season: May 11 to September 30
Sites: 9 sites with full hookups, 10 sites with no hookups
Maximum RV length: 40
Facilities: Flush toilets, water, showers, grills, tables, picnic shelter, picnic area, dump station, boat launch, playground, volleyball court, concessionaire, basketball court
Fee per night: $$–$$$
Management: Osceola County Parks
Contact: (231) 734-2588; (231) 832-6130; www.osceola-county.org/residents/county_depart ments/parks/index.php
Finding the campground: From US 131 in Reed City, go east on US 10 for 16.7 miles. Turn right (south) on 50th Avenue and the campground is 2.4 miles south on the right (west) side of the road.
GPS coordinates: N 43 51.991' / W 85 11.294'
About the campground: This county park lies on the eastern shore of Big Lake and makes a nice destination for families. The beach is grassy but beautiful, and the areas throughout the park are well maintained. A DNR boat launch is located adjacent to the park. The primitive sites are located

farthest back from the lake, and a camp map reveals the closest sites as "premium." Shade is decent but not complete.

207 Mud Lake State Forest Campground

Location: About 10 miles east of Evart
Season: Year-round
Sites: 8 sites with no hookups
Maximum RV length: 20
Facilities: Vault toilets, fire rings, water, tables, hiking/mountain biking/off-road trails
Fee per night: $$
Management: Michigan DNR–Wilson State Park
Contact: (989) 539-3021; www.michigandnr.com/parksandtrails
Finding the campground: From Evart take US 10 east 6.6 miles and turn left (north) on 20th Avenue. Go 1 mile, turn right (east) on 7 Mile Road/Brown Road, and at about 1.7 miles turn right (south) on Lee Road, which goes directly to the camp.
GPS coordinates: N 43 54.445' / W 85 04.662'
About the campground: Hikers and birders will like this little spot in the woods thanks to the mostly level Green Pine Lake Trail, a scenic path running 8.5 miles one way from Big Mud Lake to Pike Lake. The trail is OK for mountain bikers as well. Fishing might get you some bass or bluegill. The sites are shaded and mostly pretty private from each other.

The Upper Peninsula

The Upper Peninsula is so vastly different from the Lower Peninsula that it might as well be its own state. It is its own world, and one you can spend many seasons exploring. The U.P. is wilderness. In fact, it is estimated that more than 90 percent is forest. The U.P.'s prime scenery includes secluded lakes both large and small, old-growth forests, rugged rivers and hills, and the shorelines of Lakes Superior, Michigan, and Huron.

Particular local foods such as the meat and potato– (or rutabaga-) filled pasty or the spiced Italian sausage *cudaghi* are signs you are in "Yooper" country. They are holdovers from immigrant populations, especially the miners who came to descend into the earth for the rich veins of copper and taconite in the western U.P. Old mines and mining towns are now museums, and the ore docks in Marquette stand like cathedrals of industry.

In the west are the Porkies, the Porcupine Mountains and the Gogebic Range. North through Houghton, follow the Keweenaw Peninsula that juts far out into Lake Superior to Copper Harbor. Isle Royale, a national park and backcountry camper's dream, is reachable by passenger ferry from here.

The U.P. has no less than eleven National Wild and Scenic Rivers, with paddling for skill levels from beginner to advanced and many ideal places for fishing. The Two-Hearted River of Hemingway's short story empties into the big lake up here, but the description in the text is actually the Fox River, a nationally recognized trout river closer to Seney. Either one is gorgeous and a haven for anglers and canoeing enthusiasts.

The drives themselves are outstanding. Follow Lake Superior shoreline out on the Keweenaw Peninsula. Drive the Iron County Heritage Trail from Iron River to Crystal Falls. Bay de Noc along Lake Michigan on the south side offers pristine coastal areas and a scenic highway drive along US 2 that ends with a view of the Mackinac Bridge crossing to the Lower Peninsula.

The Porcupine Mountains Wilderness State Park lies between Ottawa National Forest and Lake Superior's shores to the west, and though visited by thousands each year, nothing takes away from that feeling of remote wilderness. Hike over 80 miles

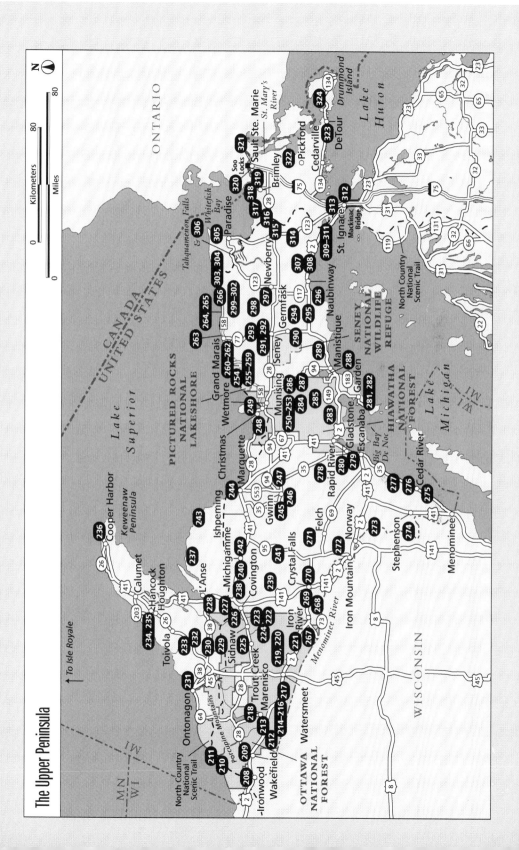

The Upper Peninsula

of trails, visit 21 miles of pristine beach, or search out the more than 90 waterfalls within its boundaries.

Near the border of Wisconsin, Sylvania Wilderness Area and its collection of lakes and portages draw paddlers looking for a bit of a Boundary Waters experience. Farther north and east check out the 95,000-acre Seney National Wildlife Refuge, with an abundance of animals ranging from 200 species of birds, river otters, and beavers to bigger beasts such as moose, wolves, and black bear.

Like the Lower Peninsula, the U.P. has its own national lakeshore. Pictured Rocks is so named for some rock outcrops of colored sandstone that stand along the Lake Superior coast east of Munising. Undeveloped beaches stretch for miles, dotted with pebbles, agates, and driftwood, and finally rising up over 300 feet into the Grand Sable Dunes. Farther inland in the park are several scenic waterfalls and, of course, excellent camping.

Lake Superior, the largest freshwater lake in the world by surface area, is a magnificent northern sea. Its color changes with its mood. Beneath the giant dunes at Grand Sable on a sunny summer day, the waters rival the turquoise brilliance of the Caribbean. After a rain, runoff can turn the lake red in some places, and at other times it becomes cold slate before a storm, or just deep, dark blue concealing the wrecks of hundreds of ships and boats that found out just how serious the mood can become.

The Great Lake Shipwreck Museum in Whitefish Point tells the tales of many such tragedies, including the infamous *Edmund Fitzgerald,* a 726-foot ore ship that sank in minutes in the wrath of a November storm in 1975 with rogue waves as high as 35 feet.

Tahquamenon Falls is the second-largest waterfall east of the Mississippi after Niagara Falls. In spring when the winter is melting away, the volume of water tumbling 50 feet over an edge 200 feet across can reach 50,000 gallons per second.

To the east is Sault Ste. Marie, the site of the Soo Locks, where the big ships are lifted and lowered between Lakes Huron and Superior. Across the St. Marys River lies Canada's version of the city. And to the farthest eastern reach of the peninsula is a smattering of islands that lie just this side of Canadian waters. Don't miss the carless Mackinac Island for a day trip at least.

The North Country National Scenic Trail continues from the Lower Peninsula at St. Ignace and heads through the eastern unit of the Hiawatha National Forest toward Tahquamenon Falls. Up here the segments are longer and the trail becomes a more serious hike in the wild, passing much of the best the U.P. has to offer, including some up-close-and-personal time with Lake Superior.

Ironwood to Copper Harbor Area/Keweenaw Peninsula

	Hookup Sites	Total Sites	Max RV Length	Hookups	Toilets	Showers	Drinking Water	Dump Station	Recreation	Fee	Reservations
208 Curry Park	25	56	50	WES	F	Y	Y	Y	N/A	$-$$$	Y
209 Eddy Park	65	75	40	WES	F	Y	Y	Y	N/A	$$-$$$$	Y
210 Black River Harbor Campground—Ottawa National Forest	0	40	40	N/A	F/NF	N	Y	Y	HSFBL	$$	N
211 Porcupine Mountains Wilderness State Park	100	227	50	E	F/NF	Y	Y	N	HSFL	$$-$$$	Y
212 Henry Lake Campground—Ottawa National Forest	0	11	35	N/A	NF	N	Y	N	FB	$$	N
213 Bobcat Lake Campground—Ottawa National Forest	0	11	35	N/A	NF	N	Y	N	SFB	$$	N
214 Moosehead Lake Campground—Ottawa National Forest	0	13	35	N/A	NF	N	Y	N	FB	$$	N
215 Pomeroy Lake Campground—Ottawa National Forest	0	17	35	N/A	NF	N	Y	N	FB	$$	N
216 Langford Lake Campground—Ottawa National Forest	0	11	35	N/A	NF	N	Y	N	FB	$$	N
217 Sylvania (Clark Lake) Campground—Ottawa National Forest	0	48	40	N/A	F/NF	Y	Y	Y	HS	$$$	N
218 Lake Gogebic State Park	105	127	45	E	F	Y	Y	Y	HSFL	$$-$$$	Y
219 Marion Lake Campground—Ottawa National Forest	0	40	60	N/A	NF	N	Y	N	SFB	$$	N
220 Imp Lake Campground—Ottawa National Forest	0	22	40	N/A	NF	N	Y	N	HFB	$$	N
221 Golden Lake Campground—Ottawa National Forest	0	22	40	N/A	NF	N	Y	N	FB	$$	N
222 Perch Lake Campground—Ottawa National Forest	0	20	40	N/A	NF	N	Y	N	FB	$$	N
223 Norway Lake Campground—Ottawa National Forest	0	27	40	N/A	NF	N	Y	N	HSFB	$$	N

	Hookup Sites	Total Sites	Max RV Length	Hookups	Toilets	Showers	Drinking Water	Dump Station	Recreation	Fee	Reservations
224 Lake Ste. Kathryn Campground–Ottawa National Forest	0	24	50	N/A	NF	N	Y	N	SFB	$$	N
225 Sparrow Rapids Campground–Ottawa National Forest	0	6	40	N/A	NF	N	Y	N	HFB	No fee	·N
226 Sturgeon River Campground–Ottawa National Forest	0	9	25	N/A	NF	N	N	N	HFB	No fee	N
227 Big Lake State Forest Campground	0	12	20	N/A	NF	N	Y	N	FO	$$	N
228 Baraga State Park	95	95	50	WES	F/NF	Y	Y	Y	HSF	$$$	Y
229 Bob Lake Campground–Ottawa National Forest	0	17	45	N/A	NF	N	Y	N	HSFB	$$	N
230 Courtney Lake Campground–Ottawa National Forest	0	21	40	N/A	NF	N	Y	N	HSFB	$$	N
231 Ontonagon Township Campground	70	70	50	WE	F	Y	Y	Y	N/A	$$$-$$$$	N
232 Emily Lake State Forest Campground	0	9	25	N/A	NF	N	Y	N	FLO	$$	N
233 Twin Lakes State Park	62	62	40	E	F	Y	Y	Y	HSFLO	$$$	Y
234 Hancock Recreation Area	58	72	30	E	F	Y	Y	Y	SFB	$$-$$$	Y
235 McLain State Park	98	98	60	E	F	Y	Y	Y	HSFB	$$$-$$$$	Y
236 Fort Wilkins Historic State Park	159	159	40	E	F	Y	Y	Y	HSFL	$$$	Y

See Amenities Charts Key on page xiii.

208 Curry Park

Location: On the west end of Ironwood next to the fairgrounds
Season: May to October
Sites: 9 sites with full hookups, 16 sites with electrical hookups, 31 sites with no hookups
Maximum RV length: 50
Facilities: Flush toilets, showers, grills, tables, dump station, playground, laundry
Fee per night: $-$$$
Management: City of Ironwood
Contact: (906) 932-5050; www.cityofironwood.org/ironwood-parks

Finding the campground: From US 2 through Ironwood, go right on Tourist Park Road on Ironwood's west side.

GPS coordinates: N 46 27.841' / W 90 11.102'

About the campground: This city park has easy access to Ironwood and makes a good place to stay for events at the Gogebic County Fairgrounds. Most of the sites are shaded by tall hardwoods in a grassy area without intervening vegetation. Some of the larger sites have no shade. The location along the highway can be bothersome with traffic noise. The park takes no reservations, and campers self-pay in a box on the side of the park building.

209 Eddy Park

Location: On Sunday Lake in Wakefield

Season: Memorial Day Weekend to the end of September

Sites: 19 sites with water, sewer, and electrical hookups; 46 sites with water, electrical hookups; 10 walk-in sites

Maximum RV length: 40

Facilities: Flush toilets, showers, tables, pavilion, dump station, boat ramp, playground, public phone

Fee per night: $$–$$$$

Management: City of Wakefield

Contact: (906) 229-5131 out of season; (906) 224-4481 in season; www.cityofwakefield.org/play

Finding the campground: From MI 28 coming into Wakefield from the north, turn right (west) on Chicago Mine Road and take the immediate first left (southwest) on Eddy Park Road. The park is on the left.

GPS coordinates: N 46 29.053' / W 89 56.708'

About the campground: Situated on the north shore of little Sunday Lake in Wakefield, opposite US 2, which passes on the south side of the lake, this is a potential urban stopover on the way to somewhere else. The street passes between the campsites, which are lakeside, and the rest of the park, which features a ball diamond just down the street. Some sites are listed as walk-in and are essentially a walk across the street from the rest of camp and into a short loop in the trees. Five sites have concrete pads, and all sites near to these are unshaded. The park land tapers with the lakeshore going west until it is about as wide as one campsite between the road and lake. These sites have good tree coverage.

210 Black River Harbor Campground– Ottawa National Forest

Location: About 19 miles north of Ironwood

Season: May 15 to September 30

Sites: 40 sites with no hookups

Maximum RV length: 40

Facilities: Flush/vault toilets, fire rings, grills, water, tables, picnic shelter, picnic area, dump station, boat ramp, hiking trails, beach, concessionaire

Fee per night: $$

Management: USDA Forest Service–Bessemer Ranger District

Contact: (906) 932-1330; www.fs.usda.gov/recarea/ottawa/recarea/?recid=12343

Finding the campground: From Ironwood go east on US 2 about 3 miles and turn left (north) on Powderhorn Road for 3 miles, then turn left (northwest) on Black River Road. Follow this 11.1 miles to the park entrance on the left.

GPS coordinates: N 46 39.532' / W 90 02.949'

About the campground: Boaters delight in one of the few public access points on Lake Superior this close to the Ironwood area. The Black River, dark with tannins, tumbles dramatically down to the lake, with 5 notable waterfalls reachable by hiking paths. The campground is to the east of the river and day-use areas. All sites have paved camping spurs and surrounding vegetation to grant privacy, but only 7 of them have lake views. A suspension bridge gives visitors access to the bridge in the day-use area as well as the North Country National Scenic Trail, from where they can continue north next to the Porcupine Mountains.

211 Porcupine Mountains Wilderness State Park

Location: About 17 miles north of Wakefield

Season: Year-round

Sites: 64 sites with no hookups, 100 sites with electrical hookups, 63 walk-in sites

Maximum RV length: 50

Facilities: Flush/vault toilets, showers, fire rings, grills, water, tables, picnic shelter, picnic area, boat launch, hiking/mountain biking trails, beach, playground, nature center, boat rental, concessionaire, telephone

Fee per night: $$-$$$

Management: Michigan DNR

Contact: (906) 885-5275; www.michigandnr.com/parksandtrails

Finding the campground: From MI 28 north of Wakefield go left (north) on Thomaston Road, which becomes CR 519/County Road. Go 2.3 miles, turn left to stay on CR 519, and continue 7.8 miles more. Then take CR 2.4 miles more and continue on Presque Isle Road for 3.5 miles. This will all be the same road heading north until you come to the campground office.

GPS coordinates: N 46 42.037' / W 89 58.479'

About the campground: This is the superstar in the Michigan State Park system, the largest undeveloped forest area in the state. "The Porkies" offer very few park roads but 87 miles of hiking trails through forest that includes stands of virgin old-growth hardwoods. But visitors flock here for the camping and the day-use areas. Despite its popularity and heavy use, the park still maintains its wilderness appeal. Legend has it the Ojibwa named this long conglomerate and basalt escarpment for its resemblance to the prickly forest resident. In addition to abundant backcountry sites, camping is in the rustic Presque Isle Campground to the west with its 50 sites, or Union Bay Campground to the east with 100 modern sites. Both are close to the Lake Superior shoreline. The North Country Trail passes through the park. Cabins in the woods are popular year-round. Don't

Lake of the Clouds inside Porcupine Mountains Wilderness Area

miss the view of Lake of the Clouds and from Summit Peak. Whole books have been written about this park.

212 Henry Lake Campground–Ottawa National Forest

Location: About 10 miles south and west from Marenisco
Season: Year-round
Sites: 11 sites with no hookups
Maximum RV length: 35 feet
Facilities: Vault toilets, fire rings, water, tables, boat ramp
Fee per night: $$
Management: USDA Forest Service–Bessemer Ranger District
Contact: (906) 932-1330; www.fs.usda.gov/recarea/ottawa/recarea/?recid=12339
Finding the campground: From Marenisco take MI 64 south for 5.5 miles and turn right (west) on FR 8100. From there go 1.1 miles and at a fork in the road with FR 8120, go right (northwest) and drive 2.9 miles to the park entrance on the right.
GPS coordinates: N 46 19.849' / W 89 47.661'
About the campground: Unusual for a small rustic camp in the Ottawa National Forest, this campground has a 144-foot accessible fishing pier. Fishing's the attraction here. Bass and bluegill occupy this deep, cold lake. A concrete-base boat ramp serves the site as well. The single camp loop has shaded sites, all separated by brush for privacy. Trees are mostly deciduous, with pine

taking over closer to the water. Some of the sites have a clear view of the sky overhead and a water view through the last trees between the sites and the lake.

213 Bobcat Lake Campground–Ottawa National Forest

Location: About 2 miles southeast of Marenisco
Season: Year-round
Sites: 11 sites with no hookups
Maximum RV length: 35
Facilities: Vault toilets, fire rings, grills, lantern posts, water, tables, picnic area, boat ramp, beach, beach house
Fee per night: $$ (no fee October 1 to May 15)
Management: USDA Forest Service–Bessemer Ranger District
Contact: (906) 932-1330; https://www.fs.usda.gov/recarea/ottawa/recarea/?recid=12338
Finding the campground: From MI 64 in Marenisco go east on Kimberly Road for 0.3 mile. Turn right (south) on FR 8500, go 1.1 miles, and turn right (south) onto the campground road.
GPS coordinates: N 46 21.515' / W 89 40.443'
About the campground: This rustic site in the Ottawa National Forest is also popular for picnics, offering a wide, grassy area with tables and grills right next to the lake. There is also a nice sandy swimming beach and a changing house. The campground, however, is almost a half mile away from this area and more shaded. All sites on this single loop have tent pads and a gravel parking spur. The brush around each site provides good privacy. Site #2 is accessible, as are 2 of the toilets. There is a boat ramp, and bass, pike, and panfish await anglers.

214 Moosehead Lake Campground– Ottawa National Forest

Location: About 15 miles south and east from Marenisco
Season: May to September
Sites: 13 sites with no hookups
Maximum RV length: 35
Facilities: Vault toilets, fire rings, water, tables, boat ramp
Fee per night: $$
Management: USDA Forest Service–Bessemer Ranger District
Contact: (906) 932-1330; www.fs.usda.gov/recarea/ottawa/recarea/?recid=12340
Finding the campground: From Marenisco head south on MI 64 about 5 miles and turn left (east) on Job Corps Road. Go 9.4 miles and turn right at a fork onto FR 6860. Go 1.5 miles and the camp is on the right.
GPS coordinates: N 46 14.498' / W 89 36.262'
About the campground: The area south of Marenisco is riddled with lakes amid the Ottawa National Forest. Reservations are not taken, but should these rustic camps be full, another may be

open just a few miles away. Moosehead, like the others, is primarily attractive to anglers. The sites are well shaded with gravel parking spurs and surrounded by intervening brush for privacy. A boat ramp is on-site, and the lake offers pike, crappie, bluegill, bass, and even muskellunge.

215 Pomeroy Lake Campground– Ottawa National Forest

Location: About 17 miles south and east of Marenisco
Season: Year-round
Sites: 17 sites with no hookups
Maximum RV length: 35
Facilities: Vault toilets, fire rings, water, tables, boat ramp
Fee per night: $$
Management: USDA Forest Service–Bessemer Ranger District
Contact: (906) 932-1330; www.fs.usda.gov/recarea/ottawa/recarea/?recid=12341
Finding the campground: From Marenisco go south on MI 64 for about 5 miles, turn left (east) on Job Corps Road, and go another 5.3 miles. Turn left (northeast) on Pomeroy Lake Road/ CR 525, follow it 3.4 miles, and turn left (northeast) on FR 6860. Go 2.3 miles and follow the curve to the right and onto CR 527 for another 0.2 mile. Turn right (southwest) on FR 6828, go 0.5 mile, and take a right (west) on Pomeroy Lake Campground Road. The entrance is 0.4 mile at the end of the road.
GPS coordinates: N 46 16.888' / W 89 34.438'
About the campground: Ottawa National Forest makes up almost one million acres here in the Upper Peninsula. It isn't hard to find rustic tranquility far from civilization. Pomeroy surely fits the bill. The directions alone keep most people away. Located on a small curve of forested land jutting out into the lake, the campground has ample shade and privacy among its 17 sites. Anglers use a concrete boat ramp in camp to get out for the muskellunge, pike, walleye, crappie, bass, and blue-gill. If this is too far out, look for other sites closer to Marenisco for a very similar experience.

216 Langford Lake Campground– Ottawa National Forest

Location: About 19 miles east and south of Marenisco
Season: Year-round
Sites: 11 sites with no hookups
Maximum RV length: 35
Facilities: Vault toilets, fire rings, water, tables, boat ramp
Fee per night: $$
Management: USDA Forest Service–Bessemer Ranger District
Contact: (906) 932-1330; www.fs.usda.gov/recarea/ottawa/recarea/?recid=12342

Finding the campground: From Marenisco go east on US 2 about 10 miles and turn right (south) on Old US 2. Go 1.9 miles, turn right (west) on CR 527, go 3.3 miles, and follow the slight left turn onto Langford Lake Road. Stay on this for 2.7 miles and the camp is on the right.

GPS coordinates: N 46 16.372' / W 89 29.533'

About the campground: Langford Lake offers 470 acres at a maximum depth of 15 feet and is a good choice for anglers. The waters offer more of a variety than some of the other Marenisco area lakes, with pike, walleye, yellow perch, crappie, bass, and bluegill among them. A boat ramp isn't far from the campsites but also has its own vault toilet. The sites all have gravel spurs for vehicles, good shade cover, and abundant understory in the trees surrounding them, making them quite private.

217 Sylvania (Clark Lake) Campground– Ottawa National Forest

Location: About 8 miles southwest of Watersmeet

Season: Year-round but open with full services from May 28 to September 30

Sites: 48 sites with no hookups

Maximum RV length: 40

Facilities: Flush/vault toilets, showers, fire rings, grills, water, tables, picnic area, dump station, boat ramp, hiking trails, beach, beach house, lantern posts

Fee per night: $$$

Management: Northwoods Property Management; USDA Forest Service

Contact: (906) 396-5428; (906) 932-1330; www.fs.usda.gov/recarea/ottawa/recarea/?recid=12332

Finding the campground: From Watersmeet take US 2 west about 4 miles and turn left (south) onto CR 535 and travel 3 miles. Turn left (south) on FR 6360 at the Sylvania Wilderness sign.

GPS coordinates: N 46 14.697' / W 89 19.077'

About the campground: The Sylvania Wilderness and Recreation Area lies just over the border from Wisconsin and is part of the Ottawa National Forest. With over 18,000 acres of pristine forest and crystal clear lakes, Sylvania is a gem in the Upper Peninsula and popular for paddlers and campers who want to disappear into the wilderness and search out one of the nearly 100 back-country camping sites. For those who prefer day trips into the primeval forest and a return to the vehicle, there are these 4 campground loops, only 2 of which have modern showers and toilets. Hikers have 26 miles of unmarked trail in the old-growth forest. Paddlers have carry-in access on Clark and Crooked Lakes.

218 Lake Gogebic State Park

Location: About 4 miles north of Marenisco

Season: Late April to early November

Sites: 105 sites with electrical hookups, 22 sites with no hookups
Maximum RV length: 45
Facilities: Flush toilets, showers, firepits, grills, water, tables, picnic shelter, picnic area, dump station, boat launch, hiking trails, beach, beach house, playground
Fee per night: $$-$$$
Management: Michigan DNR
Contact: (906) 842-3341; www.michigandnr.com/parksandtrails
Finding the campground: From Marenisco take MI 64 north 4.2 miles and the park entrance is on the right (east) side of the road.
GPS coordinates: N 46 27.410' / W 89 34.171'
About the campground: Here's a good place to get your campsite on the water. One-quarter of the sites here enjoy the lakeside perch on the largest inland lake in the Upper Peninsula. Lake Gogebic is a narrow 350 acres running north to south with a maximum depth of 30 feet. This is also Ottawa National Forest, and while the lake is perfect for fishing and paddling, there are beautiful waterfalls nearby and Lake Superior is also not far off. Hikers have a 2-mile nature loop, and the sandy beach is large and sunny and a short walk south from the campground loops.

219 Marion Lake Campground–Ottawa National Forest

Location: About 7 miles east of Watersmeet
Season: Year-round
Sites: 40 sites with no hookups
Maximum RV length: 60
Facilities: Vault toilets, fire rings, grills, water, tables, picnic area, boat ramps, beach, lantern posts
Fee per night: $$
Management: Northwoods Property Management; USDA Forest Service
Contact: (906) 396-5428; (906) 932-1330; www.fs.usda.gov/recarea/ottawa/recarea/?recid=12334
Finding the campground: From Watersmeet follow US 2 east for about 3.9 miles, turn left (north) on Marion Lake Road, and go 1.7 miles. Turn right (east) on FR 38, which becomes Dulyea Road, and go 1.1 miles to the camp entrance.
GPS coordinates: N 46 16.084' / W 89 05.183'
About the campground: Located in the Ottawa National Forest, this rustic campground is rather popular and can fill up. The sandy beach and swimming area are suitable for kids. Two boat ramps serve the campground, and the lake can get busy with fishing boats and other recreational watercraft that might spoil some campers' ideas of tranquility. The campground spreads out along the northern side of the lake, but much of it has an angle toward the west for nice sunsets over the water. The 3 loops of sites are grassy and shaded by surrounding hardwood and hemlock forest. Intervening understory and good spacing create some amount of seclusion.

220 Imp Lake Campground–Ottawa National Forest

Location: About 7 miles southeast of Watersmeet
Season: The Friday prior to Memorial Day to September 30
Sites: 22 sites with no hookups
Maximum RV length: 40
Facilities: Vault toilets, fire rings, water, tables, picnic area, boat ramp, hiking trails, beach
Fee per night: $$
Management: Northwoods Property Management; USDA Forest Service
Contact: (906) 396-5428; (906) 932-1330; www.fs.usda.gov/recarea/ottawa/recarea/?recid=12333
Finding the campground: From Watersmeet head east on US 2 for 5.4 miles and turn right (south) on FR 3978. The park entrance is on the right at 1.1 miles.
GPS coordinates: N 46 13.113' / W 89 04.271'
About the campground: Loons are the soundtrack of the north woods, and at this Ottawa National Forest campground you can expect to hear them plenty. Out in the middle of this 111-acre lake is an island where many loons typically nest each year. An accessible 1-mile interpretive trail features a boardwalk and a place to sit and watch wildlife. There's a grassy day-use area with a swimming beach as well. This is a quiet, no-wake lake, excellent for paddlers and anglers who can catch trout and panfish. The spacious and shaded sites—some of which have lake views—are arranged in 2 loops.

221 Golden Lake Campground–Ottawa National Forest

Location: About 14 miles northwest of Iron River
Season: Memorial Day Weekend through September
Sites: 22 sites with no hookups
Maximum RV length: 40
Facilities: Vault toilets, fire rings, grills, water, tables, picnic area, boat ramp, lantern posts
Fee per night: $$
Management: Northwoods Property Management; USDA Forest Service
Contact: (906) 396-5428; (906) 932-1330; www.fs.usda.gov/recarea/ottawa/recarea/?recid=12306
Finding the campground: From Iron River head west on US 2 for 13.3 miles and turn right (north) on FR 16. Go 0.7 mile to the park entrance on the left.
GPS coordinates: N 46 10.182' / W 88 52.914'
About the campground: Bass fishers know this place. The lake is 100 feet deep and cold and offers anglers a concrete boat launch and a chance at some northern pike and plenty of bass. Alternatively, Bush Creek is just northeast of here and is home to brown and brook trout. The campsites are spread out on a single loop to the east of the lake, with a few sites having water views off the back of them. The camp is shaded and offers parking spurs along with tables and fire rings. This lies halfway between Watersmeet and Iron River.

A plane lands on Perch Lake. MATT FORSTER

222 Perch Lake Campground–Ottawa National Forest

Location: About 11 miles south of Sidnaw
Season: Year-round
Sites: 20 sites with no hookups
Maximum RV length: 40
Facilities: Vault toilets, fire rings, water, tables, boat ramp
Fee per night: $$
Management: Calderwood Services; USDA Forest Service Calderwood Services;
Contact: (906) 852-3232; (906) 932-1330; www.fs.usda.gov/recarea/ottawa/recarea/?recid=12317
Finding the campground: From MI 28 in Sidnaw, go south on Ontario Street/Sidnaw South Road for 10.5 miles and turn left (east) on Perch Lake Road. Go 1.2 miles and the road goes right into the campground.
GPS coordinates: N 46 21.806' / W 88 40.514'
About the campground: A secluded rustic site, this campground on the 994-acre Perch Lake is a good base camp for anglers. Sites are on a single loop and separated by vegetation for privacy. Several sites have access to the lake, which has abundant pike, walleye, perch, and crappie. A ramp is on-site, and the Two-Hearted River and Muskallonge State Park are each less than 4 miles away. Hikers might consider this as well: The North Country National Scenic Trail is 5 miles north of here at Muskallonge.

223 Norway Lake Campground–Ottawa National Forest

Location: About 10 miles southeast of Sidnaw
Season: Year-round
Sites: 27 sites with no hookups
Maximum RV length: 40 feet
Facilities: Vault toilets, fire rings, grills, water, table, picnic shelter, picnic area, boat ramp, hiking trails, beach, beach house, lantern posts
Fee per night: $$
Management: Calderwood Services; USDA Forest Service
Contact: (906) 852-3232; (906) 932-1330; www.fs.usda.gov/recarea/ottawa/recarea/?recid=12319
Finding the campground: From MI 28 in Sidnaw go south on Ontario Street, which becomes Sidnaw South Road. Go 5.8 miles and turn left (east) on FR 2400/Norway Lake Road and continue 2.1 miles to the camp entrance on the right.
GPS coordinates: N 46 25.102' / W 88 41.078'
About the campground: Red pines are known for growing straight and reaching heights of over 100 feet. This Ottawa National Forest campground has 2 loops of sites with parking spurs in the shade of them. Sites are spaced nicely and with intervening understory for good privacy. A beach house serves the popular sandy swimming area. The boat ramp is concrete, and anglers may find walleye, bass, and panfish. The closest hiking is at Lake Ste. Kathryn, a couple miles south of here. While camping is allowed year-round, services are only provided from Memorial Day Weekend through September.

224 Lake Ste. Kathryn Campground– Ottawa National Forest

Location: About 8 miles south of Sidnaw
Season: Year-round
Sites: 24 sites with no hookups
Maximum RV length: 50
Facilities: Vault toilets, fire rings, water, tables, picnic area, boat ramp, hiking trails, beach, lantern posts
Fee per night: $$
Management: Calderwood Services; USDA Forest Service
Contact: (906) 852-3232; (906) 932-1330; www.fs.usda.gov/recarea/ottawa/recarea/?recid=12318
Finding the campground: From Sidnaw on MI 28 take Ontario Street south and continue on Sidnaw South Road for 8.1 miles. Turn right (west) on FR 2127 and go 0.3 mile to the camp entrance on the left (south) side of the road.
GPS coordinates: N 46 23.590' / W 88 43.358'

About the campground: Part of the Ottawa National Forest, this campground is set on the northern reaches of the 151-acre Lake Ste. Kathryn. The sites offer intervening understory and are spaced in such a way to maximize privacy. A few double sites can accommodate larger groups or families and even 2 bigger vehicles. Site 13 is the closest to the small beach. Hikers have 3 miles of interpretive trail to explore through pine and hardwood forest and wetlands, and anglers may find northern pike, bass, walleye, and panfish.

225 Sparrow Rapids Campground– Ottawa National Forest

Location: About 9 miles northeast of Trout Creek
Season: Year-round
Sites: 6 sites with no hookups
Maximum RV length: 40
Facilities: Pit toilet, fire rings, tables, hiking trails
Fee per night: No fee
Management: USDA Forest Service
Contact: (906) 932-1330; www.fs.usda.gov/recarea/ottawa/recarea/?recid=12320
Finding the campground: From Trout Creek take MI 28 east about 6 miles and turn left (north) on CR D-154. Go 0.3 mile, turn left (west), and go 3.4 miles on FR 1100 and the park is on the left.
GPS coordinates: N 46 30.298' / W 88 56.795'
About the campground: Normally the term "rustic" suggests at least a minimal level of park services, but here they aren't kidding. There's not much more than the pit toilet, and one must pack in water. But the location and the solitude are notable, not to mention its proximity to the scenic and wild East Branch of the Ontonagon River. Paddlers can get in here. The river offers anglers the chance to catch salmon, steelhead, and 3 trout species.

226 Sturgeon River Campground– Ottawa National Forest

Location: About 6 miles north of Sidnaw
Season: May 15 to November 30
Sites: 9 sites with no hookups
Maximum RV length: 25
Facilities: Vault toilets, fire rings, tables, hiking trails
Fee per night: No fee
Management: USDA Forest Service
Contact: (906) 932-1330; www.fs.usda.gov/recarea/ottawa/recarea/?recid=12321
Finding the campground: From Sidnaw go east on MI 28 about 0.3 mile and turn left (north) on FR 2200. Go 5 miles and the campground is on the left.

GPS coordinates: N 46 34.227' / W 88 39.351'

About the campground: This site and Sparrow Rapids are a couple of the most rustic in the book. Sturgeon River Campground's handful of sites are on a small loop just off the namesake's shore inside the Ottawa National Forest. Services are not provided; there is no water. But what you get for your troubles is a site inside the Sturgeon River Gorge Wilderness, which shows volcanic outcroppings, tumbling waters, and a depth of 350 feet. Hikers have the 7.5-mile Sidnaw Creel Trail and are not far from the North Country National Scenic Trail. In spring or when the water is high, there is paddling, but only for the experts.

227 Big Lake State Forest Campground

Location: About 9 miles north of Covington
Season: May through November
Sites: 12 sites with no hookups
Maximum RV length: 20
Facilities: Vault toilets, fire rings, water, off-road trails
Fee per night: $$
Management: Michigan DNR–Baraga State Park
Contact: (906) 353-6558; www.michigandnr.com/parksandtrails
Finding the campground: From just north of Covington at the junction of US 141 and MI 28, head west on MI 28 for 1.9 miles, go (right) north on Plains Road for 4.9 miles, and turn right (east) on Big Lake Road. Continue 1.3 miles, turn left (north) and stay left at the next fork as well, and at 0.7 mile the park road is on the left (west) side of the road.
GPS coordinates: N 46 36.672' / W 88 34.140'
About the campground: A bit tricky to find, this camp set out on a piece of land thrust into Big Lake offers shaded sites best suited for tents or smaller vehicles. ORV enthusiasts have access to Baraga Plains ORV Trail 1.5 miles to the west, which offers 28 miles of riding. Anglers can expect perch, crappie, and largemouth and smallmouth bass. Birders take note: Kirtland's warblers have been seen in the Baraga Plains.

228 Baraga State Park

Location: About 1 mile south of Baraga
Season: Late April to late October
Sites: 95 sites with electrical hookups
Maximum RV length: 50
Facilities: Flush/vault toilets, showers, firepits, grills, water, tables, picnic shelter, picnic area, pavilion, dump station, hiking trails, playground, Wi-Fi, tepee rental, telephone
Fee per night: $$$
Management: Michigan DNR

Contact: (906) 353-6558; www.michigandnr.com/parksandtrails
Finding the campground: From Baraga head south on US 41, and just outside of town find the park entrance on the right (west) side of the road.
GPS coordinates: N 46 45.640' / W 88 30.007'
About the campground: With nice views east out over Keweenaw Bay on Lake Superior, this state park lies right off the highway coming down out of the peninsula. While the campsites are separated from the lake by the highway, the park also has lake access with paths to get down to the water, but it does not have a sandy beach. The campsites themselves are grassy with only partial shade, and they include some pull-through and accessible sites. Railroad tracks run parallel to the highway and put the campground right between the two. Hiking is limited to a lollipop trail less than a mile long into the woods beyond the tracks. The park hosts an annual harvest festival in September, and the fall colors are notable.

229 Bob Lake Campground–Ottawa National Forest

Location: About 18 miles southeast of Ontonagon
Season: Year-round; services available Memorial Day Weekend to end of September
Sites: 17 sites with no hookups
Maximum RV length: 45
Facilities: Vault toilets, fire rings, water, tables, picnic area, boat ramp, hiking trail, beach, lantern posts
Fee per night: $$; no fees off-season
Management: Calderwood Services; USDA Forest Service–Ontonagon Ranger District
Contact: (906) 852-3232; (906) 884-2085; www.fs.usda.gov/recarea/ottawa/recarea/?recid=12324
Finding the campground: From Ontonagon take MI 38 east for about 17 miles, then turn right (south) on Dishneau Road. Go 4.1 miles and turn left (east) on Pori Road. Follow this 2.6 miles, turn left (east) to stay on it another 0.4 mile, and then turn right (south) on FR 1470. Go 1 mile, turn left (east) on Bob Lake Road, and the park entrance is 0.7 mile on the left.
GPS coordinates: N 46 39.738' / W 88 54.847'
About the campground: This is a nice site inside Ottawa National Forest that offers spacious and private sites, many with a lake view. Wildlife viewing is popular here, and along with birds and abundant deer, one may be lucky enough to see a bobcat, beaver, or even a rare fisher. A 1-mile interpretive trail lies just east of the campsites, and a connector trail heads for the North Country National Scenic Trail. Fishing is for walleye, perch, and smallmouth bass, and the lake is rather shallow. Services are only available during summer season; outside that there are no camping fees. There are accessible tables and toilets.

230 Courtney Lake Campground– Ottawa National Forest

Location: About 20 miles southeast of Ontonagon
Season: May 20 to October 15
Sites: 19 sites with no hookups, 2 walk-in sites
Maximum RV length: 40
Facilities: Vault toilets, fire rings, grills, water, tables, picnic area, boat launch, hiking/equestrian trails, beach, lantern posts
Fee per night: $$
Management: Calderwood Services; USDA Forest Service–Ontonagon Ranger District
Contact: (906) 852-3232; (906) 884-2085; www.fs.usda.gov/recarea/ottawa/recarea/?recid=12325
Finding the campground: From Ontonagon take MI 38 for 18.6 miles. Turn right (south) on Courtney Lake Road and follow it 0.8 mile to the camp entrance on the right.
GPS coordinates: N 46 45.332' / W 88 56.504'
About the campground: This popular rustic campground is in the northern reaches of Ottawa National Forest alongside a 33-acre lake. Sites are private and shaded, and 14 of them have views of the lake. A 2.2-mile interpretive trail offers excellent wildlife viewing opportunities and includes an observation deck overlooking wetlands. The lake is good for trout fishing, and the day-use area has a sandy beach. One of the few equestrian trails in the national forest is next door.

231 Ontonagon Township Campground

Location: About 2 miles from downtown Ontonagon
Season: Year-round
Sites: 70 sites with water and electrical hookups
Maximum RV length: 50
Facilities: Flush toilets, showers, grills, water, tables, dump station, beach, playground
Fee per night: $$$-$$$$
Management: Ontonagon Township
Contact: (906) 884-2930; www.ontonagontownshippark.com/
Finding the campground: From US 45 in downtown Ontonagon, take Houghton Street north right out of town for 1.1 miles (it becomes Lakeshore Drive) and the park is on the left.
GPS coordinates: N 46 52.995' / W 89 18.068'
About the campground: Resting right on the shores of Lake Superior, this park has serious views of both the lake and the rising Porcupine Mountains to the south. The park and the campgrounds have separate entrances, and the county road runs right through the campground, dividing it into lakeside sites—with a higher camping fee—and sites tucked into the woods across the road. The latter lose the lake view but gain a bit more seclusion. All sites are mostly grassy, with a few sandy sites, and most have some amount of shade. Be aware that some of the sites on the lake side are right off the county road.

232 Emily Lake State Forest Campground

Location: About 12 miles south of Toivola
Season: May through November
Sites: 9 sites with no hookups
Maximum RV length: 25
Facilities: Vault toilets, fire rings, water, tables, boat launch, off-road vehicle trails
Fee per night: $$
Management: Michigan DNR
Contact: (906) 288-3321; www.michigandnr.com/parksandtrails
Finding the campground: From Toivola head south on MI 26 about 9 miles and turn left (east) on Emily Lake Road, continuing 2.4 miles as it turns south and comes to the park entrance on the left (east).
GPS coordinates: N 46 51.377' / W 88 51.794'
About the campground: Not far off the highway, the deep, 54-acre Emily Lake is easy to find but a perfect, quiet campground on a lake with so few other sites. Launch a boat to fish for largemouth bass, perch, rainbow trout, and bluegill. Other lakes nearby offer more of the same for anglers. The

The Keweenaw Waterway near Hancock Recreation Area

sites here are private and shaded by a mix of pine and deciduous trees. A bit of paddling would be all right, but this spot is primarily for fishing or getting away from it all.

233 Twin Lakes State Park

Location: About 23 miles southwest of Houghton
Season: May 10 to October 31
Sites: 62 sites with electrical hookups
Maximum RV length: 40
Facilities: Flush/vault toilets, showers, fire rings, grills, water, tables, picnic shelter, picnic area, dump station, boat launch, hiking/off-road vehicle trails, beach, beach house, playground, volleyball court, horseshoe pits
Fee per night: $$$
Management: Michigan DNR
Contact: (906) 288-3321; www.michigandnr.com/parksandtrails
Finding the campground: The park is located right off MI 26, 23 miles south of Houghton. The entrance is on the east side of the road.
GPS coordinates: N 46 53.455' / W 88 51.469'
About the campground: The twin lakes in question are Lake Gerald and Lake Roland, and this campground is situated on the southwest end of the latter. Hikers have a 1.5-mile nature trail on-site that lies in the park land to the west across the highway. On clear days in winter, spring, or late fall when the trees are bare, Lake Superior can be seen from the trail. The warm waters of the lakes make the 500-foot sandy beach very popular with swimmers. Sites aren't very far apart, but they are shaded a bit by hardwood trees. Several of these sites on the eastern side of the loop are backed right up near the lakeside. Passage between the lakes is possible for paddlers. A 55-mile snowmobile trail runs right past the park parallel to the highway.

234 Hancock Recreation Area

Location: About 1 mile west of downtown Hancock
Season: May 15 to October 15
Sites: 58 sites with electrical hookups, 14 tent sites with electrical hookups
Maximum RV length: 30
Facilities: Flush toilets, showers, fire rings, water, tables, picnic area, dump station, boat launch, trails, beach, beach house, playground, volleyball court, horseshoe pits, phone, laundry, free Wi-Fi
Fee per night: $$-$$$
Management: City of Hancock
Contact: (906) 482-2720 before May 15; (906) 482-7413 after May 15; www.cityofhancock .com/recreation-beach-campground.php
Finding the campground: From downtown Hancock, follow MI 203/Jasberg Street west out of town and turn left (west) on Powder Drive. The park entrance is the first right.
GPS coordinates: N 47 07.948' / W 88 37.098'

McLain State Park lighthouse on Lake Superior

About the campground: A good place to stay if you are in the Houghton area and want to be in or near the city, the campground is right outside of Hancock. It offers 300 feet of sandy beach on this narrower portion of 26-mile-long Keweenaw Waterway. Continuing along the waterway, boats can connect to Lake Superior for big lake fishing as well. The sites are not terribly spacious but have good shade trees. Fifteen of them are only for tents.

235 McLain State Park

Location: About 10 miles north of Hancock
Season: Late April through October
Sites: 98 sites with electrical hookups
Maximum RV length: 60
Facilities: Flush/vault toilets, showers, firepits, grills, water, tables, picnic shelter, picnic area, dump station, hiking trails, beach, playground, horseshoe pits, lighthouse
Fee per night: $$$–$$$$
Management: Michigan DNR
Contact: (906) 482-0278; www.michigandnr.com/parksandtrails
Finding the campground: From Hancock take MI 203 (Jasberg Street) north 8.5 miles and the park is on the left.
GPS coordinates: N 47 14.161' / W 88 36.498'

About the campground: Situated just to the northeast of where the north end of the Keweenaw Waterway reaches Lake Superior, the state park is also halfway between Calumet and Hancock, making it a great base of operations for visiting historic mining sites in the area. The 2 miles of shore are sandy, while many other stretches on the Keweenaw Peninsula are rocky. The Keweenaw Waterway Lighthouse is near the park. The campsites are either on or near the edge of the lake. Be aware that it can be rather windy and chilly even in summer when the lake is in that sort of mood. Hikers have 4 miles of trail to explore that cross the highway and run along Bear Lake as well. Fishing is possible off the pier out to the lighthouse.

236 Fort Wilkins Historic State Park

Location: About 1 mile east of Copper Harbor
Season: April 26 to October 31
Sites: 159 sites with electrical hookups
Maximum RV length: 40
Facilities: Flush/vault toilets, showers, firepits, grills, water, tables, picnic shelter, picnic area, dump station, boat launch, hiking/mountain biking/biking trails, beach, playground, concessionaire, lighthouse
Fee per night: $$$
Management: Michigan DNR
Contact: (906) 289-4215; www.michigandnr.com/parksandtrails
Finding the campground: From Copper Harbor continue east on US 41 and the park entrance is on the right 0.9 mile out of town.
GPS coordinates: N 47 28.018' / W 87 52.310'
About the campground: It's not often you get to camp around an 1844 military outpost. Add to that a restored 1866 light station, one of Lake Superior's first lighthouses, and a historic cemetery. From June to August the fort has interpreters in period dress. This is as far north as you can camp in the peninsula. Near to the park are the Delaware Mine copper mine museum and boat service to Isle Royale. Boat tours go out for sunsets as well. The park straddles US 41 on a thin strip of land between Lake Superior to the north and Lake Fanny Hooe to the south. A creek joins the two bodies of water. There is 1 campground on the west side with 2 loops, the most western of which has the least tree coverage directly above, and another on the east side past the cemetery. Both are on the Lake Fanny Hooe side of the highway. Fishing is for walleye and splake, and a 2-mile trail circles the park with views of both lakes.

Marquette Area

	Hookup Sites	Total Sites	Max RV Length	Hookups	Toilets	Showers	Drinking Water	Dump Station	Recreation	Fee	Reservations
237 Big Eric's Bridge State Forest Campground	0	21	25	N/A	NF	N	Y	N	F	$$	N
238 King Lake State Forest Campground	0	6	30	N/A	NF	N	Y	N	FLO	$$	N
239 Deer Lake State Forest Campground	0	12	30	N/A	NF	N	Y	N	HFLO	$$	N
240 Beaufort Lake State Forest Campground	0	7	40	N/A	NF	N	Y	N	FL	$$	N
241 Squaw Lake State Forest Campground	0	15	40	N/A	NF	N	Y	N	HFLO	$$	N
242 Van Riper State Park	147	187	50	E	F	Y	Y	Y	HSFBL	$$-$$$	Y
243 Perkins Park Campground	51	75	45	WES	F	Y	Y	Y	HSF	$$-$$$$	Y
244 Marquette Tourist Park	100	110	40	WES	F	Y	Y	Y	HS	$$-$$$$	Y
245 Bass Lake State Forest Campground	0	22	40	N/A	NF	N	Y	N	HFLO	$$	N
246 Anderson Lake West State Forest Campground	0	13	40	N/A	NF	N	Y	N	HFLO	$$	N
247 Little Lake State Forest Campground	0	16	40	N/A	NF	N	Y	N	HFLO	$$	N
248 AuTrain Lake Campground–Hiawatha National Forest	0	37	40	N/A	NF	N	Y	N	HSFB	$$	Y
249 Bay Furnace Campground–Hiawatha National Forest	0	50	45	N/A	NF	N	Y	Y	HF	$$$	Y
250 Island Lake Campground–Hiawatha National Forest	0	23	30	N/A	NF	N	Y	N	HFB	$$	N
251 Council Lake Dispersed Campground–Hiawatha National Forest	0	4	20	N/A	NF	N	N	N	HSFB	$	Y
252 Pete's Lake Campground–Hiawatha National Forest	0	41	35	N/A	NF	N	Y	N	HSFB	$$$	N
253 Widewaters Campground–Hiawatha National Forest	0	34	25	N/A	NF	N	Y	N	HFB	$$	Y

	Hookup Sites	Total Sites	Max RV Length	Hookups	Toilets	Showers	Drinking Water	Dump Station	Recreation	Fee	Reservations
254 Little Beaver Lake Campground—Pictured Rocks National Lakeshore	0	8	35	N/A	NF	N	Y	N	HL	$$	Y
255 South Gemini Lake State Forest Campground	0	8	20	N/A	NF	N	Y	N	HFL	$$	N
256 North Gemini Lake State Forest Campground	0	17	20	N/A	NF	N	Y	N	HFL	$$	N
257 Canoe Lake State Forest Campground	0	4	20	N/A	NF	N	Y	N	HFL	$$	N
258 Cusino Lake State Forest Campground	0	6	20	N/A	NF	N	Y	N	HF	$$	N
259 Ross Lake State Forest Campground	0	10	20	N/A	NF	N	Y	N	HFL	$$	N
260 Kingston Lake State Forest Campground	0	16	40	N/A	NF	N	Y	N	HFL	$$	N
261 Twelvemile Beach Campground—Pictured Rocks National Lakeshore	0	36	42	N/A	NF	N	Y	N	H	$$	Y
262 Hurricane River Campground—Pictured Rocks National Lakeshore	0	21	42	N/A	NF	N	Y	N	H	$$	Y
263 Woodland Park Campground	116	149	40	WE	F	Y	Y	Y	SF	$$$-$$$$	Y
264 Lake Superior State Forest Campground	0	18	40	N/A	NF	N	Y	N	HFLO	$$	N
265 Blind Sucker State Forest Campground (No. 1 and 2)	0	45	45	N/A	NF	N	Y	N	HFLO	$$	N
266 Muskallonge Lake State Park	159	159	50	E	F	Y	Y	Y	HSFBL	$$$	Y

See Amenities Charts Key on page xiii.

237 Big Eric's Bridge State Forest Campground

Location: About 21 miles east of L'Anse
Season: April through November
Sites: 21 sites with no hookups

Maximum RV length: 25
Facilities: Vault toilets, fire rings, water, tables
Fee per night: $$
Management: Michigan DNR–Baraga State Park
Contact: (906) 353-6558; www.michigandnr.com/parksandtrails
Finding the campground: From US 41 in L'Anse take Broad Street northwest to Main Street and go right (northeast). Stay on this for 19.8 miles even as it becomes Skanee Road and then turn right (east) on Erick Road. The park is 1.2 miles on the left just before the bridge.
GPS coordinates: N 46 51.861' / W 88 05.018'
About the campground: The Big Huron River is a beauty as it tumbles north to Lake Superior through untouched wilderness and impressive geology. While experienced paddlers will enjoy river access at the campground, there are no liveries nearby. The river is rocky and shows a waterfall near the bridge. The woods are rich with birdlife, but there are no formal trails. It's a nice, rustic, scenic escape, and 7 miles north the river meets the big lake.

238 King Lake State Forest Campground

Location: About 15 miles east and south of Covington
Season: May through November

King Lake State Forest Campground

Sites: 6 sites with no hookups

Maximum RV length: 30

Facilities: Vault toilets, fire rings, water, tables, boat launch, off-road vehicle trails

Fee per night: $$

Management: Michigan DNR–Baraga State Park

Contact: (906) 353-6558; www.michigandnr.com/parksandtrails

Finding the campground: From Covington head east on US 141/MI 28 for 4.2 miles, then turn right (south) on US 41/MI 28. Go 5.4 miles, turn right (west) on King Lake Road, and go 4.9 miles to the camp entrance.

GPS coordinates: N 46 31.853' / W 88 24.133'

About the campground: Best for anglers or just those seeking solitude, these 6 rustic sites lie on the northern end of King Lake. Fishing offers northern pike, perch, crappie, and largemouth and smallmouth bass, and there is a shallow boat ramp on-site. Just 12 miles northwest of here is Canyon Falls Roadside Park, with a scenic boardwalk along the Sturgeon River.

239 Deer Lake State Forest Campground

Location: About 23 miles north of Crystal Falls

Season: Year-round

Sites: 12 sites with no hookups

Maximum RV length: 30

Facilities: Vault toilets, fire rings, water, tables, boat launch, hiking/off-road vehicles trails

Fee per night: $$

Management: Michigan DNR–Baraga State Park

Contact: (906) 353-6558; www.michigandnr.com/parksandtrails

Finding the campground: From US 2 just west of Crystal Falls, take US 141 north 12.4 miles and turn right (east) on Corral Road, which turns north onto The Grade. Go 7.4 miles and at the fork go right on 4 Corners Road for 1.1 miles. Turn right (south) on Deer Lake Road and at 0.7 mile the camp entrance is on the right.

GPS coordinates: N 46 19.502' / W 88 19.410'

About the campground: This state forest campground is nice enough, with good tree cover and a quiet little lake full of panfish. The boat ramp is right on-site, but other than that you'll need to drive a bit for other activities. Hiking is 23 miles southeast at Lake Mary Plains Trail inside Glidden Lake State Forest Campground. ATV users are 32 miles from Baraga Plains ATV Trail, and wildlife seekers go even farther to reach Deer Marsh Interpretive Trail. So come here either for day trips from home base or a low-key getaway in the woods.

240 Beaufort Lake State Forest Campground

Location: About 4 miles west of Michigamme

Season: May to November

Sites: 7 sites with no hookups

Maximum RV length: 40
Facilities: Vault toilets, fire rings, water, tables, boat launch
Fee per night: $$
Management: Michigan DNR–Van Riper State Park
Contact: (906) 339-4461; www.michigandnr.com/parksandtrails
Finding the campground: From Michigamme head west on US 41/MI 28 for 2.3 miles and turn left (southwest) onto Beaufort Lake Road, following it 1.5 miles to the entrance to the camp on the left (south) side of the road.
GPS coordinates: N 46 32.882' / W 88 11.361'
About the campground: This collection of sunny sites just off the passing road does not accept reservations. The camp has access to the 462-acre Beaufort Lake, which connects with Lakes George and Ruth. Fishing here is for walleye, pike, and perch. A nearby scenic site is Canyon Falls Roadside Park, about 12 miles northwest, which provides a boardwalk along the Sturgeon River. Otherwise there isn't much going on inside the camp itself.

241 Squaw Lake State Forest Campground

Location: About 45 miles southwest of Marquette
Season: Year-round
Sites: 15 sites with no hookups
Maximum RV length: 40
Facilities: Vault toilets, grills, water, tables, boat launch, hiking/off-road vehicle trails
Fee per night: $$
Management: Michigan DNR–Bewabic State Park
Contact: (906) 875-3324; www.michigandnr.com/parksandtrails
Finding the campground: From Marquette take US 41/MI 28 west 24 miles and go left (south) on MI 95 for 17.8 miles. Turn right (west) on Fence River Road and follow the signs to the camp.
GPS coordinates: N 46 17.466' / W 88 03.909'
About the campground: Fishing is the big attraction here, as Squaw Lake is designated as a trout lake. The campground is situated on the west side of the lake at a narrow channel point between Squaw Lake to the north and Little Squaw Lake to the south. Shade is pretty consistent, and the sites on the small loop may be better than the sites along the road to the boat ramp. No sites are on the lake proper. Most sites are for tents or small trailers, but 3 sites can handle a vehicle up to 40 feet.

242 Van Riper State Park

Location: About 35 miles west of Marquette
Season: Year-round
Sites: 147 sites with electrical hookups, 40 sites with no hookups
Maximum RV length: 50

The ruins of a mine and part of a mining museum in Ishpeming near Van Riper State Park

Facilities: Flush/vault toilets, showers, grills, water, tables, picnic shelter, picnic area, dump station, boat launch, hiking/biking trails, beach, beach house, playground, nature center, fishing pier, concessionaire

Fee per night: $$-$$$

Management: Michigan DNR

Contact: (906) 339-4461; www.michigandnr.com/parksandtrails

Finding the campground: From Champion head west on US 41/MI 28 for about 1 mile and find the park entrance on the left (south) side of the highway.

GPS coordinates: N 46 31.250' / W 87 59.091'

About the campground: The park system designates this park as a Watchable Wildlife site, which is not surprising, as this is where moose were introduced into the wild in the Upper Peninsula. While you are not guaranteed to see one by any means, other mammals and birds are abundant. The campground is modern and even offers Wi-Fi throughout. There is a sandy beach on Lake Michigamme and access to the Peshekee River. The modern sites are arranged in 2 long parallel loops with some tree shade but not a lot of privacy, while the rustic sites have their own loop to the west of those, with similar tree cover.

243 Perkins Park Campground

Location: About 26 miles north of Marquette

Season: May through September

Sites: 30 sites with full hookups, 21 sites with electrical hookups, 24 sites with no hookups

Maximum RV length: 45

Facilities: Flush toilets, showers, grills, water, tables, picnic area, dump station, boat launch, hiking trail, beach, playground, fishing pier, fish-cleaning station, Wi-Fi, tent rental

Fee per night: $$-$$$$

Management: Marquette County

Contact: (906) 345-9353; www.co.marquette.mi.us/departments/planning/perkins_park/index.php

Finding the campground: Head north from Marquette on Big Bay Road/CR 550 for 24.3 miles and just before Big Bay find the campground on the right (east) side of the road.

GPS coordinates: N 46 48.648' / W 87 43.702'

About the campground: Situated on the shores of Lake Independence, this county park offers good fishing and some nice wildlife observation. The beach has lifeguards—a rarity—and hikers have a walking trail and observation deck of the wetlands area. This is camping with some modern conveniences and, as it is just off the county highway, good access to town. Some of the sites are on the lakefront, and there are 6 pull-throughs. Tents are also rentable. Accessible walkways connect restrooms, the playground, and the lake.

A mile from Marquette Tourist Park are some Superior views at Presque Isle Park.

244   Marquette Tourist Park

Location: Just north of downtown Marquette
Season: Mid-May to mid-October
Sites: 58 sites with electrical hookups, 38 sites with full hookups, 4 sites with electrical and water hookups, 10 sites with no hookups
Maximum RV length: 40
Facilities: Flush toilets, showers, barbecue pits, water, tables, picnic area, dump station, hiking/biking trails, beach, playground, softball diamond, ball field, cooking facilities
Fee per night: $$-$$$$
Management: City of Marquette
Contact: (906) 228-0465; (906) 228-0460 off-season; www.marquettemi.gov/departments/community-services/parks-and-recreation/tourist-park
Finding the campground: From US 41/MI 28 enter Marquette on Washington Street heading east. Go left (north) on 4th Street/Presque Isle Avenue and turn left (west) on Wright Street. Turn right (north) on Sugar Loaf Avenue, and the park entrance is on the left (west) at Power Mill Road.
GPS coordinates: N 46 34.152' / W 87 24.389'
About the campground: This modern campground is comfortable and clean, making this a perfect place to enjoy the Marquette area. Sites are shaded and spacious. The excellent city bike path runs past the park, and Lake Superior's shores are a mile away. This is the site of the Hiawatha Traditional Music Festival each year. A fishing area created by a dam on the Dead River is shore accessible and offers a beach and pier as well.

245 Bass Lake State Forest Campground

Location: About 11 miles west of Gwinn
Season: Year-round
Sites: 22 sites with no hookups
Maximum RV length: 40
Facilities: Vault toilets, fire rings, water, tables, boat launch, hiking/off-road vehicle trails
Fee per night: $$
Management: Michigan DNR–Escanaba Field Office
Contact: (906) 786-2351; www.michigandnr.com/parksandtrails
Finding the campground: From Gwinn head west on MI 35 for 4.7 miles and turn left (west) on CR Eo/Horseshoe Lake Road. Go 0.9 mile, take the slight left on Chain Lake Trail (still CR Eo), and follow this road 5.1 miles as it winds around as CR Ett/Crooked Lake Lane until you come to Spring Lake Lane. Go right for 0.2 mile and the camp entrance is on the left.
GPS coordinates: N 46 15.775' / W 87 35.064'
About the campground: Ironically, the catch here at Bass Lake is typically rainbow trout. Three other lakes nearby—Big and Little Shag Lakes, Pike Lake—are also good fishing spots, all of which have boat ramps. Hikers and bikers have to head for Anderson Lake 8 miles off for some trails, but the 26-mile Bass Lake Motorcycle Trail is only 1 mile east. While the maximum vehicle length is 40 feet, only 10 of these sites can handle that. Sites are arranged in a single loop, with scattered pine and hardwood trees providing some shade.

246 Anderson Lake West State Forest Campground

Location: About 6 miles south of Gwinn
Season: Year-round
Sites: 13 sites with no hookups
Maximum RV length: 40
Facilities: Vault toilets, fire rings, water, tables, boat launch, hiking/mountain biking/off-road vehicle trails
Fee per night: $$
Management: Michigan DNR–Escanaba Field Office
Contact: (906) 786-2351; www.michigandnr.com/parksandtrails
Finding the campground: From MI 35 in Gwinn head south on Serenity Drive for 1.4 miles and turn left (south) on CR 557. Go 2.7 miles and turn right (west) on Anderson Lake Lane. At 0.6 mile a dirt road to the right leads you another mile into the camping area.
GPS coordinates: N 46 13.360' / W 87 29.725'
About the campground: This quiet lake located amid a smattering of lakes in the area of Gwinn State Forest offers something for anglers and trail seekers alike. The lake has bluegill and a carry-in boat launch to get to them. Just 5 miles north near Gwinn is a ramp for the Escanaba River for trout fishing. Hikers have 6 miles of rolling land that is also accessible to mountain bikers. The sites are very well shaded and have good privacy.

247 Little Lake State Forest Campground

Location: About 6 miles east of Gwinn
Season: Year-round
Sites: 16 sites with no hookups
Maximum RV length: 40
Facilities: Vault toilets, fire rings, water, tables, boat launch, hiking/mountain biking/off-road trails
Fee per night: $$
Management: Michigan DNR–Escanaba Field Office
Contact: (906) 786-2351; www.michigandnr.com/parksandtrails
Finding the campground: From Gwinn head east on MI 35 for about 5 miles and turn right (south) on Little Lake Road. The campground entrance is 0.2 mile on the right (west) side of the road.
GPS coordinates: N 46 16.866' / W 87 19.961'
About the campground: Just a single loop of rustic sites and a boat landing, this campground located at the northeast end of Little Lake is easy to get to and good for anglers and paddlers. Fishing targets include walleye and perch. Only 6 sites can fit big rigs, otherwise these are all tent and small trailer sites.

248 AuTrain Lake Campground– Hiawatha National Forest

Location: About 10 miles west of Munising
Season: May 15 to September 30
Sites: 37 sites with no hookups
Maximum RV length: 40
Facilities: Vault toilets, grills, fire rings, water, tables, picnic area, boat launch, hiking trails, beach, boat rental
Fee per night: $$
Management: USDA Forest Service
Contact: (906) 428-5800; Reservations: (877) 444-6777; www.fs.usda.gov/recarea/hiawatha/recarea?recid=13283
Finding the campground: From the intersection of CR 3 and MI 28 in AuTrain, drive south 4.2 miles on CR 3 to FR 2276. Turn left (east) and drive 0.7 mile to FR 2596. Turn left (north) and drive 1.4 miles to the campground.
GPS coordinates: N 46 23.500' / W 86 50.284'
About the campground: This popular campground is situated on the shore of AuTrain Lake at Buck Bay and bordered to the east by Buck Creek. Sites are wooded with good shade and privacy, and each is staggered with the site across the park road. Activities on the 830-acre lake include waterskiing, fishing, and paddling. Some sites are reservable.

249 Bay Furnace Campground– Hiawatha National Forest

Location: At the west edge of the town of Christmas
Season: May 15 to September 30
Sites: 50 sites with no hookups
Maximum RV length: 45
Facilities: Vault toilets, grills, fire rings, water, tables, picnic area, dump station, hiking trails
Fee per night: $$
Management: USDA Forest Service
Contact: (906) 428-5800; Reservations: (877) 444-6777; www.fs.usda.gov/recarea/hiawatha/recarea?recid=13284
Finding the campground: From MI 28 head west of Christmas and find Bay Furnace Road on the north side of the road.
GPS coordinates: N 46 26.300' / W 86 42.500'
About the campground: Located on Bay Furnace of Lake Superior, about 2 miles west of the ferry crossing to Grand Island, this campground offers some fine lake views with sites shaded by tall pine. The layout facing north means one can see both sunrise and sunset here. The beach is a bit rocky. Ruins of an old iron furnace are nearby. This is a nice option for base camp for visits to Pictured Rocks National Lakeshore, plus there is a campsite for divers exploring the shipwrecks of the Alger Underwater Preserve.

250 Island Lake Campground– Hiawatha National Forest

Location: About 14 miles south of Munising
Season: May 15 to September 8
Sites: 23 sites with no hookups
Maximum RV length: 30
Facilities: Vault toilets, firepits, water, tables, ORV trails
Fee per night: $$
Management: USDA Forest Service
Contact: 906-428-5800; Reservations: (877) 444-6777; www.fs.usda.gov/recarea/hiawatha/recarea?recid=13285
Finding the campground: From Munising head south on MI 94 for about 6.5 miles and go left (south) on 16 Mile Lake Road/CH 513 for only 0.2 mile. Take a left (southeast) on FR 2254 and go 6.2 miles to turn right (south) on Island Lake Road/FR 2557. The camp entrance is 0.6 mile on the left.
GPS coordinates: N 46 16.243' / W 86 39.098'
About the campground: Here is some nice solitude off the beaten path where paddlers or ORV enthusiasts will find the most pleasure. The sites are arranged into 2 loops that lie on either end of

the northern tip of the lake. Canoe access is carry in. Sites are nicely shaded, and many of them overlook the lake. This campground is also one of the few campgrounds that allow ORV riding in the campground, and there is direct access to the ORV trail system. The camp gets light traffic.

251 Council Lake Dispersed Campground– Hiawatha National Forest

Location: About 11 miles south of Wetmore
Season: Year-round
Sites: 4 sites with no hookups
Maximum RV length: 20
Facilities: Vault toilets, firepits, grills, tables, picnic area, hiking trails, beach
Fee per night: $
Management: USDA Forest Service
Contact: (906) 428-5800; Reservations: (877) 444-6777; www.fs.usda.gov/recarea/hiawatha/recarea/?recid=13316
Finding the campground: From MI 94/MI 28 head south 9.2 miles from Wetmore on Connors Road/NF-13. Turn right (west) on USFS-2334 and go 1.1 miles (staying on this road as it becomes USFS-2262), then turn right (west) on Boy Scout Road and the camp is 0.7 mile more at the end of the road.
GPS coordinates: N 46 14.495' / W 86 38.825'
About the campground: Deep in Hiawatha National Forest, this camp has some nice privacy but is very rustic. Located on the south shore of Council Lake in a mixed forest of beech and other hardwoods, the sites are shaded and popular with anglers here to find perch, bass, bluegill, pike, and crappie in this 12-acre lake, part of a chain of lakes. Paddlers also will enjoy this. Be aware there is no water or toilet paper here, and reservations are required.

252 Pete's Lake Campground– Hiawatha National Forest

Location: About 11 miles south of Wetmore
Season: May 15 to September 30
Sites: 41 sites with no hookups
Maximum RV length: 35
Facilities: Vault toilets, grills, water, tables, picnic area, hiking/biking trails, beach, change house, boat ramp, fishing pier
Fee per night: $$$
Management: USDA Forest Service
Contact: (906) 428-5800; Reservations: (877) 444-6777; www.fs.usda.gov/recarea/hiawatha/recarea/?recid=13286

Finding the campground: From Wetmore head south on NF-13 nearly 10 miles. Turn left (east) on NF-2173 and then right (south) on Pete's Lake Road to get to the park entrance.

GPS coordinates: N 46 13.852' / W 86 36.186'

About the campground: Though rustic, the campground has paved roads and is a bit more accessible than some of the other campgrounds deep in the woods. The 160-acre lake is good for fishing (bass, walleye, perch, and pike), and there is an accessible pier on-site. Campsites here are shaded by the woods, spacious, and offer privacy. The 9-mile Bruno's Run trail that connects here is a loop suitable for hikers and bikers that passes along the Indian River and among the lakes of the area.

253 Widewaters Campground– Hiawatha National Forest

Location: About 13 miles south of Wetmore

Season: May 15 to September 30

Sites: 34 sites with no hookups

Maximum RV length: 25

Facilities: Vault toilets, grills, water, tables, boat launch, hiking/biking trails

Fee per night: $$

Management: USDA Forest Service

Contact: (906) 428-5800; Reservations: (877) 444-6777; www.fs.usda.gov/recarea/hiawatha/recarea/?recid=13287

Finding the campground: From Westmore go south on NF-13 about 11 miles and turn right (west) on FR 2262. Go 0.7 mile and the park entrance is on the left (west).

GPS coordinates: N 46 13.166' / W 86 37.700'

About the campground: While the road to the park separates these shaded sites from Irwin Lake, the Indian River runs along the west side of the campground and offers benches for hikers on the wilderness trail. Anglers come for bass, pike, bluegill, and crappie and have access to the 60-acre Fish Lake at the north-end boat ramp; the Indian River, which is good for brook trout; and Irwin Lake. Hikers and bikers have a spur trail to the 9-mile loop Bruno's Run, which passes area lakes and goes along the Indian River.

254 Little Beaver Lake Campground– Pictured Rocks National Lakeshore

Location: About 20 miles northeast of Munising

Season: Year-round

Sites: 8 sites with no hookups (1 disabled-accessible site)

Maximum RV length: 35

Facilities: Vault toilets, fire rings, water, tables, lantern poles, boat ramp, hiking trails

Pictured Rocks National Lakeshore

Fee per night: $$
Management: Pictured Rocks National Lakeshore National Park Service
Contact: (906) 387-2607; Reservations: (877) 444-6777; www.nps.gov/piro/planyourvisit/camping.htm
Finding the campground: From Munising head east on CR 58 for 19 miles and turn left (north) on Little Beaver Lake Road. Follow this 2.9 miles right into camp.
GPS coordinates: N 46 33.491' / W 86 21.790'
About the campground: This small collection of rustic sites offers a bit of shade at each site. Half of the sites are right up the bank from the lake. There is a boat launch for the little lake, but only electric motors are allowed. Take a turn around the 1-mile interpretive trail, or hike 1.5 miles out to Lake Superior's shoreline and connect with the North Country National Scenic Trail. Sites go fast in summer and reservations are required. Fees are lower from November through April.

255 South Gemini Lake State Forest Campground

Location: About 24 miles east of Munising
Season: Year-round
Sites: 8 sites with no hookups
Maximum RV length: 20
Facilities: Vault toilets, grills, water, tables, boat launch, hiking/mountain biking trails
Fee per night: $$
Management: Michigan DNR

Contact: (906) 341-2355; www.michigandnr.com/parksandtrails

Finding the campground: From Munising go east on CR 58 for 13.5 miles and turn right (east) on Cusino Road. Continue 3.3 miles and turn left (north) on CH 454. Go 1.1 miles and turn right (west) on what becomes CH 454/Creighton Road. Go another 3.1 miles and the camp entrance is on the left (north) side of the road.

GPS coordinates: N 46 28.840' / W 86 18.190'

About the campground: These sites are similar to North Gemini Lake: nice and private, spacious, and good backup options for those coming to see Pictured Rocks National Lakeshore during high-season weekends in summer when one hasn't made a reservation and so many of the other camps are full. Sites are well shaded, and several are right on the lake. The lake has bass, walleye, perch, and bluegill. Cusino Lake is 3 miles southeast of here. North Gemini Lake is an option when this is full. The roads back here are like washboards at times. From Munising this still might be close to an hour's drive.

256 North Gemini Lake State Forest Campground

Location: About 23 miles east of Munising
Season: Year-round

North Gemini Lake

Sites: 17 sites with no hookups
Maximum RV length: 20
Facilities: Vault toilets, grills, water, tables, boat launch, hiking/mountain biking trails
Fee per night: $$
Management: Michigan DNR
Contact: (906) 341-2355; www.michigandnr.com/parksandtrails
Finding the campground: From Munising go east on CR 58 for 21 miles and turn right (south) on Fox River Long Lake Cutoff. At 0.9 mile turn right (south) on Long Lake Road and continue 0.5 mile to turn left (east) on Twin Lake Road. Follow this 0.7 mile and the camp is on the right (west).
GPS coordinates: N 46 29.480' / W 86 18.205'
About the campground: These sites are nice and private, and they are good backup options for those coming to see Pictured Rocks National Lakeshore during high-season weekends in summer when one hasn't made a reservation and so many of the other camps are full. It is a nice, well-shaded camp of 2 loops. Some sites are right on the water on a high bank. The lake has bass, walleye, perch, and bluegill. Cusino Lake is 3 miles southeast of here. South Gemini Lake is an option when this is full. The roads back here are like washboards at times. From Munising this still might be close to an hour's drive.

257 Canoe Lake State Forest Campground

Location: 23 miles east of Munising
Season: Year-round
Sites: 4 sites with no hookups
Maximum RV length: 20
Facilities: Vault toilets, fire rings, water, tables, boat launch, hiking trails
Fee per night: $$
Management: Michigan DNR
Contact: (906) 341-2355; www.michigandnr.com/parksandtrails
Finding the campground: From Munising go east 13.7 miles on CR 58. Turn right (east) on Cusino Road and continue 3.3 miles to turn left (north) on CR 454/Creighton Road. Take this 2.3 miles to Wolf Lake Road and turn right (south), driving 2.3 miles, and the park entrance is on the left (north) side of the road.
GPS coordinates: N 46 27.383' / W 86 17.434'
About the campground: These sites are best for anglers or perhaps for those coming to see Pictured Rocks National Lakeshore during high-season weekends in summer when one hasn't made a reservation and so many of the other camps are full. It is a nice, well-shaded, and private rustic area. Canoe Lake has perch and pike, while nearby Cusino Lake has muskie, perch, and bluegill. Gemini Lakes are 3 miles northwest of here, with slightly larger and similar rustic camps. The roads back here are like washboards at times.

258 Cusino Lake State Forest Campground

Location: About 24 miles east of Munising
Season: Year-round
Sites: 6 sites with no hookups
Maximum RV length: 20
Facilities: Vault toilets, water, hiking/mountain biking trails
Fee per night: $$
Management: Michigan DNR
Contact: (906) 341-2355; www.michigandnr.com/parksandtrails
Finding the campground: From Munising head about 13 miles east on CR 58. Turn right (east) on Cusino Road and go 3.3 miles to turn left (north) on CR 454. Go 1.1 miles and continue on CR 454/Creighton Road for another 2.3 miles. Turn right (south) on Wolf Lake Road and drive 4 miles to the campground.
GPS coordinates: N 46 27.008' / W 86 15.634'
About the campground: This campground is well off the beaten path and is best for those looking for some solitude. These are also an option for those coming to see Pictured Rocks National Lakeshore during high-season weekends in summer when one hasn't made a reservation and so

Grand Sable Dunes near Grand Marais

many of the other camps are full. It is well shaded and private. Cusino Lake has muskie, perch, and bluegill fishing. Also nearby are Canoe Lake and Gemini Lakes, 3 miles northwest of here, with similar rustic sites. The roads back here are like washboards at times, with sandy patches in some places. That 24-mile drive should take you at least an hour.

259 Ross Lake State Forest Campground

Location: About 26 miles east of Munising
Season: Year-round
Sites: 10 sites with no hookups
Maximum RV length: 20
Facilities: Vault toilets, water, boat launch, hiking/mountain biking trails
Fee per night: $$
Management: Michigan DNR
Contact: (906) 341-2355; www.michigandnr.com/parksandtrails
Finding the campground: From Munising go east 23.5 miles on CR 58 and turn right (south) on Russ Lake Road, which becomes Crooked Lake Road. Follow this 2.8 miles south and the park entrance will be on the left (east) side of the road.
GPS coordinates: N 46 29.206' / W 86 15.735'
About the campground: This is one of several area rustic campgrounds situated on lakes. This one, however, has a boat launch about a quarter mile outside the park. Anglers come for pike, bluegill, bass, and perch. Sites are nicely shaded and spacious. This is still within striking distance of Pictured Rocks National Lakeshore to the north. Gemini, Cusino, and Canoe Lakes are similar options.

260 Kingston Lake State Forest Campground

Location: About 19 miles southwest of Grand Marais
Season: May through November
Sites: 16 sites with no hookups
Maximum RV length: 40
Facilities: Vault toilets, fire rings, water, tables, boat launch, hiking/mountain biking trails
Fee per night: $$
Management: Michigan DNR-Indian Lake State Park
Contact: (906) 341-2355; www.michigandnr.com/parksandtrails
Finding the campground: From Grand Marais head west on CR 58 for about 18 miles and watch for the camp entrance road on the right (west).
GPS coordinates: N 46 35.184' / W 86 13.616'
About the campground: Situated on what is almost an island in this little sprawling lake, the campground is nicely shaded and rustic. Anglers will find walleye, pike, muskie, bass, perch, and bluegill here, and there is a boat ramp in camp to get to them. Hikers and mountain bikers share

Au Sable Lighthouse along Pictured Rocks National Lakeshore and the North Country National Scenic Trail

over 27 miles of trails that connect Kingston Lake to Fox River State Forest Campground. This is a good home base for exploring Pictured Rocks National Lakeshore, but it is not on Lake Superior.

261 Twelvemile Beach Campground– Pictured Rocks National Lakeshore

Location: About 15 miles west of Grand Marais
Season: Year-round; May 15 to October 31 services available and fees collected
Sites: 36 sites with no hookups (2 wheelchair-accessible sites)
Maximum RV length: Single vehicles no more than 36 feet and vehicle/trailer combined length no more than 42 feet
Facilities: Vault toilets, fire rings, water, tables, picnic area, hiking trails, beach, interpretive amphitheater
Fee per night: $$
Management: Pictured Rocks National Lakeshore National Park Service
Contact: (906) 387-2607; Reservations: (877) 444-6777; www.nps.gov/piro/planyourvisit/camping.htm
Finding the campground: From Grand Marais take CR 58 west for 15 miles and the camp entrance is on the right (north) side of the road and leads another mile to the sites.

GPS coordinates: N 46 38.134' / W 86 12.424'

About the campground: As the name suggests, this is a superb place for a long walk down a sandy portion of Lake Superior's coastline. Set within the national park, the campground is nicely shaded and lines up along the shore but on a sandy ridge above it. Sites along the lakeside of the campground go fast. Reservations are required. Fees are lower from November through April. Generators are not allowed in the west loop. The North Country National Scenic Trail passes through, and there is a 2-mile interpretive trail as well.

262 Hurricane River Campground– Pictured Rocks National Lakeshore

Location: About 12 miles west of Grand Marais
Season: Year-round
Sites: 21 sites with no hookups (2 wheelchair-accessible sites)
Maximum RV length: 42 (36 for single vehicle)
Facilities: Vault toilets, water, fire rings, tables, picnic area, hiking trails
Fee per night: $$
Management: Pictured Rocks National Lakeshore National Park Service
Contact: (906) 387-2607; Reservations: (877) 444-6777; www.nps.gov/piro/planyourvisit/camping.htm
Finding the campground: From Grand Marais take CR 58 west about 12 miles and the park road is on the right (north).
GPS coordinates: N 46 39.850' / W 86 09.931'
About the campground: Set in the woods right along the shore of Lake Superior inside the national park, the camp is situated where the namesake river empties into Lake Superior. The North Country National Scenic Trail passes through here, and a 1.5-mile hike passes shipwreck remains in the lake and connects to the historic Au Sable Light Station. Sites are nicely separated by shade trees and understory for privacy and divided into an upper and lower loop. Reservations are required. Fees are lower from November through April. Some sites do not allow generators.

263 Woodland Park Campground

Location: Right at the edge of Grand Marais on Lake Superior
Season: April through October
Sites: 116 sites with water and electrical hookups, 33 sites with no hookups
Maximum RV length: 40
Facilities: Flush toilets, showers, grills, water, tables, picnic area, pavilion, dump station, beach, playground, fish-cleaning station, Wi-Fi, laundry facilities, tennis and basketball courts
Fee per night: $$$-$$$$
Management: Burt Township

Lake Superior near Woodland Park

Contact: (906) 494-2613, park phone from April to October; (906) 494-2381, Burt Township Office; www.burttownship.com/recreation/woodland-park-campground

Finding the campground: From CR 58 through Grand Marais, go north on Lake Avenue 1 block to turn left on Brazel Street. The park entrance is 3 blocks on the right (north) side of the street.

GPS coordinates: N 46 40.377' / W 85 59.450'

About the campground: Come here for beautiful views of Lake Superior. Just 3 blocks from the businesses and marina in Grand Marais, the historic campground is set up with a shoreline location on the big lake. Sites are grassy with only partial shade and arranged in rows parallel to the beach. The lakefront sites are about $1 more per night and overlook the beach. The primitive sites are the cheapest but unfortunately are also the farthest from the lake and backed up against Brazel Street. There is another area designated primitive that lies east of the park pavilion and offers 17 sites in a lakeside location away from the rest of camp. A couple stairways lead from the camp to the beach. Reservations are not taken, and there are no pull-through sites.

264 Lake Superior State Forest Campground

Location: About 11 miles east of Grand Marais
Season: Year-round
Sites: 18 sites with no hookups
Maximum RV length: 40 feet
Facilities: Vault toilets, fire rings, water, tables, boat launch, hiking/off-road vehicle trails

Fee per night: $$
Management: Michigan DNR
Contact: (906) 658-3338; www.michigandnr.com/parksandtrails
Finding the campground: From Grand Marais head east on CR 58/Grand Marais Avenue for 11.3 miles and the camp entrance is on the left.
GPS coordinates: N 46 40.595' / W 85 45.828'
About the campground: You may lose your fillings on the drive. Expect a serious washboard of a road coming from Grand Marais, but if your intention is to be away from it all, this will be worth it. Be aware that the nearest gas is back in town, and they can have consistency problems in peak season. Also, sites near the vault toilet have odor issues. But the beach is pristine, stretching miles in either direction, and the sunrises and sunsets are as attractive as the agates you might find on the shore. This park is typically full throughout July and August and takes no reservations. Blind Sucker Flooding is nearby to the south. The North Country National Scenic Trail runs right through the campground. Pine Ridge and Two-Heart ATV trails are 2 and 20 miles away, respectively.

265 Blind Sucker State Forest Campground (No. 1 and 2)

Location: About 13 miles east of Grand Marais
Season: Year-round
Sites: 45 sites with no hookups
Maximum RV length: 45
Facilities: Vault toilets, fire rings, water, tables, boat launch, hiking trails
Fee per night: $$
Management: Michigan DNR
Contact: (906) 658-3338; www.michigandnr.com/parksandtrails
Finding the campground: From Grand Marais head east on CR 58 for 12.7 miles and turn right (south) on Deer Park Road. The camp entrance is at 0.8 mile on the right.
GPS coordinates: N 46 40.120' / W 85 45.348'
About the campground: Blind Sucker Flooding was created with a dam on the Blind Sucker River to create habitat for Canada geese years ago when they were threatened. Go figure; now the state swarms with them in migration periods. The flooding has excellent fishing for pike, perch, bass, and bluegill. Lake Superior is less than a mile north. There are 2 campgrounds here, but Campground No. 1 has 13 rustic sites, while No. 2 (to the east of No. 1 and marked by GPS here) has 32 sites. The latter camp is preferred, as the sites are actually on the water and offer better shade and privacy. The North Country National Scenic Trail runs through both, and the Pine Ridge ATV trail is 2 miles east of here.

266 Muskallonge Lake State Park

Location: About 18 miles east of Grand Marais
Season: May through October
Sites: 159 sites with electrical hookups
Maximum RV length: 50
Facilities: Flush toilets, grills, water, tables, showers, picnic area, dump station, boat launch, hiking trails, beach, playground
Fee per night: $$$
Management: Michigan DNR
Contact: (906) 658-3338; www.dnr.state.mi.us/parksandtrails
Finding the campground: From Grand Marais follow Grand Marais Avenue/CR 58 east 12.7 miles. Turn left on CR 407/Deer Park Road and go 5.6 miles to the campground, which is on the right (south) side of the road.
GPS coordinates: N 46 40.641' / W 85 37.639'
About the campground: Once a Native American settlement and then a lumber town, this park lies along Lake Muskallonge and on the south side of the road from Lake Superior. There are many places to visit in this area, including Pictured Rocks National Lakeshore, lighthouses, Kingston Plains, and the Seney National Wildlife Refuge. Seven loops of sites run north to south and parallel to each other. Shade is partial, and privacy isn't the best. The North Country National Scenic Trail passes through the park. There are stairs to the beach on Lake Superior across the county highway.

Iron River to Bay de Noc

	Hookup Sites	Total Sites	Max RV Length	Hookups	Toilets	Showers	Drinking Water	Dump Station	Recreation	Fee	Reservations
267 Lake Ottawa Recreation Area–Ottawa National Forest	0	32	40	N/A	F	N	Y	Y	HSFB	$$$	N
268 Pentoga Park	100	100	40	WE	F	Y	Y	Y	SFB	$$$	Y
269 Bewabic State Park	123	130	50	E	F	Y	Y	Y	HSFBL	$$-$$$	Y
270 Glidden Lake State Forest Campground	0	23	30	N/A	NF	N	Y	N	HFLO	$$	N
271 Gene's Pond State Forest Campground	0	14	40	N/A	NF	N	Y	N	HFLO	$$	N
272 Carney Lake State Forest Campground	0	16	40	N/A	NF	N	Y	N	HFL	$$	N
273 Sturgeon Bend Campground	0	11	45	N/A	NF	N	Y	N	HFL	$	N
274 Shakey Lakes Park	111	139	50	E	F/NF	Y	Y	Y	HSFBL	$$$	Y
275 Kleinke Park	31	31	50	E	F/NF	Y	Y	Y	SFBL	$$$	N
276 J. W. Wells State Park	150	150	45	E	F/NF	Y	Y	Y	HFSB	$$$	Y
277 Cedar River North State Forest Campground	0	18	40	N/A	NF	N	Y	N	HFLO	$$	N
278 Gladstone Bay Campground	64	74	50	WES	F	Y	Y	Y	SC	$$-$$$$	Y
279 Pioneer Trail Park and Campground	78	98	40	WE	F	Y	Y	Y	HF	$$$$	Y
280 Little Bay de Noc Campground–Hiawatha National Forest	0	38	40	N/A	NF	N	Y	N	HSFBL	$$$	Y
281 Fayette Historic State Park	61	61	50	E	NF	N	Y	N	HSFBL	$$$	Y
282 Portage Bay State Forest Campground	0	23	30	N/A	NF	N	Y	N	HF	$$	N
283 Flowing Well Campground–Hiawatha National Forest	0	10	40	N/A	NF	N	Y	N	FB	$$	Y
284 Corner Lake Campground–Hiawatha National Forest	0	9	40	N/A	NF	N	Y	N	SFB	$$	Y
285 Camp Seven Lake Campground–Hiawatha National Forest	0	41	40	N/A	NF	N	Y	N	HSFB	$$$	Y

	Hookup Sites	Total Sites	Max RV Length	Hookups	Toilets	Showers	Drinking Water	Dump Station	Recreation	Fee	Reservations
286 Colwell Lake Campground–Hiawatha National Forest	5	35	40	E	NF	N	Y	Y	HSFB	$$-$$$	Y
287 Little Bass Lake Campground–Hiawatha National Forest	0	12	40	N/A	NF	N	Y	N	SFB	$	N
288 Indian Lake State Park	217	217	50	E	F/NF	Y	Y	Y	HSFBL	$$-$$$	Y

See Amenities Charts Key on page xiii.

267 Lake Ottawa Recreation Area– Ottawa National Forest

Location: About 6 miles southwest of Iron River

Season: May through September

Sites: 32 sites with no hookups

Maximum RV length: 40

Facilities: Flush toilets, fire rings, grills, water, tables, picnic shelter, picnic area, dump station, boat launch, hiking trails, beach, fishing pier, ball field

Fee per night: $$$

Management: Northwoods Property Management; USDA Forest Service

Contact: (906) 396-5428; (906) 932-1330; www.fs.usda.gov/recarea/ottawa/recreation/camping-cabins/recarea/?recid=12305&actid=29

Finding the campground: From US 2 on the west side of Iron River, go southwest on MI 73 for 0.8 mile and turn right (west) on Lake Ottawa Road. Follow this 4.1 miles to the park entrance on the right.

GPS coordinates: N 46 04.634' / W 88 45.518'

About the campground: This campground is located inside the recreation area and surrounded almost entirely by national forest. The loops are in the woods with good shade and spaced out very nicely for privacy and a quiet camping experience. Some of the sites have lake views. The park offers a few easy trails but also a more strenuous trek along 9 miles of the Ge-Che Trail. Down by the swimming beach is also a long T-shaped fishing pier. Log buildings and stone fireplaces in the picnic area were built by the Civilian Conservation Corps back in the 1930s.

268 Pentoga Park

Location: About 12 miles south and west of Crystal Falls
Season: May 15 to September 30
Sites: 100 sites with water and electrical hookups
Maximum RV length: 40
Facilities: Flush toilets, showers, fire rings, water, tables, picnic area, pavilion, dump station, boat launch, beach, playground, fish-cleaning station, volleyball court, horseshoe pits, shuffleboard, concessionaire, public phone
Fee per night: $$$
Management: Iron County
Contact: (906) 265-3979; www.pentogapark.com
Finding the campground: From Crystal Falls head south 2.2 miles on US 2/US 141 and turn right (west) on CR 424. Follow this 9.2 miles and the park entrance is on the right.
GPS coordinates: N 46 02.309' / W 88 30.631'
About the campground: Within the boundaries of this land, there are Anishinaabe (Ojibwa) burial sites. Iron County purchased the land in 1922 in order to preserve this sacred historic site. The park lies on the southern end of Chicaugon Lake. Fishing is for bass, muskie, walleye, and lake trout. The beach is good for swimming, and the campgrounds have plenty of shade. The playground and sporting equipment give everyone plenty to do, plus there is the George Young Golf Course just west of here. The fall colors in the park are wonderful.

269 Bewabic State Park

Location: About 4 miles west of Crystal Falls
Season: Mid-April to mid-October
Sites: 123 sites with electrical hookups, 7 walk-in sites
Maximum RV length: 50
Facilities: Flush/vault toilets, showers, fire rings, grills, water, tables, picnic shelter, picnic area, dump station, boat launch, hiking trails, beach, beach house, playground, volleyball court, tennis court, horseshoe pits
Fee per night: $$-$$$
Management: Michigan DNR
Contact: (906) 875-3324; www.michigandnr.com/parksandtrails
Finding the campground: From Crystal Falls follow US 2 east 4.5 miles and the park entrance is on the left (south) side of the highway.
GPS coordinates: N 46 05.662' / W 88 25.525'
About the campground: Just off US 2, this easy-to-find state park is part of the Iron County Heritage Trail System, a 14-mile stretch from Iron River to Crystal Falls. This makes a good base camp for exploring the sites, which range from museums to Native American burial grounds. The park has a great beach on Fortune Lake (also known as First Lake, as this is a chain of lakes) and a hiking trail that connects the campground to the day-use area. The sites are divided into 3 loops, all of

Fog lifts in the forest at Bewabic State Park. MATT FORSTER

which are well shaded by trees that offer some startling colors in fall. Sites are mostly well spaced, and many have intervening understory to grant some privacy.

270 Glidden Lake State Forest Campground

Location: About 5 miles east of Crystal Falls
Season: Year-round
Sites: 23 sites with no hookups
Maximum RV length: 30
Facilities: Vault toilets, fire rings, water, tables, boat launch, hiking/mountain biking/off-road vehicles trails
Fee per night: $$
Management: Michigan DNR
Contact: (906) 875-3324; www.michigandnr.com/parksandtrails
Finding the campground: From Crystal Falls head east on MI 69 4.5 miles and turn right (south) on Lake Mary Road. The park is 1.1 miles south on the right.
GPS coordinates: N 46 04.226' / W 88 14.249'
About the campground: While there's a boat ramp in the campground to get anglers in for panfish, one might consider a night here to be within a couple miles of Paint River, which is excellent for paddlers and also shows some pike and walleye. Canoe rentals can be had in Crystal Falls. Hikers and bikers have 3 loops of trail in Lake Mary Plains through the state forest, totaling 10 miles, and there's a trailhead right at camp. The sites are private and moderately sized, with a decent amount of shade and some sandy areas.

271 Gene's Pond State Forest Campground

Location: About 10 miles north of Felch
Season: Year-round
Sites: 14 sites with no hookups
Maximum RV length: 40
Facilities: Vault toilets, fire rings, water, tables, boat launch, hiking/mountain biking
Fee per night: $$
Management: Michigan DNR–Escanaba Field Office
Contact: (906) 786-2351; www.michigandnr.com/parksandtrails
Finding the campground: From MI 69 just west of Felch, go north on CR 581/Norway Lake Road for 6.1 miles. Turn left (west) on Leeman Road, go 1.4 miles, and turn left onto Gene's Pond Road to follow that 1.3 miles right into camp.
GPS coordinates: N 46 04.470' / W 87 51.922'
About the campground: To be honest, 734 acres might seem a bit more than just a "pond." Anglers have a hard-surface ramp to get in here for the walleye, bass, and panfish, but paddlers will also enjoy the scenery of the nooks and crannies of the shoreline. The wetlands around the pond are rich with birdlife, including loons, herons, bald eagles, and ospreys. The forest has 2.3

miles of trail that works well for both hikers and mountain bikers. The sites are nicely shaded, and the park itself is down its own road and feels secluded.

272 Carney Lake State Forest Campground

Location: About 14 miles north and east of Iron Mountain
Season: Year-round
Sites: 16 sites with no hookups
Maximum RV length: 40
Facilities: Vault toilets, fire rings, water, tables, boat launch
Fee per night: $$
Management: Michigan DNR
Contact: (906) 875-3324; www.michigandnr.com/parksandtrails
Finding the campground: From Iron Mountain head north on MI 95 about 7 miles and turn right (east) on Sportsmens Club Road. Go 2.6 miles, turn right (south) on Carney Lake Road, and follow that 4.1 miles to the camp entrance.
GPS coordinates: N 45 53.583' / W 87 56.547'

The morning mists hug the edges of Carney Lake. MATT FORSTER

About the campground: Deep in Copper Country State Forest lies this heavily wooded lakeside campground. Sites are private and quite shaded. Fishing here is good for walleye, panfish, and pike, and a boat launch is on-site. While there are no trails connected here, one can drive to Merriman East 4 miles to the north for 9.5 miles of trails suitable for both hikers and mountain bikers. Birders will want to go south 5 miles and check out Fumee Lake Natural Area or 10 miles north to Groveland Mine Wetland.

273 Sturgeon Bend Campground

Location: About 17 miles south of Norway
Season: May to November
Sites: 11 sites with no hookups
Maximum RV length: 45
Facilities: Vault toilets, fire rings, water, picnic area, boat launch, hiking trails
Fee per night: $
Management: American Legion
Contact: Jim Wash with the American Legion, (906) 438-2236
Finding the campground: In Vulcan, just east of Norway on US 2, go west on Main Street for 0.1 mile and go left (south) on CR 577/River Road. Stay on CR 577 for 9.5 miles and then continue on State Road for 2.2 miles. Turn right (west) on Lake Drive for 0.2 mile and take the next left (south) on State Road again. Go 2.8 miles, turn right on Lane 34.5, and it goes right into camp.
GPS coordinates: N 45 36.982' / W 87 47.012'
About the campground: This campground is a short swim to Wisconsin. A township park, Sturgeon Bend is a nice roughing-it experience. Rough may also describe the drive to get here, as it is down a dirt road often resembling a washboard or a collection of potholes. A few of the sites will, however, take a bigger rig if you want to bring one in. The policy is "leave no trace," so campers are expected to carry out everything they carried in. There is river access at the end of the campground, and if there is any traffic here at all, it will likely be a day-use angler. Sites are grassy and open to the sky but surrounded by woods and secluded. This is perfectly quiet with nice views of the Menominee River, which is the border between Michigan and Wisconsin. Close to Peminee Falls with a neat lookout.

274 Shakey Lakes Park

Location: About 11 miles west of Stephenson
Season: Year-round
Sites: 111 sites with electrical hookups, 28 sites with no hookups
Maximum RV length: 50
Facilities: Flush/vault toilets, showers, fire rings, water, tables, picnic area, pavilion, dump station, boat launch, hiking trails, beach, beach house, playground, fishing pier, fish-cleaning station, volleyball court, horseshoe pits, boat rental, concessionaire
Fee per night: $$$

Management: Menominee County

Contact: (906) 753-4582; www.menomineecounty.com/departments

Finding the campground: From the center of Stephenson, head south on US 41 and turn right (west) on CR 352/G 12. Go 10.5 miles and turn right (north) on River Road, go 0.4 mile, take the slight right, and follow Shakey Lane 0.4 mile right into the campground.

GPS coordinates: N 45 24.947' / W 87 49.217'

About the campground: Shakey Lakes is a collection of 6 lakes all connected to each other and centered on the campground, which is on what almost seems like an island, as there is water in nearly all directions. It is connected to the outside world by a bridge. A good number of campsites, especially primitive ones, are right by the shore of one of the lakes. Boat ramps are on either side of the park entrance, giving access to Bass and Resort Lakes. No generators are allowed, and a 10 p.m. curfew is in effect. There is a park entrance fee as well. This is just inside the central time zone.

275 Kleinke Park

Location: About 18 miles north of Menominee

Season: Year-round

Sites: 30 sites with electrical hookups

Maximum RV length: 50

Facilities: Flush/vault toilets, showers, fire rings, water, tables, picnic area, pavilion, dump station, boat launch, beach, playground

Fee per night: $$$

Management: Menominee County

Contact: (906) 753-4582; www.menomineecounty.com/departments/

Finding the campground: From Menominee, head north 18 miles on M35 and the park entrance is on the right (east).

GPS coordinates: N 45 19.363' / W 87 25.761'

About the campground: For some camping right along the shores of Lake Michigan, this county park often flies under the radar. A nice sandy beach runs the length of the park, offering good swimming but no lifeguard on duty. All sites have 50-amp service, and both firewood and ice are for sale. This is just inside the central time zone. A service building, sinks, flush toilets, coin-op showers, and a dump station are on-site. Road noise and a rumble strip on the highway may annoy some campers.

276 J. W. Wells State Park

Location: About 1 mile south of Cedar River

Season: Mid-April through October

Sites: 150 sites with electrical hookups

Maximum RV length: 45

Facilities: Flush/vault toilets, showers, fire rings, grills, water, tables, picnic shelter, picnic area, dump station, hiking trails, beach, beach house, playground, volleyball court, horseshoe pits

Fee per night: $$$

Management: Michigan DNR

Contact: (906) 863-9747; www.michigandnr.com/parksandtrails

Finding the campground: From Cedar River on MI 35, go south 1.3 miles and the park entrance is on the left (east) side of the highway.

GPS coordinates: N 45 23.725' / W 87 22.040'

About the campground: Situated on the shores of Lake Michigan's Green Bay, the park has fantastic lake views and a 3-mile sandy beach. The park is named for a pioneer lumberman, whose children donated this land to the State of Michigan in 1925. Many of the park buildings date back to the work programs of the 1930s and 1940s. The campground is a double loop, with the sites on the lane farthest east backed up right on the lake. There's no boat ramp at camp, but find one in Cedar River Harbor just across the mouth of said river to the north of the park. Sites are grassy, and most have at least partial shade.

277 Cedar River North State Forest Campground

Location: About 7.6 miles north of Cedar River

Season: Year-round

Sites: 14 sites with no hookups, 4 walk-in sites

Maximum RV length: 40

Facilities: Vault toilets, fire rings, water, tables, boat launch, hiking/mountain biking/off-road vehicle trails

Fee per night: $$

Management: Michigan DNR

Contact: (906) 863-9747; www.michigandnr.com/parksandtrails

Finding the campground: From MI 35 just north of Cedar River, turn left on CR 551, follow it 5.8 miles, and the park road is on the left.

GPS coordinates: N 45 29.988' / W 87 22.949'

About the campground: The Cedar River takes its name from the trees along the banks. This slow-flowing, tannin-rich waterway makes its way south to the larger waters of Green Bay and is a pleasant paddle. Area outfitters serve those who need a canoe or kayak, and apparently they deliver. Campsites are grassy and packed dirt, with some right on the water and shaded by the cedars, as well as tamarack and birch. A few steps grant carry-in access for paddlers. Hikers have access to the 8-mile Cedar River Pathway. The river has bass and trout for anglers but isn't so great for a swim.

278 Gladstone Bay Campground

Location: Inside the City of Gladstone

Season: Year-round

Sites: 25 sites with full hookups, 17 sites with electrical and water hookups, 22 sites with electrical hookups, 10 tent sites with no hookups
Maximum RV length: 35
Facilities: Flush toilets, showers, fire rings, water, tables, beach, playground, horseshoe pits, firewood, ice, free bicycle use, Wi-Fi
Fee per night: $$–$$$$
Management: City of Gladstone
Contact: (906) 428-1211; off-season (906) 428-9222; www.gladstonemi.org/community/parks_and_recreation/gladstone_bay_campground.php
Finding the campground: From US 2/41 MI 35 in Gladstone, head east on Hill Road (or Lake Shore Drive if coming from the south), then follow Lake Shore Drive 1.1 miles northeast along the lake and continue onto 9th Street. At 0.2 mile, turn right (east) on Michigan Avenue and continue 0.7 mile to the park entrance on the right.
GPS coordinates: N 45 50.827' / W 87 0.378'
About the campground: Set along the shore of Little Bay de Noc, this city park offers a bit of beach and decent modern services. Some pull-through sites are full service, but they are mostly unshaded and set closely alongside each other. A bike path runs along the park edge and back into town, and there is a shoreline boardwalk and viewing deck.

279 Pioneer Trail Park and Campground

Location: On the north side of Escanaba
Season: Year-round
Sites: 78 with water and electrical hookups, 20 tent sites with no hookups
Maximum RV length: 40
Facilities: Flush/vault toilets, showers, fire rings, water, tables, picnic area, pavilions, dump station, boat ramp, disc golf course, hiking trails, playground, Wi-Fi
Fee per night: $$$$
Management: Delta County
Contact: (906) 786-1020; www.deltacountyparks.com/pioneer-trail-park.html
Finding the campground: From Escanaba on US 2/US 41 go north across the Escanaba River and the park entrance is on the right.
GPS coordinates: N 45 47.713' / W 87 04.214'
About the campground: The Escanaba River flows 52 miles south to empty into Little Bay de Noc on Lake Michigan. This park sits across the river from the City of Escanaba and just east of the last dam before the lake. Paddlers enjoy the slow waters farther upstream, and anglers can fish from the bank in the park. Most of the campsites are large and grassy and offer the shade of hardwoods, but only 6 are considered riverside. A cemetery from the pioneer days lies along the park's historic hiking trail. Because of the playground and sporting fields and equipment, this is a popular recreation park for locals.

280 Little Bay de Noc Campground– Hiawatha National Forest

Location: About 8 miles south of Rapid River
Season: May 15 to October 7
Sites: 38 sites with no hookups
Maximum RV length: 40
Facilities: Vault toilets, grills, water, tables, picnic area, boat launch, hiking trails, beach
Fee per night: $$$
Management: USDA Forest Service
Contact: (906) 428-5800; Reservations: 877-444-6777; www.fs.usda.gov/recarea/hiawatha/recarea/?recid=13282
Finding the campground: From Rapid River drive 2.4 miles east on US 2 to CR 513. Turn right (southwest) on CR 513 and drive 5.5 miles to the campground road.
GPS coordinates: N 45 50.443' / W 86 58.579'
About the campground: This bay is at the upper reaches of Green Bay at the top of Lake Michigan and is 10 miles west of Big Bay de Noc. The sites are laid out in 3 loops: Maywood, the northernmost, and Oaks and Twin Springs loops down along the southern curve of the shore. Despite the loop layout, all sites are on the western side of the westernmost road of the loop, thus every site is lakeside and has a trail down to the beach. All sites are wooded with oak and hemlock for shade and privacy, except those in Twin Springs, which offer open, grassy areas. Expect stellar sunsets over the bay. While anglers may catch salmon, perch, pike, and bass, the bay is most famous for its abundance of walleye.

281 Fayette Historic State Park

Location: About 7 miles southwest of Garden
Season: May 4 to December 2
Sites: 61 sites with electrical hookups, 11 of them pull-through sites
Maximum RV length: 50
Facilities: Vault toilets, fire rings, grills, water, tables, picnic shelter, picnic area, boat launch, hiking trails, beach, playground, scuba diving
Fee per night: $$$
Management: Michigan DNR
Contact: (906) 644-2603; www.michigandnr.com/parksandtrails
Finding the campground: From Garden head south on MI 183 for 7.7 miles and find the park entrance on the right (west) side of the road.
GPS coordinates: N 45 43.079' / W 86 38.933'
About the campground: Between 1867 and 1891 an iron smelting operation was on these park grounds. The massive furnace complex can be seen, and the town has been redone as a sort of living museum. The park overlooks Big Bay de Noc from the eastern side and Snail Shell Harbor. The campground is also along the shore but to the south of the historic site. The forest is maple

The historic iron smelting buildings are preserved at Fayette Historic State Park.
MATT FORSTER

and beech and offers 5 miles of trails with Lake Michigan scenic overlooks. Fishing is good from shore, but there is also a boat launch not far from the camp. Scuba diving affords a look at some artifacts in the harbor. The second Saturday of August hosts an annual heritage day celebration.

282 Portage Bay State Forest Campground

Location: About a 36-mile journey south of Manistique
Season: Year-round
Sites: 23 sites with no hookups
Maximum RV length: 30
Facilities: Vault toilets, fire rings, water, tables, hiking trails
Fee per night: $$
Management: Michigan DNR
Contact: (906) 644-2603; www.michigandnr.com/parksandtrails
Finding the campground: From Manistique take US 2 west to Bay de Noc and turn right (south) on MI 183. Take this 13.7 miles and turn left (southwest) on LI Road where it splits from 14th Road. Go 1.3 miles and turn left (east) on 12.75 Lane, which weaves 4.7 miles to the camp entrance.
GPS coordinates: N 45 43.432' / W 86 32.104'

About the campground: For some guaranteed seclusion, check out the Garden Peninsula, the finger of land reaching down into Lake Michigan toward Wisconsin's Door County Peninsula. This row of shaded rustic sites lines up with a remote beach facing east to the open water. Sites have little more than a fire ring and table and are steps from the sand. What keeps this place quiet and nearly empty at times is the drive to get here. The road in is a narrow, low-clearance, tight-turn, single-lane gravel road winding nearly 10 miles to the campground. Some have gotten in here with big rigs but likely left without some paint or even a mirror. Kayakers can jump right in and go.

283 Flowing Well Campground– Hiawatha National Forest

Location: About 16 miles east of Rapid River
Season: May 15 to December 1
Sites: 10 sites with no hookups
Maximum RV length: 40
Facilities: Vault toilets, fire rings, grills, water, tables, picnic area
Fee per night: $$
Management: USDA Forest Service
Contact: (906) 428-5800; Reservations: (877) 444-6777; www.fs.usda.gov/recarea/hiawatha/recarea/?recid=13279
Finding the campground: From Rapid River drive east 13.4 miles on US 2 to FR 13. Turn left (north) on FR 13 and go 2.8 miles to the campground.
GPS coordinates: N 45 56.133' / W 86 42.461'
About the campground: With a location along the western banks of the Sturgeon River, the camp is an obvious choice for paddlers, and this is a carry-in access point for the 41-mile canoe trail through the Hiawatha National Forest. However, it is also known for an abundance of wildflowers in the summer. All sites but #1, #3, and #5 are on the river side of the single campground lane, and they are all shady and private. The Flowing Well is exactly what the name suggests, and the water is tested regularly to ensure its safety.

284 Corner Lake Campground– Hiawatha National Forest

Location: About 30 miles from Rapid River
Season: April 15 to early October
Sites: 9 sites with no hookups
Maximum RV length: 40
Facilities: Vault toilets, fire rings, water, tables, boat launch, beach
Fee per night: $$
Management: USDA Forest Service

Contact: (906) 428-5800; www.fs.usda.gov/recarea/hiawatha/recarea/?recid=13278

Finding the campground: Head east about 14 miles from Rapid River on US 2 and take FR 13 north 18.7 miles to CR 440. Turn right (east) on CR 440 and drive 1.1 miles to the campground road.

GPS coordinates: N 46 08.950' / W 86 36.857'

About the campground: This Hiawatha National Forest campground has a nice sandy beach and a shallow, slow-sloping, and roped-off swimming area. The sites are few but quite spacious for good family camping under some tall shade trees. Fishing on the 100-acre lake turns up the usual suspects: pike, largemouth bass, bluegill, walleye, and perch. There is a boat ramp right in camp as well. All sites are wheelchair accessible.

285 Camp Seven Lake Campground– Hiawatha National Forest

Location: About 30 miles east and north of Rapid River

Season: May 15 to October 7

Sites: 41 sites with no hookups

Maximum RV length: 40

Facilities: Vault toilets, fire rings, water, tables, picnic area, boat launch, hiking trails, beach, fishing pier

Fee per night: $$$

Management: USDA Forest Service

Contact: (906) 428-5800; Reservations: (877) 444-6777; www.fs.usda.gov/recarea/hiawatha/recarea/?recid=13276

Finding the campground: From Rapid River head east 14 miles on US 2 and go left (north) on FR 13 for 8.4 miles. Turn right (east) on CR 442 and drive 7.8 miles to the campground road on the left (north).

GPS coordinates: N 46 03.304' / W 86 32.915'

About the campground: Camp Seven Lake lies within the Hiawatha National Forest and offers 60 acres for boaters, paddlers, and swimmers to enjoy. The campground is situated at the east end of the lake. Hikers have a 2-mile trail along the lake. There are 2 boat ramps, 1 exclusively for campers, and anglers head out for smallmouth bass, bluegill, and perch. The campsites are arranged in 3 long rows, and 10 of them on the westernmost lane look out toward the lake through the trees. Trails head down to the shore.

286 Colwell Lake Campground– Hiawatha National Forest

Location: About 25 miles north of Manistique

Season: May 15 to October 7

Sites: 5 sites with electrical hookups, 28 sites with no hookups, 2 walk-in sites

Maximum RV length: 40

Facilities: Vault toilets, fire rings, grills, water, tables, picnic area, dump station, boat launch, hiking trails, beach, lantern posts

Fee per night: $$–$$$

Management: USDA Forest Service

Contact: (906) 428-5800; Reservations: (877) 444-6777; www.fs.usda.gov/recarea/hiawatha/recarea/?recid=13277

Finding the campground: On MI 94 in Manistique drive north 25 miles to FR 2246. Turn right (east) and drive 0.5 mile to the campground road.

GPS coordinates: N 46 13.300' / W 86 26.250'

About the campground: Located within the Hiawatha National Forest, the campground is situated on the eastern shore of a 145-acre lake. The campsites are arranged on either side of a park road that follows the curve of the shore, giving about half of all the sites a perfect perch over the water. A couple of walk-in sites make for an easy backpacker experience not far from the vehicle. Anglers can expect largemouth bass, northern pike, crappie, sunfish, perch, and bluegill. Hiking is partly along the lake, with 2 miles of easy trail. The beach is large and sandy, making this a popular swimming hole.

287 Little Bass Lake Campground– Hiawatha National Forest

Location: About 30 miles north and west of Manistique

Season: May 15 to October 7

Sites: 12 sites with no hookups

Maximum RV length: 40

Facilities: Vault toilets, fire rings, water, tables

Fee per night: $

Management: USDA Forest Service

Contact: (906) 428-5800; Reservations: (877) 444-6777; www.fs.usda.gov/recarea/hiawatha/recarea/?recid=13281

Finding the campground: From Manistique take US 2 west about 5.4 miles and turn right (west) on MI 149. Take this 8.1 miles to CR 437/Thunder Lake Road and go right (north) for 12.6 miles. Turn right on FR 2213 and go 1.1 miles, take the soft left on Bass Lake Road, and stay on this for 2.7 miles. Turn left onto the park road and the camp is another 0.7 mile on the left.

GPS coordinates: N 46 09.842' / W 86 26.975'

About the campground: The tangled roads to get here may deter some, but then that's what keeps this place deep in the Hiawatha National Forest so secluded—that and the nice arrangement of the sites in a loop and staggered so they don't face each other across the road. Intervening brush adds to the privacy. There's carry-in access to the 84-acre lake, and anglers often catch largemouth bass, crappies, sunfish, perch, bluegill, and even northern pike.

288 Indian Lake State Park

Location: About 5 miles west of Manistique
Season: Mid-April to November
Sites: 217 sites with electrical hookups
Maximum RV length: 50
Facilities: Flush/vault toilets, showers, fire rings, grills, water, tables, picnic shelter, picnic area, dump station, boat launch, hiking trails, beach, beach house, playground, boat rental
Fee per night: $$–$$$
Management: Michigan DNR
Contact: (906) 341-2355; www.michigandnr.com/parksandtrails
Finding the campground: From Manistique head west on CR 442/Deer Street for 4.5 miles and the park entrance of the southern unit will be on the right (north) side of the road.
GPS coordinates: N 45 56.466' / W 86 19.953'
About the campground: At a length of 6 miles and a widest point of 3 miles, Indian Lake is one of the biggest inland lakes in the Upper Peninsula. Despite its size it is rather shallow and thus makes a good swimming lake. The state park is divided into 2 separate units set 3 miles from each other. The largest section is spread out along the southern shore of the lake. The west unit offers semimodern sites along the west shore of the lake. The variety of fish here is notable and includes sturgeon, muskie, and brown trout, and Lake Michigan is only 3 miles away to the southeast. Sites are grassy and not always shaded.

Sault Ste. Marie Area

	Hookup Sites	Total Sites	Max RV Length	Hookups	Toilets	Showers	Drinking Water	Dump Station	Recreation	Fee	Reservations
289 Merwin Creek State Forest Campground	0	10	40	N/A	NF	N	Y	N	FL	$$	N
290 Mead Creek State Forest Campground	0	9	35	N/A	NF	N	Y	N	FL	$$	N
291 Fox River State Forest Campground	0	7	40	N/A	NF	N	Y	N	FHC	$$	N
292 Seney Township Campground	15	25	40	E	NF	Y	Y	N	HF	$$$	N
293 East Branch of Fox River State Forest Campground	0	19	40	N/A	NF	N	Y	N	HFLO	$$	N
294 South Manistique Lake State Forest Campground	0	29	40	N/A	NF	N	Y	N	FLO	$$	N
295 Milakokia Lake State Forest Campground	0	35	40	N/A	NF	N	Y	N	HFLO	$$	N
296 Big Knob State Forest Campground	0	23	40	N/A	NF	N	Y	N	HFLO	$$	N
297 Natalie State Forest Campground	0	12	40	N/A	NF	N	Y	N	HFLO	$$	N
298 Bass Lake State Forest Campground (Luce)	0	18	40	N/A	NF	N	Y	N	HFLO	$$	N
299 Pretty Lake State Forest Campground	0	23	40	N/A	NF	N	Y	N	HFO	$$	N
300 Holland Lake State Forest Campground	0	15	40	N/A	NF	N	Y	N	HFLO	$$	N
301 High Bridge State Forest Campground	0	7	35	N/A	NF	N	Y	N	HFO	$$	N
302 Perch Lake State Forest Campground	0	35	40	N/A	NF	N	Y	N	HFLO	$$	N
303 Mouth of Two-Hearted River State Forest Campground	0	39	40	N/A	NF	N	Y	N	HFLO	$$	N
304 Bodi Lake State Forest Campground	0	20	40	N/A	NF	N	Y	N	HFLO	$$	N
305 Andrus Lake State Forest Campground	0	25	40	N/A	NF	N	Y	N	FL	$$	N
306 Tahquamenon Falls State Park	260	296	50	E	F	Y	Y	Y	HFBL	$$-$$$	Y
307 Garnet Lake State Forest Campground	0	10	30	N/A	NF	N	Y	N	FO	$	N

	Hookup Sites	Total Sites	Max RV Length	Hookups	Toilets	Showers	Drinking Water	Dump Station	Recreation	Fee	Reservations
308 Hog Island Point State Forest Campground	0	50	40	N/A	NF	N	Y	N	HFLO	$$	N
309 Little Brevoort Lake– North State Forest Campground	0	20	40	N/A	NF	N	Y	N	HFL	$$	N
310 Brevoort Lake Campground–Hiawatha National Forest	0	70	45	N/A	F	N	Y	N	HSFB	$$$	Y
311 Lake Michigan Campground–Hiawatha National Forest	0	35	40	N/A	F/NF	N	Y	N	HSFB	$$$	Y
312 Straits State Park	255	270	50	E	F	Y	Y	Y	HS	$$-$$$$	Y
313 Carp River Campground–Hiawatha National Forest	0	20	40	N/A	NF	N	Y	N	HF	$$	Y
314 Trout Lake Township Park	60	83	45	E	F	Y	Y	Y	SL	$$$-$$$$	Y
315 Three Lakes Campground–Hiawatha National Forest	0	10	40	N/A	NF	N	Y	N	HSFB	$$	Y
316 Soldier Lake Campground–Hiawatha National Forest	0	44	40	N/A	NF	N	Y	N	HSFB	$$$	Y
317 Bay View Campground– Hiawatha National Forest	0	24	35	N/A	NF	N	Y	N	FS	$$	Y
318 Monocle Lake Campground–Hiawatha National Forest	0	42	40	N/A	NF	N	Y	N	HSFB	$$	N
319 Brimley State Park	237	237	50	E	F	Y	Y	Y	HSFBL	$$$$	Y
320 Sherman Park	0	25	45	N/A	NF	N	Y	N	H	$$$	Y
321 Aune Osborn Campground	100	100	50	WE	F	Y	Y	Y	FL	$$$$	Y
322 Munuscong River State Forest Campground	0	26	40	N/A	NF	N	Y	N	HFLO	$$	N
323 DeTour State Forest Campground	0	21	40	N/A	NF	N	Y	N	HFLO	$$	N
324 Drummond Island Township Park	34	46	31	E	NF	N/A	Y	N	HL	$$	N

See Amenities Charts Key on page xiii.

289 Merwin Creek State Forest Campground

Location: About 11 miles northeast of Manistique
Season: Year-round
Sites: 10 sites with no hookups
Maximum RV length: 40
Facilities: Vault toilets, fire rings, water, tables, boat launch
Fee per night: $$
Management: Schoolcraft County
Contact: (906) 341-3618; www.michigandnr.com/parksandtrails
Finding the campground: From Manistique go east on US 2 for about 7 miles and turn left (north) on Town Line Road. Go 2.2 miles, turn left (west) on River Road, and continue 0.5 mile. Turn right (north) on Merwin Creek Road and go 0.9 mile to the campground.
GPS coordinates: N 46 01.877' / W 86 07.370'
About the campground: The Seney National Wildlife Refuge offers astounding nature watching, and the Manistique River on its 60-mile route to Lake Michigan is a nice vantage point. South of the refuge are this campground and the similar Mead Creek Campground, which is about a 30-mile drive north. Merwin Creek is closer to Lake Michigan. Anglers fish for lake trout, lake herring, pike, bass, walleye, perch, muskie, and bluegill. A gravel ramp gets medium-size boats into the water. The campground is on the east side of the river and offers privacy and at least partial shade.

290 Mead Creek State Forest Campground

Location: About 7 miles southwest of Germfask
Season: Year-round
Sites: 9 sites with no hookups
Maximum RV length: 35
Facilities: Vault toilets, fire rings, water, tables, boat launch
Fee per night: $$
Management: Michigan DNR
Contact: (906) 341-2355; www.michigandnr.com/parksandtrails
Finding the campground: From Germfask take MI 77 south for about 2 miles and turn right (west) on CR 436/River Road. Go 3.5 miles, continue on Floodwoods Road for another 1.5 miles, and the campground entrance is on the right.
GPS coordinates: N 46 10.805' / W 85 59.168'
About the campground: The Manistique River passes through the scenic Seney National Wildlife Refuge, and paddlers come for hours or days to enjoy some of its 60-mile journey to Lake Michigan. Just south of the refuge are this campground and the similar Merwin Creek Campground, but this is the first takeout for paddlers. The fishing is good for a variety of species: lake trout, lake herring, pike, bass, walleye, perch, muskie, and bluegill. A gravel ramp gets medium-size boats into the water. The campground is on the east side of the river and offers privacy and good shade.

291 Fox River State Forest Campground

Location: About 6 miles northwest of Seney
Season: Year-round
Sites: 7 sites with no hookups
Maximum RV length: 40
Facilities: Vault toilets, fire rings, water, tables, hiking/biking trails
Fee per night: $$
Management: Michigan DNR
Contact: (906) 341-2355; www.michigandnr.com/parksandtrails
Finding the campground: From Seney head west on MI 28 for about 0.4 mile and take a slight right northwest onto Fox River Road. Follow this 6.4 miles to the camp entrance on the right.
GPS coordinates: N 46 24.357' / W 86 02.748'
About the campground: Much like the East Branch of Fox River Campground, paddlers will appreciate the on-site river access, and anglers will come for the brook trout. The trail on-site follows the Little Fox and Fox Rivers, covering 27.5 miles between here and Kingston Lake State Forest Campground. The campsites are spacious, with shade trees but also some space for sun to come in. From here the Seney National Wildlife Refuge is just 10 miles south. This is on the west side of the river, while the East Branch camp is on the east side of that eastern branch.

292 Seney Township Campground

Location: About 1 mile northwest of Seney
Season: Year-round
Sites: 15 sites with electrical hookups, 10 sites with no hookups
Maximum RV length: 40
Facilities: Vault toilets, showers, tables, hiking trails
Fee per night: $$$
Management: Township of Seney
Contact: (906) 499-3491; www.michigan.org/property/seney-township-campground
Finding the campground: From MI 28 in Seney take School Street, which becomes Fox River Road, northwest for 0.7 mile and the park is on the right.
GPS coordinates: N 46 21.184' / W 85 57.772'
About the campground: Hemingway fans take note: The Two-Hearted River of the short story was actually the Fox River here outside Seney. This little loop of sites just west of the river is ideal for anglers looking to get into the Fox. Hemingway fans can follow in Nick Adams's footsteps on a 27-mile hiking trail that begins at the camp, follows the Fox, and ends at Kingston Lake near Pictured Rocks National Lakeshore. Seney was a lumber town and has a museum open in the summer months with colorful stories of the rough-and-tumble days. The campground is popular, so get there early or have a backup plan.

293 East Branch of Fox River State Forest Campground

Location: About 9 miles north of Seney
Season: Year-round
Sites: 19 sites with no hookups
Maximum RV length: 40
Facilities: Vault toilets, fire rings, water, tables, boat launch, hiking/off-road vehicle trails
Fee per night: $$
Management: Michigan DNR–Indian Lake State Park
Contact: (906) 341-2355; www.michigandnr.com/parksandtrails
Finding the campground: From Seney head north on MI 77 for 8.3 miles and turn left (west) at the park sign.
GPS coordinates: N 46 27.931' / W 85 56.696'
About the campground: Paddlers will appreciate this riverside camp in the Lake Superior State Forest with carry-in access on the Fox River. The river is known for brook trout and its nice scenery. A trail on-site follows the Little Fox and Fox Rivers, covering 27.5 miles between Kingston Lake and Fox River State Forest Campgrounds. The campsites are spacious, with shade trees but also some space for sun to come in. From here the Seney National Wildlife Refuge is just 10 miles south.

294 South Manistique Lake State Forest Campground

Location: About 12 miles southeast of Germfask
Season: Year-round
Sites: 29 sites with no hookups
Maximum RV length: 40
Facilities: Vault toilets, fire rings, water, tables, boat launch, off-road vehicle trails
Fee per night: $$
Management: Michigan DNR–Tahquamenon Falls State Park
Contact: (906) 492-3415; www.michigandnr.com/parksandtrails
Finding the campground: From Germfask take MI 77 south about 2 miles and turn left (east) on CR 436/Ackley Road. Go 4 miles and turn right (south) on McGahn Road. Go 1.5 miles and turn left (east) on Curtis Road. Go 1.8 miles and turn right on Long Pointe Road, driving 1 mile and turning right (west) on Sherman Road. Go 0.7 mile and go left on Randal Road 0.7 mile to the campground.
GPS coordinates: N 46 10.478' / W 85 47.481'
About the campground: With just over 4,000 acres, South Manistique is pretty big, but not as big as "Big" Manistique Lake nearby to the north, which has more than 10,000 acres. Boating activity is the main attraction here, and there are ramps on both lakes, including one right inside the campground. Anglers may catch walleye, pike, bass, perch, bluegill, muskie, or lake herring. The sites are shaded and not far from the lake edge. Though spacious and private, not all of them can handle the indicated 40-foot vehicle maximum limit.

295 Milakokia Lake State Forest Campground

Location: About 29 miles east of Manistique
Season: Year-round
Sites: 35 sites with no hookups
Maximum RV length: 40
Facilities: Vault toilets, fire rings, water, tables, boat launch, hiking/mountain biking/off-road vehicle trails
Fee per night: $$
Management: Michigan DNR–Tahquamenon Falls State Park
Contact: (906) 492-3415; www.michigandnr.com/parksandtrails
Finding the campground: From Manistique head east on US 2 about 27 miles and turn right (south) on Milakokia Lake Road. Go 0.2 mile and turn left (east) on Pike Lake Grade. Drive 1.3 miles and the campground road is on the right.
GPS coordinates: N 46 05.201' / W 85 47.334'
About the campground: This 1,956-acre lake lies just south of US 2 and about 16 miles west of where that highway becomes a scenic route right along Lake Michigan. Its proximity to US 2 makes it a good overnight stop between here and there, but anglers have a hard boat ramp and decent fishing. The closest hiking of note is 16 miles to Big Knob, and the Seney National Wildlife Refuge is 25 miles west. Some of the sites are too small for the big rigs, but they are all shaded and line up along the park road backed up to the lake on one side.

296 Big Knob State Forest Campground

Location: About 14 miles southwest of Naubinway
Season: Year-round
Sites: 23 sites with no hookups
Maximum RV length: 40
Facilities: Vault toilets, fire rings, water, tables, boat launch, hiking/mountain biking/off-road vehicle trails, beach
Fee per night: $$
Management: Michigan DNR–Tahquamenon Falls State Park
Contact: (906) 492-3415; www.michigandnr.com/parksandtrails
Finding the campground: From Naubinway head west on US 2 about 7.6 miles and turn left (south) on Big Knob Road. Follow it 5.8 miles all the way to the campground.
GPS coordinates: N 46 02.340' / W 85 35.635'
About the campground: This is a secluded, rustic campground down a 6-mile country road that gets campers out on the edge of Lake Michigan. The beach has modest dunes, with much of the beach covered with grasses out to the narrow strip of golden sand along the water, but it stretches for miles in both directions. The water is shallow a good distance out, making it nice for kids to play in. The campsites are shaded and separated nicely from each other. A short hiking trail visits a marsh pond and the beach.

A trail in the sand leads out to Lake Michigan at Big Knob State Park. MATT FORSTER

297 Natalie State Forest Campground

Location: About 4 miles west of Newberry
Season: Year-round
Sites: 12 sites with no hookups
Maximum RV length: 40
Facilities: Vault toilets, fire rings, water, tables, boat launch, hiking/mountain biking/off-road vehicle trails
Fee per night: $$
Management: Michigan DNR–Tahquamenon Falls State Park
Contact: (906) 492-3415; www.michigandnr.com/parksandtrails
Finding the campground: From MI 123 in Newberry head west on McMillan Avenue, which becomes CR 405 on its way out of town. After the curve south, turn right (west) on Natalie Road and follow it 1.6 miles to the campground entrance on the right.
GPS coordinates: N 46 21.005' / W 85 34.880'
About the campground: Great for paddlers, the Tahquamenon River flows past on its way to its dramatic falls about 35 miles northeast of here. The campground is a forest loop located just before the boat launch area, so it is not right on the river, but the backwaters of the Dallarville Flooding are near. Hikers and bikers have 14 miles of the Canada Lake Pathway that has its trailhead on-site. The river and flooding offer anglers a shot at walleye, muskie, bass, perch, and pike. Seney National Wildlife Refuge is 25 miles west of here, so the camp does have good potential as a base of operations for more than just the neighboring river.

298 Bass Lake State Forest Campground (Luce)

Location: About 15 miles north and west of Newberry
Season: Year-round
Sites: 18 sites with no hookups
Maximum RV length: 40
Facilities: Vault toilets, fire rings, water, tables, boat launch, hiking/off-road vehicle trails
Fee per night: $$
Management: Michigan DNR–Tahquamenon Falls State Park
Contact: (906) 492-3415; www.michigandnr.com/parksandtrails
Finding the campground: From Newberry head north on MI 123 for 4.4 miles and turn left (west) on CR 407. Go 4.3 miles and turn left (west) on Carlson Camp Road/CR 455 and stay on this for 6.9 miles until the camp entrance on the right.
GPS coordinates: N 46 27.719' / W 85 42.513'
About the campground: This rustic state forest campground offers ramp access to the lake and carry-in access on nearby Murray and Buckeye Lakes. Fishing might get you bass, perch, bluegill, or pike. The campground is across the road from the boat landing and lake. Some of the sites are wide, grassy, and open to the skies, while the others are well shaded and surrounded by understory. Other activities require a bit of driving: 25 miles to Seney National Wildlife Refuge, 19 miles to Canada Lake for some good hiking, and about an hour's journey to Tahquamenon Falls State Park.

299 Pretty Lake State Forest Campground

Location: About 25 miles north of Newberry
Season: Year-round
Sites: 18 sites with no hookups, 5 walk-in sites
Maximum RV length: 40
Facilities: Vault toilets, fire rings, water, tables, hiking/off-road vehicle trails
Fee per night: $$
Management: Michigan DNR
Contact: (906) 658-3338; www.michigandnr.com/parksandtrails
Finding the campground: From Newberry head north on MI 123 for 4.4 miles and turn left (west) on CR 407. Drive 17.6 miles and turn left (west) on Holland Lake Road. Go 2.7 miles and turn left (south) on Pretty Lake Road. Continue 0.8 mile to the campground.
GPS coordinates: N 46 36.238' / W 85 39.483'
About the campground: This is an ultimate get-away-from-it-all spot amid a small collection of lakes that nearly connect. Five hike-in sites even allow campers to get away from the vehicle. The lake is great for paddling, but boats must be nonmotorized. Portaging to 4 other lakes is possible, all of them as clear and pristine as this one. Canoe campsites are located at each portage pathway. Large pines and some hardwoods shade the campground sites, and there is a sandy beach/carry-in access. The North Country National Scenic Trail is 5 miles north.

300 Holland Lake State Forest Campground

Location: About 25 miles north of Newberry
Season: Year-round
Sites: 15 sites with no hookups
Maximum RV length: 40
Facilities: Vault toilets, fire rings, water, tables, boat launch, hiking/off-road vehicle trails
Fee per night: $$
Management: Michigan DNR
Contact: (906) 658-3338; www.michigandnr.com/parksandtrails
Finding the campground: From Newberry head north on MI 123 for about 4.4 miles, turn left (west) on CR 407, and go 17.6 miles. Turn left (west) on Holland Lake Road, go 2.7 miles, and the camp entrance is on the right.
GPS coordinates: N 46 36.923' / W 85 39.383'
About the campground: This camp might best be suited for off-road enthusiasts, as the 49-mile Pine Ridge Trail connects here and farther on to the Two-Heart Trail. While fishing on-site is good for brook trout, anglers should note that no motors are allowed. Nearby is Pretty Lake and its complex of small, clear lakes—also with motorless rules. Just a half mile south of here hikers can get on the North Country National Scenic Trail. The camp here is pretty standard: partial shade from surrounding trees, adequate privacy, and a boat ramp.

301 High Bridge State Forest Campground

Location: About 22 miles north of Newberry
Season: Year-round
Sites: 7 sites with no hookups
Maximum RV length: 35
Facilities: Vault toilets, fire rings, water, tables, hiking/off-road vehicle trails
Fee per night: $$
Management: Michigan DNR
Contact: (906) 658-3338; www.michigandnr.com/parksandtrails
Finding the campground: From Newberry drive north on MI 123 for 4.4 miles and turn left (west) on CR 407. Continue 17.3 miles and take a right (east) on Rut Lane to find the campground.
GPS coordinates: N 46 36.463' / W 85 36.128'
About the campground: The Two-Hearted River was made famous by Ernest Hemingway in one of his short stories, but it was actually this river only in name. The Fox River was the actual setting described. Nevertheless, this stream is known for its good fishing for brook trout and steelhead. The camp is right on it, with a handful of secluded and shaded rustic sites. Hikers can get to the North Country National Scenic Trail just 5 miles north of here, and 2 ATV trails are even closer. Many other campgrounds are in the area.

302 Perch Lake State Forest Campground

Location: About 24 miles north of Newberry
Season: Year-round
Sites: 35 sites with no hookups
Maximum RV length: 40
Facilities: Vault toilets, fire rings, water, tables, boat launch, hiking/off-road vehicle trails
Fee per night: $$
Management: Michigan DNR
Contact: (906) 658-3338; www.michigandnr.com/parksandtrails
Finding the campground: From Newberry drive north on MI 123 for 4.4 miles and turn left (west) on CR 407. Continue 18.7 miles and take a right (east) on Rut Lane to find the campground.
GPS coordinates: N 46 37.745' / W 85 35.472'
About the campground: Anglers hit this lake for bluegill and largemouth bass, and with the Two-Hearted River and Muskallonge Lake both nearby, fishing is likely the biggest draw. Steps lead down to a modest sandy beach. The North Country National Scenic Trail is at Muskallonge Lake's park, Blind Sucker Flooding is 9 miles northeast, and ATV riders will seek out Pine Ridge Trail's 49 miles just a few minutes south of here. And the biggest lake of them all, Superior, is right up the road.

303 Mouth of Two-Hearted River State Forest Campground

Location: About 30 miles north of Newberry
Season: May through October
Sites: 39 sites with no hookups
Maximum RV length: 40
Facilities: Vault toilets, fire rings, water, tables, boat launch, hiking/mountain biking/off-road vehicle trails
Fee per night: $$
Management: Michigan DNR–Tahquamenon Falls State Park
Contact: (906) 492-3415; www.michigandnr.com/parksandtrails
Finding the campground: From Newberry take MI 123 north 4 miles to Four Mile Corner. Turn left (west) on CR 407. Take CR 407 for 14 miles to CR 414. Turn right on CR 414 and go 10 miles to CR 423. Turn left on CR 423 and go just over 4 miles to the campground entrance on the left.
GPS coordinates: N 46 41.806' / W 85 25.138'
About the campground: Rated one of the top trout streams in the country, the scenic Two-Hearted River of Hemingway fame meets Lake Superior here. The paddling and fishing are exceptional. The rustic sites are in 2 loops in the forest. A suspension bridge offers a path over the river to the sandy shore of the big lake. Don't let the miles fool you. The condition of the road may take you twice as long as you expect. Don't try to outsmart the directions with Google. They don't have

You'll find the camping rustic at Bodi Lake. MATT FORSTER

accurate judgment of good roads. Rainbow Lodge is out here. It is a reliable resource and runs canoe trips and sells gas and provisions.

304 Bodi Lake State Forest Campground

Location: About 30 miles north of Newberry
Season: Year-round
Sites: 20 sites with no hookups
Maximum RV length: 40
Facilities: Vault toilets, fire rings, water, tables, boat launch, hiking/mountain biking/off-road vehicles trails
Fee per night: $$
Management: Michigan DNR–Tahquamenon Falls State Park
Contact: (906) 492-3415; www.michigandnr.com/parksandtrails
Finding the campground: From Newberry head north for 18.5 miles on MI 123, turn left (north) on CR 500, and continue 10.8 miles, following the turns of the county road. At the fork with CR 437/Bodi Lake Road, stay right and continue 1.2 miles, turn right, and the campground is 0.2 mile down the road.
GPS coordinates: N 46 42.270' / W 85 20.239'
About the campground: Bodi Lake is tucked into the Lake Superior State Forest and just about a 2-mile drive from the big lake. Bodi makes for some good fishing for pike, bass, walleye, perch,

and bluegill, and Little Lake and Culhane Lake are nearby as well. Hikers have just over a mile on-site of trail through pine and oak forest, or they can head 1.5 miles west to pick up the North Country National Scenic Trail. The sites here are well shaded and private, a real forest experience, and a decent home base to visit Tahquamenon Falls, 13 miles away.

305 Andrus Lake State Forest Campground

Location: About 5 miles north of Paradise
Season: Year-round
Sites: 25 sites with no hookups
Maximum RV length: 40
Facilities: Vault toilets, fire rings, water, tables, boat launch, fishing pier
Fee per night: $$
Management: Michigan DNR–Tahquamenon Falls State Park
Contact: (906) 492-3415; www.michigandnr.com/parksandtrails
Finding the campground: From Paradise head north 5.1 miles on Whitefish Point Road. Turn left (west) on Vermillion Road and go 0.4 mile to the campground entrance on the left.
GPS coordinates: N 46 42.189' / W 85 02.150'
About the campground: This could be just another state forest camp on a good fishing lake (never a bad thing) if it weren't for its location. These shaded and private sites in the woods along the northwestern shore of Andrus Lake are perfect for home base for day trips up to Whitefish Point for the Great Lake Shipwreck Museum, or south to Tahquamenon Falls, or for Lake Superior shoreline visits just half a mile east. Birders must check out Whitefish Point Bird Observatory as well as the wetlands above Shelldrake Dam. Fishing is good here, at Shelldrake, and on Superior.

306 Tahquamenon Falls State Park

Location: About 14 miles west of Paradise
Season: Year-round
Sites: 260 sites with electrical hookups, 36 sites with no hookups
Maximum RV length: 50
Facilities: Flush/vault toilets, showers, fire rings, grills, water, tables, picnic shelter, picnic area, dump station, boat launch, hiking trails, playground, fishing pier, boat rental, concessionaire, telephone, amphitheater
Fee per night: $$-$$$
Management: Michigan DNR
Contact: (906) 492-3415; www.michigandnr.com/parksandtrails
Finding the campground: From Paradise on MI 123 head east for 13.9 miles and the park entrance is on the left (south).
GPS coordinates: N 46 34.946' / W 85 15.279'
About the campground: Half a million visitors check in here each year, and for good reason. The Upper Falls drops 50 feet and drains more water than any other vertical drop east of the

Tahquamenon Falls

Mississippi other than Niagara Falls—up to 50,000 gallons per second in spring. The Lower Falls 4 miles downriver is a collection of smaller falls that pass around an island. With over 46,000 acres, this is also Michigan's second-largest state park. There are 3 main campgrounds besides the group area: Lower Falls with 188 mostly modern sites, Rivermouth with 72 more modern sites, and Rivermouth Pines with 36 rustic sites. The North Country National Scenic Trail passes through, and there is a privately owned microbrewery and restaurant right inside the park.

307 Garnet Lake State Forest Campground

Location: About 12 miles east and north of Naubinway
Season: Year-round
Sites: 10 sites with no hookups
Maximum RV length: 30
Facilities: Vault toilets, fire rings, water, tables, off-road vehicle trails
Fee per night: $
Management: Hudson Township
Contact: (906) 595-7202; www.michigandnr.com/parksandtrails
Finding the campground: From US 2 about 6 miles east of Naubinway, go north on Borgstrom Road. Drive 4.6 miles and turn right (east) on Park Road. The camp entrance is 1 mile east on the left.
GPS coordinates: N 46 09.315' / W 85 17.971'

About the campground: As state forest management aimed to close some campgrounds due to budget cuts, several communities came forward to take over the management to keep them open. Such is the case with this 10-site rustic camp on the southern shore of Garnet Lake. Newberry-Rexton Trail is a mile away and offers 66 miles of off-road motorcycle pathway. Anglers will find pike and perch in the lake. The sites are mostly shaded and offer seclusion just 6 miles north of the Lake Michigan Scenic Highway.

308 Hog Island Point State Forest Campground

Location: About 7 miles east of Naubinway
Season: Year-round
Sites: 50 sites with no hookups
Maximum RV length: 40
Facilities: Vault toilets, fire rings, water, tables, boat launch, hiking/off-road vehicle trails
Fee per night: $$
Management: Michigan DNR–Straits State Park
Contact: (906) 643-8620; www.michigandnr.com/parksandtrails
Finding the campground: From Naubinway follow US 2 east for 7.4 miles and the camp entrance is on the right (south).
GPS coordinates: N 46 04.946' / W 85 18.276'
About the campground: This popular state forest camp is unfortunately just off the highway. While that makes it a great stopover for a night, it can also mean traffic noise. As many of the sites are near the water, however, a bit of wave action might eliminate that intrusion. The beach along Lake Michigan is sandy and attractive, but most campers are here and gone, on their way to somewhere else. Lake fishing might get you trout or steelhead. Ramp access, however, is 7 miles away in Naubinway. Big Knob campground isn't far off and offers a very secluded, remote experience.

309 Little Brevoort Lake– North State Forest Campground

Location: About 24 miles west of St. Ignace
Season: Year-round
Sites: 20 sites with no hookups
Maximum RV length: Some will accommodate 40-foot vehicle/trailer
Facilities: Vault toilets, fire rings, water, tables, boat launch, hiking/mountain biking trails
Fee per night: $$
Management: Michigan DNR–Straits State Park
Contact: (906) 643-8620; www.michigandnr.com/parksandtrails
Finding the campground: From St. Ignace take US 2 20.9 miles west and turn right (north) on Ozark Road/Schoolhouse Road. Go 0.6 mile and turn right (east) on Word Road, following it 1.1 miles to the park road on the right. Follow that 0.6 mile into the campground.

GPS coordinates: N 46 01.177' / W 85 01.048'

About the campground: The camp and lake are within a state natural area, and in this case the nature you can see is wildflowers. Head 6 miles west to Cut River Bridge for all sorts of floral species and some good birding as well. The camp is a single loop that ends at the lakeside. A couple of miles of trails, which are shared by hikers and bikers, start at camp. Fishing on the lake is good for pike, crappie, walleye, bass, bluegill, and perch, but no motors are allowed. The sites are partly shaded and moderately spacious, but not all can accommodate the 40-foot vehicles or trailers.

310 Brevoort Lake Campground– Hiawatha National Forest

Location: About 20 miles west of St. Ignace
Season: May 6 to September 30
Sites: 70 sites with no hookups
Maximum RV length: 45
Facilities: Flush toilets, fire rings, water, tables, picnic area, dump station, boat launch, hiking trails, beach, concessionaire
Fee per night: $$$
Management: USDA Forest Service
Contact: (906) 428-5800; Reservations: (877) 444-6777; www.fs.usda.gov/recarea/hiawatha/recarea/?recid=13292
Finding the campground: From St. Ignace go about 17 miles west on US 2, turn (right) north on FR 3108/Brevoort Camp Road, and drive 1.2 miles to FR 3473. Turn right (east) on FR 3473 and drive to the camp entrance.
GPS coordinates: N 46 00.454' / W 84 58.335'
About the campground: Up the Lake Michigan lakeshore west of the Mackinac Bridge and along the scenic highway, this campground lies about a mile inland on the southern shore of the 4,233-acre Brevoort Lake. A camp loop extends into the lake on a peninsula sheltered by woods, while another strip of 21 sites—half of which are along the water—lies along the lakeshore to the west. There are some sandy swimming areas here on the lake, and the sites are rather private thanks to intervening brush. Hikers will enjoy the Sand Dunes Cross Country, Ridge, and North Country National Scenic Trails that pass through the campground.

311 Lake Michigan Campground– Hiawatha National Forest

Location: About 16 miles west of St. Ignace
Season: Early May through September
Sites: 35 sites with no hookups
Maximum RV length: 40

The Mackinac Bridge between Lower and Upper Peninsula, Michigan

Facilities: Flush/vault toilets, fire rings, water, tables, boat launch, beach
Fee per night: $$$
Management: USDA Forest Service
Contact: (906) 428-5800; Reservations: (877) 444-6777; www.fs.usda.gov/recarea/hiawatha/recarea/?recid=13293
Finding the campground: From the intersection of US 2 and I-75, drive west 16 miles on US 2 to Lake Michigan Campground on the left (south) side.
GPS coordinates: N 45 59.158' / W 84 58.283'
About the campground: This is a lovely string of sites just off the highway and lined up along Lake Michigan. The waves crashing along shore are fun, and swimming is possible. Be alert of conditions for riptides. Dunes up to 30 feet high characterize this stretch of Lake Michigan shoreline, and the campsites are well above the waterline with sloping trails down to the beach. Many of the sites are best for tent campers, although half of the sites are still workable for trailers and RVs. Highway noise is present, but wind and waves can often drown that out.

312 Straits State Park

Location: Right inside St. Ignace
Season: April 1 to November 30 (April 1 to October 29 for waterfront sites)
Sites: 255 sites with electrical hookups, 15 sites with no hookups
Maximum RV length: 50
Facilities: Flush/vault toilets, showers, fire rings, grills, water, tables, picnic area, dump station, hiking trails, playground
Fee per night: $$-$$$$
Management: Michigan DNR
Contact: (906) 643-8620; www.michigandnr.com/parksandtrails
Finding the campground: From I-75 north of the Mackinac Bridge, take exit 344(A) and go east on I-75 Business to Church Street. Go right (south) on Church Street about 0.2 mile and the park entrance is on the right.
GPS coordinates: N 45 51.305' / W 84 43.168'
About the campground: The Mackinac Bridge is an impressive structure connecting the Upper and Lower Peninsulas of Michigan, and from this park one can admire it and the passing ship traffic from the beach, campsites, and a special viewing platform. The beach area is shallow and good for swimming, while anglers will prefer to go west of the big bridge for the best lake fishing. The modern campground is set back from the lake, and with 255 sites it has the bulk of them. Along the waterfront is another collection of 15 sites, which have no hookups. Sault Ste. Marie is another hour north of here. At 80 miles away, Tahquamenon Falls is a potential day trip, and local ferries connect to Mackinac Island.

313 Carp River Campground–Hiawatha National Forest

Location: About 13 miles north of St. Ignace
Season: Mid-May through September
Sites: 20 sites with no hookups
Maximum RV length: 40
Facilities: Vault toilets, fire rings, water, tables, boat launch, hiking trails
Fee per night: $$
Management: USDA Forest Service
Contact: (906) 428-5800; Reservations: (877) 444-6777; www.fs.usda.gov/recarea/hiawatha/recarea/?recid=13295
Finding the campground: From St. Ignace head north on I-75 for 6.8 miles and take exit 352. Turn right (east) to drive a few hundred feet on MI 123 and then turn left (north) on CR H63/Mackinac Trail. Drive 5.3 miles, turn left (west) on FR 3445, and the campground entrance is 400 feet farther on the left side of the road.
GPS coordinates: N 46 02.020' / W 84 43.142'
About the campground: The Carp River is a scenic trout river that offers paddlers a decent flow throughout the season but an experienced paddler's current in June. The river empties into Lake Huron. This campground offers 2 loops of spacious, private, and shaded sites. Steps lead down to the river in two places, and a trail between sites 8 and 10 has carry-in access. Paddling not your thing? The North Country National Scenic Trail is 8 miles west. The camp is close to the highway, so noise may be a distraction for some.

314 Trout Lake Township Park

Location: About 31 miles northwest of St. Ignace
Season: May 15 to October 15
Sites: 60 sites with electrical hookups, 23 sites with no hookups
Maximum RV length: 45
Facilities: Flush toilets, showers, grills, water, tables, picnic area, pavilion, dump station, boat ramp, beach, playground, volleyball court, horseshoe pits, ball field
Fee per night: $$$–$$$$
Management: Trout Lake Township
Contact: (906) 569-3299; www.troutlaketownship.com/township-park
Finding the campground: From I-75 about 7 miles north of St. Ignace, take MI 123 22.5 miles and turn left (west) on Trout Lake Road. Go 1 mile and the park entrance is on the left (south).
GPS coordinates: N 46 11.536' / W 85 02.561'
About the campground: This is a grassy open park along the north shore of 560-acre Trout Lake. The best sites are #31–36 right along the lake and next to the beach area. These are the only lakeside sites. Some sites have partial shade, but many are exposed. Railroad tracks run right behind the last row of campsites #1–20 plus #90–91. Electric and water are shut off after October 15. This is a developed lake, and park activities are numerous. Some may choose to use this campground as a central point for day trips to the various regional attractions.

315 Three Lakes Campground– Hiawatha National Forest

Location: About 39 miles west of Sault Ste. Marie
Season: May 13 to September 30
Sites: 10 sites with no hookups
Maximum RV length: 40
Facilities: Vault toilets, fire rings, grills, water, tables, picnic area, hiking trails, ball field
Fee per night: $$
Management: USDA Forest Service
Contact: (906) 428-5800; Reservations: (877) 444-6777; www.fs.usda.gov/recarea/hiawatha/recarea/?recid=13291
Finding the campground: From I-75 about 8 miles south of Sault Ste. Marie, take MI 28 west 26.7 miles and turn left (south) on Strongs Road. Continue 1.9 miles and the campground entrance is on the left.
GPS coordinates: N 46 19.249' / W 84 58.939'
About the campground: This campground in the Hiawatha National Forest is so named for its location amid 3 small fishing lakes: Brown, Whitmarsh, and Walker. Sites are shaded by spruce, pine, and maple trees and in close proximity to Walker Lake. In fact, some of them back right up to the lake. However, the most secluded are along the back (north) side of the loop. The Walker Loop Trail circles that lake in just over a mile. Boat access is carry-in, and no motors are allowed. While swimming is possible, there is no beach area.

316 Soldier Lake Campground– Hiawatha National Forest

Location: About 32 miles south and east of Sault Ste. Marie
Season: May 13 to September 30
Sites: 44 sites with no hookups
Maximum RV length: 40
Facilities: Vault toilets, fire rings, grills, water, tables, picnic shelter with fireplace, picnic area, hiking trails, beach
Fee per night: $$$
Management: USDA Forest Service
Contact: (906) 428-5800; Reservations: (877) 444-6777; www.fs.usda.gov/recarea/hiawatha/recarea/?recid=13290
Finding the campground: From I-75 about 8 miles south of Sault Ste. Marie, take MI 28 west 21.4 miles and turn left (south) on FR 3138. Follow it 0.7 mile to Soldier Lake Road and stay on that 0.2 mile to arrive at the park entrance.
GPS coordinates: N 46 20.964' / W 84 52.216'

About the campground: This 15-acre lake is OK for bass and perch fishing, and because of its small size, the campground nearly encompasses it. The best sites along the water are #1–24, with a couple that are across the road. All other sites lie in a loop to the southwest and have the park road between them and the lake. However, they are spaced nicely and have no facing sites across the road. Pine, aspen, and maple provide nice shade for campsites and a bit of color in fall. A quarter-mile spur trail connects hikers to the vast North Country National Scenic Trail.

317 Bay View Campground–Hiawatha National Forest

Location: About 25 miles west from Sault Ste. Marie
Season: May 13 to September 30
Sites: 24 sites with no hookups
Maximum RV length: 35
Facilities: Vault toilets, fire rings, grills, water, tables, picnic area, boat launch, beach
Fee per night: $$
Management: USDA Forest Service
Contact: (906) 428-5800; Reservations: (877) 444-6777; www.fs.usda.gov/recarea/hiawatha/recarea/?recid=13288
Finding the campground: From I-75 south of Sault Ste. Marie, head west on MI 28 for 15.5 miles and turn right (north) on Ranger Road for 6.3 miles. Turn left (west) on Lakeshore Drive, continue 1.9 miles, and Bay View Camp Road is on the right (north).
GPS coordinates: N 46 27.021' / W 84 46.594'
About the campground: The lake that Native Americans called Gitche Gumme is Lake Superior, the largest freshwater lake by surface area in the world. This campground is parked right on its shore. Sites are staggered along the single park road for good privacy, and tree cover provides shade. The sandy beach stretches for miles in either direction, and the sites on the north side of the strip are just steps from it. The shore faces north-northwest, so sunsets are brilliant. A host is on-site in summer months.

318 Monocle Lake Campground– Hiawatha National Forest

Location: About 7 miles north of Brimley
Season: May 13 to September 30
Sites: 42 sites with no hookups
Maximum RV length: 40
Facilities: Vault toilets, fire rings, grills, water, tables, picnic area, boat launch, hiking trails, beach, lantern posts
Fee per night: $$
Management: USDA Forest Service

The good life includes fishing on Monocle Lake. MATT FORSTER

Contact: (906) 428-5800; Reservations: (877) 444-6777; www.fs.usda.gov/recarea/hiawatha/recarea/?recid=13289

Finding the campground: From MI 221 in Brimley, take Iroquois Road/Lakeshore Drive west 6.2 miles. Turn left (west) on Park Road and follow it 0.9 mile to the campground entrance on the right.

GPS coordinates: N 46 28.184' / W 84 38.328'

About the campground: Set amid a forest of maple, birch, and aspen, this lakeside campground is a stunner in fall. The location, not far from where Whitefish Bay on Lake Superior narrows into the channel to Sault Ste. Marie, is convenient as well. The city of the Soo Locks isn't far, nor is Tahquamenon Falls State Park, and Point Iroquois Lighthouse is 2 miles away. The lake has 172 acres and is good for bass, pike, perch, and walleye, and the park's interpretive trail runs 14.5 miles. The sites are in a loop along the lakeshore, but all of them have at least the park road or more between them and the water.

319 Brimley State Park

Location: About 14 miles west of Sault Ste. Marie
Season: Mid-April to late October
Sites: 237 sites with electrical hookups
Maximum RV length: 50

Facilities: Flush/vault toilets, showers, fire rings, grills, water, tables, picnic shelter, picnic area, dump station, hiking trails, beach, beach house, playground

Fee per night: $$$

Management: Michigan DNR

Contact: (906) 248-3422; www.michigandnr.com/parksandtrails

Finding the campground: From Sault Ste. Marie head south out of the city on CR H63 for about 3.1 miles. Turn right (west) on 6 Mile Road and drive 8.1 miles to the park entrance on the right (north).

GPS coordinates: N 46 24.765' / W 84 33.373'

About the campground: Set along the shore of Whitefish Bay on Lake Superior, Brimley was founded in 1923, one of the first state parks in the Upper Peninsula. Unlike some of the other regional parks, fishing and hiking are not on-site, but the area offers plenty of trout streams and access to Lake Superior. The beach is the main attraction, and families will appreciate this park for its warm waters and long stretches of sand. The sites are laid out in parallel loops with good shade but no lake views. While there are trees spread throughout, overhead shade isn't common among these spacious sites.

320 Sherman Park

Location: On the west side of Sault Ste. Marie

Season: May 15 to October 15

Sites: 25 sites with no hookups

Maximum RV length: 45 feet

Facilities: Vault toilets, fire rings, grills, water, tables, picnic area, pavilion for rent, hiking trails, beach, changing rooms, playground volleyball court, horseshoe pits, boccie courts

Fee per night: $$$

Management: City of Sault Ste. Marie

Contact: (906) 632-5768; www.saultcity.com/sherman-park

Finding the campground: From I-75 take exit 394 in Sault Ste. Marie and head west on Easterday Avenue. This will become 4th Avenue. Follow it to the end, turn left (south) on 24th Street, and the park entrance is on the right.

GPS coordinates: N 46 29.225' / W 84 24.975'

About the campground: Sault Ste. Marie is home to the Soo Locks, where the big boats make the 21-foot difference between Lakes Superior and Huron via the St. Marys River. Visitors watch from a viewing platform. The city is famous for fudge and its own little brewery. This city park feels more like camping than the Aune-Osborn Campground on the east side of town thanks to nice tree coverage and its rustic nature. This park also has a swimming beach, walking trails, and more activities.

321 Aune Osborn Campground

Location: On the eastern side of Sault Ste. Marie

Season: May 15 to October 15

The Soo Locks

Sites: 100 sites with water and electrical hookups
Maximum RV length: 50
Facilities: Flush toilets, showers, fire rings, water, tables, dump station, boat launch, playground, fish-cleaning station, phones, laundry. Wi-Fi
Fee per night: $$$$
Management: City of Sault Ste. Marie
Contact: (906) 632-3268; www.saultcity.com/aune-osborn-campground
Finding the campground: Coming into Sault Ste. Marie, take the I-75 Business spur right downtown to Portage Avenue and go right (east). The camp is just over 2 miles along Portage Avenue on the left (north) side.
GPS coordinates: N 46 29.309' / W 84 18.624'
About the campground: The big boats—freighters, ore ships—make the 21-foot vertical journey between Lake Superior and Lake Huron at the Soo Locks using the St. Marys River to get from the locks to Huron's open water. This campground has front-row seats for watching the ships passing on the river. Sites are grassy and have no shade. There are 24 premium sites at the river's edge, but no tents are allowed in that row for safety reasons. Still, there are benches for campers to sit and watch water traffic. This is a good spot for special city events, such as late June's annual tugboat race. The Soo Locks are open for viewing as well.

322 Munuscong River State Forest Campground

Location: About 8 miles northeast of Pickford
Season: Year-round
Sites: 26 sites with no hookups
Maximum RV length: 40
Facilities: Vault toilets, fire rings, water, tables, boat launch, hiking/mountain biking/off-road vehicle trails
Fee per night: $$
Management: Michigan DNR–Brimley State Park
Contact: (906) 248-3422; www.michigandnr.com/parksandtrails
Finding the campground: From Pickford take MI 48/MI 129 north about 2 miles and turn right (east) on 22 Mile Road. Go 3 miles and turn left (north) on Riverside Drive. Go 1 mile and turn right (east) on 21 Mile Road. Continue 1 mile, turn left (north), and the road takes you 0.7 mile to the campground entrance.
GPS coordinates: N 46 12.792' / W 84 16.839'
About the campground: The Munuscong River feeds into the lake of the same name, which is actually part of the St. Marys River connecting Superior to Huron. The lake area is good for wildlife watching. The campground lies south of the river about 2 miles from its outlet. The boat ramp then gives access to the river as well as the lake beyond. The closest hiking is 15 miles away at Pine Bowl Pathway, and off-road trails aren't much closer. Fishing is good for pike, muskie, bass, walleye, perch, and crappie. The sites are mostly shaded and spacious, with only a few that cannot accommodate a 40-foot vehicle or trailer.

323 DeTour State Forest Campground

Location: About 18 miles east of Cedarville
Season: Year-round
Sites: 21 sites with no hookups
Maximum RV length: 40 feet
Facilities: Vault toilets, fire rings, water, tables, boat launch, hiking/off-road vehicle trails
Fee per night: $$
Management: Michigan DNR–Brimley State Park
Contact: (906) 248-3422; www.michigandnr.com/parksandtrails
Finding the campground: From Cedarville head east along MI 134 for 17.9 miles and the park entrance is on the right (south).
GPS coordinates: N 45 57.693' / W 84 00.591'
About the campground: Located along the sandy shore of Lake Huron, the park offers boat access. Hikers should head north a mile to explore the Cranberry Lake Flooding, a wetland area. Wildlife is abundant in the Munuscong Wildlife Area nearby. The sites are shaded mostly by pine, and a number of sites have trails out to the beach. Only 3 sites can handle a 40-foot RV. Catch the sunrise over Lake Huron each morning.

324　Drummond Island Township Park

Location: About 6 miles east of the ferry crossing from DeTour
Season: Year-round
Sites: 34 sites with electrical hookups, 12 sites with no hookups
Maximum RV length: 31 feet
Facilities: Vault toilets, fire rings, water, tables, picnic area, pavilion, boat ramp, hiking trails, beach, concessionaire, outhouses
Fee per night: $$
Management: Drummond Island Township
Contact: (906) 322-4246; www.visitdrummondisland.com/campgrounds.html
Finding the campground: Take the ferry from DeTour Village 1 mile to Drummond Island. Continue on MI 134 5.8 miles and the park entrance is on the left.
GPS coordinates: N 45 59.676' / W 83 46.768'
About the campground: Just a short ferry ride from the rest of the Upper Peninsula, Drummond Island is one of Lake Huron's largest. The township park offers a 3-mile heritage trail. The beach is sandy, and the water is shallow a long way out. In fact, you can walk to a nearby island. Restaurants and provisions are just 2 miles east of here. The wildlife and especially birdlife are quite varied on the island, as it has 13 ecosystems. Migration routes pass here in spring and fall. The campsites are private and well shaded by the forest. Sunsets are nice from the beach area.

Campsite Index

About the Author

Kevin Revolinski is a freelance writer/photographer writing mainly about travel and the outdoors. He is the author of several books, and his work has appeared in the *New York Times*, the *Chicago Tribune*, and the *Sydney Morning Herald*. His year teaching abroad in Turkey became the subject of his first book, *The Yogurt Man Cometh*. He did his first guidebook work for Rough Guides and has since written several Wisconsin travel and outdoor guides. As the author of *Wisconsin's Best Beer Guide,* he was invited on *The Today Show* to sample beers with Al Roker at Lambeau Field. He maintains a website called The Mad Traveler (TheMadTraveler.com and is an avid camper, hiker, paddler, and craft beer drinker. He has traveled to more than seventy-five countries and lived for a year each in Italy, Guatemala, Turkey, Panama, and Thailand. He currently makes base camp in Madison, Wisconsin. His author site is KevinRevolinski.com.

Other works by Kevin Revolinski:
The Yogurt Man Cometh: Tales of an American Teacher in Turkey
Best Easy Day Hikes Milwaukee
Best Easy Day Hikes Grand Rapids
Wisconsin's Best Beer Guide
Michigan's Best Beer Guide
Minnesota's Best Beer Guide
60 Hikes Within 60 Miles of Madison
Backroads and Byways of Wisconsin
Best Rail Trails Wisconsin
Insiders' Guide Madison
Best in Tent Camping Wisconsin
Stealing Away: Stories
Paddling Wisconsin
Hiking Wisconsin